THE EVERYTHING
MEDITERRANEAN
SLOW COOKER COOKBOOK

Dear Reader,

We're delighted to invite you on a journey of flavor and fresh ingredients. This journey will take you to far-off places. To Italy and Egypt. To rolling Tuscan hills and the bustling streets of Greece. But mostly, it will take you home. Where you will prep a meal in the morning and later return to home-cooked, preservative-free, healthy eating, whenever you want.

Inspired by the rich flavors and naturally healthy approach to cooking so often found in Mediterranean food, we've combined the favorite foods of the area into this delicious cookbook. Within these pages, you'll find recipes for everything from breakfast to dessert. Many recipes use familiar ingredients—foods you already love and have on hand. Others will push you to try something new. Perhaps you'll buy a packet of anchovies for the first time, or learn to cook lamb. We encourage you to try all of the recipes! They're packed with flavor, nutrition, and all the love of Mediterranean cuisine—from our kitchen to yours.

Opa!

Launie and Brooke

Welcome to the EVERYTHING. Series!

These handy, accessible books give you all you need to tackle a difficult project, gain a new hobby, comprehend a fascinating topic, prepare for an exam, or even brush up on something you learned back in school but have since forgotten.

You can choose to read an Everything® book from cover to cover or just pick out the information you want from our four useful boxes: e-questions, e-facts, e-alerts, and e-ssentials.

We give you everything you need to know on the subject, but throw in a lot of fun stuff along the way, too.

We now have more than 400 Everything® books in print, spanning such wide-ranging categories as weddings, pregnancy, cooking, music instruction, foreign language, crafts, pets, New Age, and so much more. When you're done reading them all, you can finally say you know Everything®!

QUESTION

Answers to common questions

FACT

Important snippets of information

ALERT

Urgent warnings

ESSENTIAL

Quick handy tips

PUBLISHER Karen Cooper

MANAGING EDITOR, EVERYTHING® SERIES Lisa Laing

COPY CHIEF Casey Ebert

ASSISTANT PRODUCTION EDITOR Alex Guarco

ACQUISITIONS EDITOR Lisa Laing

SENIOR DEVELOPMENT EDITOR Brett Palana-Shanahan

EVERYTHING® SERIES COVER DESIGNER Erin Alexander

Visit the entire Everything® series at *www.everything.com*

THE
EVERYTHING®
MEDITERRANEAN
SLOW COOKER
COOKBOOK

Brooke McLay and Launie Kettler

Adamsmedia
Avon, Massachusetts

For Mom, Dad, Grammy, and Jedd. Thank you for teaching me to love food. —L.K.

To Grandma Brown.
For waking every morning and anticipating what was for dinner. —B.M.

An Everything® Series Book.
Everything® and everything.com® are registered trademarks of F+W Media, Inc.

Published by
Adams Media, a division of F+W Media, Inc.
57 Littlefield Street, Avon, MA 02322. U.S.A.
www.adamsmedia.com

Contains material adapted and abridged from *The Everything® Gluten-Free Slow Cooker Cookbook* by Carrie S. Forbes, copyright © 2012 by F+W Media, Inc., ISBN 10: 1-4405-3366-0, ISBN 13: 978-1-4405-3366-2; *The Everything® Healthy Slow Cooker Cookbook* by Rachel Rappaport, copyright © 2010 by F+W Media, Inc., ISBN 10: 1-4405-0231-5, ISBN 13: 978-1-4405-0231-6; *The Everything® Mediterranean Cookbook* by Dawn Altomari-Rathjen, LPN, BPS and Jennifer M. Bendelius, MS, RD, copyright © 2003 by F+W Media, Inc., ISBN 10: 1-58062-869-9, ISBN 13: 978-1-58062-869-3; and *The Everything® Slow Cooking for a Crowd Cookbook* by Katie Thompson, copyright © 2005 by F+W Media, Inc., ISBN 10: 1-59337-391-0, ISBN 13: 978-1-59337-391-7.

ISBN 10: 1-4405-6852-9
ISBN 13: 978-1-4405-6852-7
eISBN 10: 1-4405-6853-7
eISBN 13: 978-1-4405-6853-4

Printed in the United States of America.

10   9   8   7   6   5   4   3   2   1

Cover photographs by Brooke McLay.
Interior photographs by Launie Kettler and Brooke McLay.
Nutritional statistics by Nicole Cormier, RD, LDN.

This book is available at quantity discounts for bulk purchases.
For information, please call 1-800-289-0963.

Contents

Acknowledgments

From Launie: To my family and friends, especially Jedd, who makes me laugh and who laughs the perfect amount in return. Thanks for taste testing everything I make—sometimes over and over and over and over and over and over—until I'm happy with it. To my parents, who believe in me and taught me to laugh, and who let me travel to Spain—where I first fell in love with Mediterranean food. Thanks to P.J. for spreading the word and the light reflector; it made all the difference. To Li'l Evie, who makes the cayenne-based tincture that keeps my fingers nimble. To Colleen Brennan, who was an invaluable wine resource. To Amy Frame and her cohorts, who gave me some Sundays. To the Farm wives and husbands— music wouldn't be quite the same without you. To Jan, because you're my laughter doppelganger and inspiration. For Steve, who gave me and my typewriter our first writer's nook. And of course to my grandmother, who forgave me for the "rice soup incident" of 1984. You're a sweet and patient woman.

And of course, thanks to Brooke. You're an amazing sweetheart! Also, thanks to Lisa Laing. Oh, and because I anthropomorphize everything— thanks to my slow cooker, "Leslie." You've done well.

Acknowledgments

From Brooke: This cookbook arrived thanks to the gentle encouragement and patient organization of two wonder darlings—editor Lisa Laing and co-writer herself, Mizz Thang, Launie K. These two women have been a joy to work with, and I can't thank them enough for making such divine coworkers on this project.

There was a day, many moons ago, when I was walking through the vibrant streets of Barcelona. Rich architecture rose colorful and carved in vast arches overhead. The streets pulsed with children, gray-skirted women in sharp heels, crooked graying men wearing tweed caps. I fell in love with people there. And the smells. The smell of ocean, the smell of herbs and wine wafting on the wind, the smell of food and family and all that is good in life. I thank that day for teaching me that food could be so many things—healing and life-giving and full of celebration. It is the Mediterranean approach to eating that has inspired me in so very much of my own cooking at home. To friends, to family, to food. *La vida es delicioso!*

Introduction

THE MEDITERRANEAN DIET IS like the land and sea it springs from—vibrantly hued and beautiful. It's also effortlessly filled with health and nutrition. The residents of the Mediterranean infuse their meals with vitamin- and antioxidant-rich vegetables and grains, and they eat a lot of them. And when they do indulge in red meat they consume it in moderation, and use heart-healthy olive oil instead of butter.

There are other notably nutritious aspects to Mediterranean cooking. The use of beans—white beans, chickpeas, lentils—is common and abundant. Herbs, rich and varied, are sprinkled into tomato- and wine-based sauces, imbuing them with deep, satisfying flavor. Sugar is rarely turned to—even for desserts. The end of a Mediterranean meal may include a bite of fruit-and-nut-based goodness, perhaps drizzled with the natural sweetness of honey, but mounds of white sugar aren't spooned into overly sweet batters or frostings. Mediterranean eating is simple, fresh, filling, and generally low in the processed sugars and carbohydrates that have been linked to obesity, cancer, and other chronic or fatal health conditions. In fact, Mayo Clinic recognizes Mediterranean foods as a "heart-healthy eating plan" (*www.mayoclinic.org/healthy-living/nutrition-and-healthy-eating/in-depth/mediterranean-diet/art-20047801*).

Of course, the idea of Mediterranean cooking sounds ideal, but changing from familiar, traditional comfort recipes, embracing a new way of eating, can be difficult at first. Learning to cook a new food style can feel overwhelming, as it often calls for unfamiliar ingredients, spices, and combinations. The newness of the process requires work and learning—it's not automatic in the same way grabbing a box of tacos or broiling a breast of chicken once was. It can be time consuming to learn which ingredients go together, which taste good with chicken or beef, and which work best with pasta.

The Everything® Mediterranean Slow Cooker Cookbook seeks to simplify the process, making it easy and fun to learn a new way to cook. It turns more than 300 delicious, healthy Mediterranean-style recipes into breakfasts, lunches, dinners, desserts, and more—all made in a slow cooker.

The use of a slow cooker dramatically reduces the typical prep and "stove-watching" time associated with many traditional Mediterranean dishes. Where classic sauces, meats, and stews once took a dedicated housewife a full day of preparation time, the slow cooker delivers the same sort of slow-simmered goodness without all the watch time. Simply set the slow cooker and let it do the rest.

The flavors—and health benefits—of Mediterranean cuisine are undeniable and incredibly delicious. When made in the slow cooker, they become easier than ever to prepare and enjoy. With the hundreds of simple recipes included in this book, healthy Mediterranean cooking has never been so simple! Set that slow cooker, eat . . . and enjoy!

CHAPTER 1

Everything Mediterranean

Mediterranean cuisine is more than just a way of cooking; it's a way of life. It's a slower pace of life, it's long, slow-simmered cooking served around a rustic farm table, it's deep flavors and rich spices, it's lean meats and fresh-caught fish full of vital nutrients, fats, and vitamins. And what a wonderful thing that is! After all, to change your diet is one thing. To change your focus, priorities, and start molding your life to a lifestyle known for its health benefits won't just give you a flatter stomach; it will give you a fresh, new way of approaching every day. As you dive deep into these pages, keep in mind your diet is a reflection of your values, your schedule, and the way you view what's important. Embracing the simple values of health, flavor, vibrancy, community, and connection—all associated with the Mediterranean way—may prove to be just as invigorating as the fresh, beautiful flavors you'll taste as you make the recipes in this book.

What Is Mediterranean Cuisine?

To put it very simply, Mediterranean food is good food. Meals that are inspired by the sea, chock-a-block with fresh gorgeous vegetables and fruit along with fish, whole grains, nuts, and legumes. And maybe even a glass of red wine along with a healthy pasta dish. The diet is light on meat and sweets and uses heart-healthy olive oil instead of butter or lard.

Legendary Italian actress Sophia Loren once famously said, "Everything I have I owe to spaghetti." And pasta tossed with olive oil along with fresh vegetables and herbs is a staple in the Mediterranean diet. Though olive oil is high in fat, it's filled with monounsaturated fatty acids, which are the "good" type of fatty acid for the heart. That, combined with the benefits of a diet that's low in sugar and doesn't rely on processed food or copious amounts of meat, means that it has health benefits ranging from heart health to glucose control. Also, people who eat the Mediterranean diet have lower reported incidences of Alzheimer's and Parkinson's diseases.

The Mediterranean Way

In the middle of living a bustling American life, more and more families are turning to the relaxed simplicity of Mediterranean cuisine. The mere mention of Mediterranean cuisine conjures an idea that is likely two parts fantasy and half reality—oversized wooden farm tables surrounded by families, everyone sun-kissed and wearing loose gauzy clothes, wide-opened windows overlooking the Mediterranean, sea air wafting gently through homespun curtains.

The Mediterranean area is just mysterious enough, old enough, and far away enough to intrigue us. Of course, that intrigue becomes all the more interesting when there are real life reports from a multitude of studies that indicate Mediterranean countries experience lower rates of coronary disease, and lower rates of some diet-related cancers, than there are in the United States.

The Mediterranean lifestyle does have a focus on family, siestas, big-hearted enjoyment of life, and balanced work hours, which makes the consumer-driven fast-paced American lifestyle look overwhelming and unsustainable. And the fresh, simple flavors and nutrition-packed foods of the area complement this lifestyle.

FACT

Many Mediterranean dishes are made with low-cost ingredients. Look for recipes in this book that focus on beans versus meat and that use affordable vegetables (like carrots, onions, and potatoes) to bulk up a diet without breaking the bank.

The popularity of the Mediterranean diet in recent years must be attributed to more than just the ingredients listed in a cookbook. A focus on Mediterranean eating is a focus on fresh and local, slow and savory—on flavorful food grown by hand, by farmers in your own village (or at least in your own state). It's about food made to be shared with a table full of people, as simple and satisfying as feeding a crowd with a bowl of pasta.

Mediterranean eating is a call to slow down, to stop the madness, to fill body and schedule with less and more: Less processed food, more produce. Less microwaving, more oven baking. Less beef, more seafood. Less hurry up, more sip and breathe and enjoy. Mediterranean food is as much about the flavor combinations as it is about the focus on priorities.

With this in mind, and recognizing that lifestyle and diet changes take time, cooking Mediterranean-inspired foods in the slow cooker is an excellent first step toward a healthier whole-food, whole-body approach to daily living. The slow cooker offers a simple way to prepare fresh ingredients and have a home-cooked meal ready and waiting at the end of a long day. Quick and easy prep steps leave you with precious leisure time during the workweek.

The Mediterranean way invites a fuller focus on true health. It's about the food—brightly colored vegetables, rich sauces, fresh fish, flavorful herbs. But it's also about the culture of community and connection. It is the sewing together of the nostalgic comfort of a simpler time with the obvious demands of modern living. A way to bring past and present into one healthful, vibrant human experience in a way that is approachable, enjoyable, and utterly delicious.

Why Eat Mediterranean?

In a simplified nutshell, food has undergone a lot of trends over the last several years. French cooking was popularized by Julia Child in the 1970s and 1980s, and beloved for its rich, flavorful approach to cuisine. Unfortunately, French cooking wasn't always approachable. Coq au vin, often considered one of the finest French food experiences, typically takes more than an hour and forty-five minutes to prep, cook, and complete.

There was the hippie, simplistic approach to food in the '70s, with chefs like Alice Waters beginning the move toward fresh, local eating. The comfort, farm-food from the 1950s continued to grace American tables (mashed potatoes, gravy, steak, grits, fried chicken, casseroles) and while there was some focus on the connection between health and diet, fitness superstars like Jack Lalanne were still somewhat of an entertaining anomaly.

In the 1980s, fat-free eating enjoyed a brief rise in popularity, but began to lose ground when researchers found that fat-free food wasn't the magic fountain to health and wellness. In some instances, weight loss happened when fat was dropped from diets, but health and wellness rates were not rising. In fact, obesity rates began to rise, leading to the reconsideration of the USDA dietary guidelines, where grains and produce formed a healthful, fresh, natural base to a well-balanced diet. Fats were reintroduced as an important aspect to healthful eating, and the focus shifted to the rich flavors and simple preparations often seen in Mediterranean cooking.

Here, diet has found a happy combination of the best aspects of previous favorite diet fads. With rich, comforting, satisfying flavors, and scientific studies to back up the nutritious reality of Mediterranean diets, eaters can experience the best of all worlds, while experiencing a whole new level of health. In fact, the Mayo Clinic reports: "An analysis of more than 1.5 million healthy adults demonstrated that following a Mediterranean diet was associated with a reduced risk of death from heart disease and cancer, as well as a reduced incidence of Parkinson's and Alzheimer's diseases."

Plus, the food is delicious! With vibrant fruits and vegetables, a rich variety of spices and herbs, and slow-cooked meat as part of every meal, the flavors sit deeply and happily upon your tongue. The natural lack of sugar in the diet pulls the focus away from sweet, and satisfies with robust savory flavors instead. Less sugar and the addition of healthy fats (like olive oil) in a diet tends to result in weight loss. So, Mediterranean eating wins on three major counts—tastes great, less filling, and full of scientifically proven vitality!

The Flavors of the Region

The Mediterranean area is home to a large variety of cuisines. Italian food is, perhaps, one of the more familiar menus, but Mediterranean flavors range from Greek to Israeli cooking, from Moroccan to Albanian. Though the foods vary tremendously between areas, the primary focus of diets from each of the Mediterranean areas is vegetables, grains, and olive oil, with meat used sparingly, and sugar used even less.

The countries of the Mediterranean are numerous and varied. Though many of the same ingredients can be found in different countries' cuisines, some of the cuisines stand out as having a particular flavor profile. Knowing that there are distinctive spices or ingredient combinations in some of the more vibrant menus can help when you are putting together an entire menu, or swapping out spices and other ingredients in recipes.

Here are a few of the more familiar cuisines and the essential ingredients that go with each:

- **Italy:** Pasta, risotto, Parmesan cheese, olive oil, tomatoes, garlic, seafood, whole grains, beans, dark greens, nuts, red wine
- **Greece:** Olives, lemons, honey, Greek yogurt, cheese, sea salt, cucumbers, chickpeas, lamb, tomatoes, greens
- **France:** Bread, leeks, olive oil, shallots, cheese, tarragon, vinegar, wine, onions, celery, carrots, thyme, broths (chicken, beef, and veal), eggs
- **Morocco:** Almonds, olives, sesame seeds, lemons, wheat, barley, couscous, dried beans, dried fruits, honey, green tea
- **Egypt and Israel:** Barley, couscous, pasta, rice, wheat, tahini, olive oil, dates, figs, grapes, citrus, raisins, almonds, nuts, eggs, cheese, yogurt

Traditional Mediterranean Foods

Though there are dozens (maybe even hundreds!) of local variations on the Mediterranean Diet (Moroccan food, for example, is quite unique from Italian food), there are many overarching similarities in ingredients used between the regions. Many of the same fruits, vegetables, herbs, and spices grow abundantly throughout the region. And though they may be combined in unique ways depending on the regional recipes and traditional flavor combinations, this basic list of traditional foods is a good place to start in understanding the sorts of foods worth focusing on in a Mediterranean-style diet.

Grains

When cooking the Mediterranean way, you will find many recipes focused on whole grains, like barley, buckwheat, bulgur, farro, millet, oats, polenta, rice, couscous, and pasta. These grains supply valuable nutrients needed in a healthy diet, including vitamins, minerals, and fiber.

Vegetables

Mediterranean cuisine puts a huge emphasis on vegetables. Fresh, cooked vegetables bulk up meals and increase satiety. Vegetables used include artichokes, arugula, beets, broccoli, Brussels sprouts, cabbage, carrots, celery, collard greens, cucumbers, eggplants, fennel, kale, leeks, mushrooms, onions, peppers, potatoes, pumpkins, radishes, root vegetables, scallions, shallots, spinach, sweet potatoes, tomatoes, turnips, and zucchini.

Fruits

Fresh fruit and unsweetened or lightly sweetened cooked fruit is abundant in diets common to Mediterranean areas. Traditional recipes focus on honey as a sweetening agent for fruit-based desserts. Common fruits included in many recipes are apples, apricots, berries, cherries, dates, figs, grapes, melons, nectarines, oranges, pears, and tangerines.

Nuts, Beans, and Legumes

Mediterranean dishes are bulked up with the healthy fats, protein, and fiber naturally contained in nuts, beans, and legumes. Some of these often included in Mediterranean dishes are almonds, cannellini beans, cashews, chickpeas, fava beans, green beans, hazelnuts, kidney beans, lentils, pine nuts, pistachios, sesame seeds, split peas, tahini sauce, and walnuts.

Herbs and Spices

A variety of deeply aromatic spices are common to Mediterranean cuisine—adding flavor without adding calories or fat. Many of these spices are rich in antioxidants and natural minerals. Herbs and spices common to the Mediterranean diet are further detailed in the following section, but include basil, bay leaf, cardamom, cloves, cumin, curry, fennel, garlic, rosemary, saffron, tarragon, and thyme.

Cheese and Yogurt

Cheese and yogurt are included in low and moderate amounts in Mediterranean eating. They add protein and calcium to the diet, increase satiety, and lend flavor to many dishes—even when used in small amounts. Dairy commonly used in Mediterranean cooking includes brie, feta, goat cheese, Greek yogurt, Parmesan, pecorino, and ricotta.

Fish and Shellfish

A focus on fish and shellfish is often seen in Mediterranean eating, a natural extension of the very name of the diet itself, which comes from the areas around the Mediterranean Sea. Seafood common to the area includes clams, crab, flounder, mussels, octopus, oysters, salmon, sardines, sea bass, shrimp, squid, tilapia, and tuna.

Eggs

Eggs add filling protein to many Mediterranean recipes. They lend essential nutrition—especially to vegetarian diets, which might otherwise be void of vitamin B_{12}. In the areas surrounding the Mediterranean, chicken, duck, and quail eggs are often added to dishes.

Meats

Lean cut meat is the preferred option when cooking Mediterranean. Look for red meat, lamb, and pork with the fats trimmed, and the lowest fat percentage, for the most healthful options. White chicken breast is preferable over the darker meats of the bird, since it's lower in calories and packs a wallop of protein.

Olives and Olive Oil

Olives and olive oil are used plentifully in Mediterranean menus. Olive oil is used for cooking, baking, and drizzling over salads and vegetables. It lends flavor and healthy fat to dishes, and comes is a variety of "strengths"—with light olive oil lending a more mild flavor to dishes and cooking, and extra-virgin olive oil having a bolder, stronger flavor.

Olive oil is commonly used in Mediterranean cooking, but should be watched when heating in a skillet. If the oil reaches burning point—about 405°F—that can change the taste and texture and decrease the nutritional benefits of the oil.

Wines

When it comes to Mediterranean living, it's not just the food that inspires the residents—it's the wine too. The Mediterranean diet makes ample use of red, white, and sparkling wines, in sauces and stews or as flavorful sides to any meal.

If the idea of pairing wine with food feels overwhelming, remember one wine tip: If a specific food is grown in the area, it will pair well with wine grown there. So, if you're making a recipe like Tuscan Chicken and White Beans (Chapter 5), you can confidently pair it with a good Tuscan wine in your price range.

Though many dieters become concerned about the caloric content of alcohol, red and white wine typically contain just 100 calories per 5-ounce serving, so the addition of wine to dishes can be considered an indulgence worth making. Lots of flavor, not very many calories at all!

Chianti, Bordeaux, Champagne, and Burgundy, for example, are types of wines made from grapes grown in the region that gives them their name.

Essential Mediterranean Herbs

Having a pantry of herbs that complement cooking styles is a good way to encourage home cooking. When all ingredients are well stocked and ready for recipes, it's easier to find the motivation to cook from scratch.

Mediterranean cooking uses a broad variety of fragrant herbs and spices. Many may be new to cupboards accustomed to traditional cooking, so this list includes several uncommon herbs and spices that may need to be purchased for a Mediterranean-friendly spice cupboard:

- **Basil:** Sweet and peppery, basil is used in many Italian dishes. It's best when fresh, as dried basil often loses its vibrancy.
- **Bay leaves:** Bay leaves are often added to soups and stews, giving a deep sage-like flavor to recipes. Remove bay leaves before serving; they are not for consumption.
- **Caraway seeds:** These are peppery and perfect for breads, lentil and vegetable dishes, or even homemade pickles.
- **Cardamom:** Crushed pods create an aromatic, spicy-sweet powder perfect for both sweet and savory recipes, particularly those made with Moroccan flavors.
- **Coriander:** From the cilantro plant, but entirely unlike the cilantro flavor, coriander is warm and sweet, with a slight citrus scent.
- **Curry:** Yellow curry powder is mild and pungent. It is often cooked into a vegetable-based curry sauce, or stirred into soups for added flavor. Powdered curries come in a variety of heats, but the yellow curry powder typically found in most grocery stores is fairly mild and makes a delicious mix-in where curry is requested in a recipe.
- **Fennel:** Fennel seeds add a mild black-licorice flavor to everything from seafood to tomato dishes.
- **Marjoram:** With a taste like a light version of oregano, marjoram is often used in Greek, Italian, and French dishes. It lends a slight mint flavor to vegetables, sauces, and stews.
- **Saffron:** The bright red stigmas of the crocus flower, saffron lends a pungent, earthy flavor to dishes, and is often used in sauces, salad dressings, and as a complement to seafood and poultry.
- **Sage:** From the mint family, sage lends a mild, pine-and-herb-like aroma to meats, seafood, soups, breads, and salads. It is most

commonly used in Italian sauces to lend traditional Italian-herb flavor to recipes.

- **Sea salt:** Sea salt lends rich minerals to a Mediterranean diet. Varying in color and coarseness, sea salt enhances flavors of just about any savory dish, including meats, cooked and pickled vegetables, sauces, and dressings.
- **Tarragon:** Most often found in French food, tarragon is commonly used to add licorice-like flavor to sauces, dressings, vinegars, and meats. It is often blended with other herbs to create an aromatic spice blend.
- **Thyme:** Native to the Mediterranean region, thyme lends a pungent minty flavor to meats, sauces, stews, and marinades. Fresh thyme is most flavorful, but dried thyme retains the original flavor and can be easily stored in the pantry.
- **Turmeric:** This deep yellow spice adds vibrant color and a warm, mild flavor to everything from egg dishes to vegetables and sauces. The spice tastes of mild ginger, and can be used in place of saffron for some dishes.

ALERT

When adding new spices to a pantry, always write the date of purchase on the bottom of the spice bottle with a permanent marker. Doing so makes it easy to know how fresh the spices are, since some of them may not be used as quickly as others.

Slow Cooking the Mediterranean Way

Although Mediterranean cooking is associated with fresh food prepared quickly, that doesn't mean that it doesn't also have roots in slow cooking. For instance, Spanish paella is a dish that combines meat and rice, which requires time to develop its rich flavors. So does Greek kapama, a chicken dish that is warmly scented with cinnamon. And a beautiful Italian ragu Bolognese is a perfect fit for a slow cooker. So even though it may seem counterintuitive at first, fresh Mediterranean food and slow cooking really are a perfect combination.

ESSENTIAL

Healthy eating isn't just about the ingredients. It's also about the experience. Take time to slow down at dinnertime, rather than just rushing through it. Set a table, light candles to encourage relaxation, pour a glass of wine, and purposefully enjoy a slow meal. Doing so allows the brain to process fullness levels, so overeating is significantly reduced, and stress hormones are minimized when relaxation at mealtime is mindfully approached.

Slow Cooker Start Kit

Get ready for the recipes in this book by stocking up on the following items. This brief list includes the basics needed to make most of the recipes in this book.

- 4- to 5-quart slow cooker
- Nonstick spray
- Parchment paper
- Wooden spoons
- Slotted spoons
- Meat thermometer

Slow Cooker Features

Whether you pay $15 or $350 for your slow cooker unit, you'll generally get the following basics out of your unit. Most units produce essentially the same results, with the temperature on the low setting generally 190°F, and the temperature on high generally cooking at 250°F.

- **Slow cooker.** This portion of the unit is the electric part. It comes with a plug and dials for selecting the settings. Most units allow you to set the unit to OFF, WARM, LOW, or HIGH. While higher-end units offer digital features, consumer-priced units will use a dial to move between settings on the slow cooker. This portion of the slow cooker should never be immersed in water, and can be wiped clean with a damp rag once it's been disconnected from any electrical outlets.

- **Stoneware crock.** Inside the slow cooker unit is a stoneware crock. This ceramic bowl generally has easy-to-grab handles, making removal of the crock quick and simple. Most stoneware crocks are glazed with a nonstick glaze for ease of cleaning: many are dishwasher safe. Check the manufacturer instructions included with each unit to determine if yours is dishwasher safe. The crock can be removed from the slow cooker unit for serving, and should always be removed from the unit and allowed to cool to room temperature before immersing in water or cleaning.
- **Lid.** A glass lid should always be used when slow cooking, unless otherwise specified in a recipe. Lids are always included with slow cooker units, and help keep any moisture inside the crock as food cooks inside the slow cooker. They also help prevent splatter on walls or countertops. Because they're generally made of glass, lids can break. Most slow cooker manufacturers offer replacement lids for separate purchase at a minimal cost. Check the manufacturer's website for replacement part details, if desired.

QUESTION

Is it a slow cooker or a Crock-Pot?
Slow cookers and Crock-Pots are the same thing! The difference is Crock-Pot is a trademarked name. Dozens of companies manufacture slow cookers in a variety of sizes, colors, and styles. However, most slow cookers have the same basic features.

Slow Cooker Sizes

There are dozens of slow cooker sizes and options, but three basic models worth considering when purchasing a slow cooker are:

- **Family size (6-quart slow cooker):** Large enough to double most of the recipes in this book, a 6-quart slow cooker is great for making big batches. Feed a whole family, effortlessly host a potluck, or make enough to freeze as leftovers. The large slow cooker is perfect for people who traditionally cook for a crowd.

- **Standard (3- to 4-quart slow cooker):** Perfect for recipes made for 2–6 people, the medium or "standard" sized slow cooker is big enough to feed a small family, and small enough to easily store in kitchen cabinets since it's about the size of a large bowl. Most of the recipes in this book were created for this medium size of slow cooker.
- **Small (16-ounce):** This tiny slow cooker is perfect for making hot dips for parties, or small amounts of cheese or chocolate fondue. The smaller version is likewise perfect for singles looking for a simple way to cook one-serving meals in a slow cooker.

Tips and Tricks for Slow Cookers

With a slow cooker ready for use in your kitchen, there are a few ways to get the most out of your unit. From cooking food evenly to keeping your slow cooker clean and well maintained, these insider tips and tricks will help you master the art of slow cooker cooking!

- **Don't overfill the slow cooker.** That can keep meat from not cooking all the way through, and could cause a potential food threat. Whenever possible, use a meat thermometer to check the temperature of the meat or poultry. And when using very large cuts of meat, such as a whole chicken, make sure you cut it into pieces first.
- **Don't peek!** As tempting as it is to check up on the meal—don't. Opening the lid means that you lose 20–30 minutes of heat that needs to build back up again. Only lift the lid to check when the dish is close to being done, about 15–20 minutes before the specified cooking time.
- **Temperature is important,** because 1 hour on high equals 2 hours on low. For some recipes it's preferable to cook on low so the dish won't get dried out if you think you may be running late.
- **Trim excess fat** off of meats to avoid any greasiness in the finished dish.
- **Keep it clean.** Keep slow cookers clean by spraying them with a coat of nonstick olive oil cooking spray before making *any* recipe.

Alternately, line slow cookers with parchment or aluminum foil to keep cleanup easy.

ESSENTIAL

Keep slow cookers in good shape by wiping the stoneware crock clean. If splatters of food get on the outside of the slow cooker, wipe them immediately with a warm, wet rag to avoid burned bits of food sticking permanently to the outside of the cooker.

Pantry Essentials

Stock the pantry with these items and you'll be ready to make just about every recipe in this book! The following list includes shelf-stable ingredients commonly used in this book. Before making any recipe, be sure to check the ingredient list to confirm that all items needed for the recipe are in your kitchen!

- Arborio rice
- Beans, canned or dried
- Black peppercorns and a grinder
- Brown rice
- Chives
- Cinnamon
- Dried basil
- Dried cherries
- Dried cranberries
- Dried oregano
- Dried rosemary
- Dried thyme
- Fresh basil
- Fresh flat-leaf parsley
- Fresh lemons
- Fresh limes
- Fresh oregano
- Fresh rosemary

- Garlic
- Goat cheese
- Kalamata olives
- Kosher salt
- Lemon juice
- Lime juice
- Manzanillo olives
- Niçoise olives
- Olive oil
- Onions
- Pasta
- Polenta
- Potatoes
- Rice, brown and wild
- Saffron or turmeric
- Sea salt
- Shallots
- Tomatoes, fresh and canned
- Tomato paste
- Walnuts
- Wild rice

Let's Get Started!

With these insights into the basics of Mediterranean cuisine and the basics of slow cooking, all that's needed for a beautiful dinner is a book full of recipes. The next fifteen chapters detail everything from breakfast to dessert, all created with the healthy Mediterranean diet in mind. Whether you need a hearty frittata at the beginning of the day or a hot dinner at the end of the day, the 300 recipes in this book will invite Mediterranean cooking—quickly, easily, and vibrantly—into any kitchen.

CHAPTER 2

Breakfast

Potato Frittata with Cheese and Herbs

Use both nonstick spray and butter in this recipe, or the starch in the potatoes will stick. Add chopped fresh herbs, additional shredded cheese, or sour cream to garnish the frittata before serving.

INGREDIENTS | SERVES 4

1 large Yukon gold potato, peeled

4 teaspoons butter, melted

Nonstick olive oil cooking spray

6 large eggs

½ cup grated Parmesan cheese

6 sage leaves, minced

½ teaspoon kosher salt

½ teaspoon ground black pepper

An Untraditional Frittata

Usually frittatas are open omelets that are started in a heavy skillet on the stove and then finished by broiling in the oven. Using this slow cooker method you can put together the frittata the night before, then get up early and place it in the slow cooker—2 hours later, breakfast is hot and ready!

1. Using a mandoline, slice the potato as thinly as possible. Grease a 4- to 5-quart slow cooker with melted butter and a spritz of nonstick cooking spray and place the potatoes on the bottom in a thin layer.

2. In a medium bowl, beat the eggs well. Add the cheese, sage, salt, and pepper; stir to combine. Pour over the potatoes.

3. Cover and cook on high for 2 hours or on low for 4 hours.

4. Cut into squares and serve at once.

PER SERVING: Calories: 290 | Fat: 18g | Protein: 16g | Sodium: 580mg | Fiber: 2g | Carbohydrates: 16g | Sugar: 2g

Spinach with Baked Eggs and Cheese

*This is an excellent brunch, lunch, or supper. Everyone loves it,
and even after a tough day, it's easy to put together.*

INGREDIENTS | SERVES 4

Nonstick olive oil cooking spray

1½ cups cornbread crumbs

3 (10-ounce) packages frozen spinach, thawed, moisture squeezed out

2 tablespoons butter or margarine, melted

½ cup shredded Swiss cheese

½ teaspoon nutmeg

1 teaspoon kosher salt

½ teaspoon ground black pepper

1 cup heavy cream

8 large eggs

Herbs and Spices

People often confuse herbs with spices. Herbs are green and are the leaves of plants—the only herb (in Western cooking) that is a flower is lavender. Frequently used herbs include parsley, basil, oregano, thyme, rosemary, cilantro, and mint. Spices are roots, tubers, barks, berries, or seeds. These include pepper, cinnamon, nutmeg, allspice, cumin, turmeric, ginger, cardamom, and coriander.

1. Grease a 4- to 5-quart slow cooker with nonstick cooking spray. Sprinkle cornbread crumbs on the bottom of the slow cooker.

2. In a medium bowl, mix the spinach, butter, cheese, nutmeg, salt, and pepper together. Stir in the cream. Spread the spinach-cheese mixture on top of the cornbread crumbs.

3. Using the back of a tablespoon, make 8 depressions in the spinach mixture. Break open the eggs and place one egg in each hole.

4. Cover and cook on low for 3 hours or on high for 1½–2 hours until the yolks are cooked through, but not hard.

PER SERVING: Calories: 578 | Fat: 43g | Protein: 26g | Sodium: 935mg | Fiber: 7g | Carbohydrates: 26g | Sugar: 3g

Breakfast Spanish Tortilla

Traditionally served as tapas or an appetizer in Spanish restaurants and bars, this version of the Spanish tortilla removes a lot of the fat and makes a healthy breakfast casserole. Conventionally it does not contain cheese, but feel free to sprinkle some on top in the last 30 minutes of cooking.

INGREDIENTS | SERVES 6

3 tablespoons olive oil

2 small onions, peeled and finely diced

10 large eggs

1 teaspoon kosher salt

1 teaspoon ground black pepper

4 teaspoons butter, melted

Nonstick olive oil cooking spray

3 large baking potatoes, peeled and thinly sliced

1. Heat olive oil in a skillet over medium heat. Slowly cook onions in olive oil until lightly brown and caramelized, about 5–6 minutes.

2. In a large bowl, whisk together the eggs, salt, and pepper.

3. Grease a 4- to 5-quart slow cooker with melted butter and a spritz of nonstick cooking spray and place half the potatoes on the bottom in a thin layer. Pour half the eggs over the potato layer. Repeat layers, adding onions, ending with the last of the whisked eggs.

4. Cover and cook on low for 6–7 hours or on high for 3½–4 hours.

PER SERVING: Calories: 367 | Fat: 18g | Protein: 15g | Sodium: 520mg | Fiber: 3g | Carbohydrates: 36g | Sugar: 3g

Eggs Florentine

Freshly ground black pepper goes well in this dish. You can use up to a teaspoon in the recipe. If you prefer to go lighter on the seasoning to accommodate individual tastes, be sure to have a pepper grinder at the table for those who want to add more.

INGREDIENTS | SERVES 4

Nonstick olive oil cooking spray

9 ounces (2 cups) grated Cheddar cheese, divided

1 (10-ounce) package frozen spinach, thawed

1 (8-ounce) can sliced mushrooms, drained

1 small onion, peeled and diced

6 large eggs

1 cup heavy cream

½ teaspoon Italian seasoning

½ teaspoon garlic powder

½ teaspoon freshly ground black pepper

Make It Dairy-Free

To make egg casseroles dairy-free, replace the cream with full-fat coconut milk. For the Cheddar cheese, there are many dairy-free alternatives available now; one in particular called Daiya is sold in shreds and melts beautifully in dishes like this.

1. Grease a 4- to 5-quart slow cooker with nonstick spray. Spread 1 cup of the grated cheese over the bottom of the slow cooker.

2. Drain the spinach and squeeze out any excess moisture; add a layer on top of the cheese. Next add the drained mushrooms in a layer and then top them with the onion.

3. In a small bowl, beat together the eggs, cream, Italian seasoning, garlic powder, and pepper. Pour over the layers in the slow cooker. Top with the remaining cup of cheese.

4. Cover and cook on high for 2 hours or until eggs are set.

PER SERVING: Calories: 611 | Fat: 51g | Protein: 30g | Sodium: 810mg | Fiber: 4g | Carbohydrates: 11g | Sugar: 3.5g

Baklava Oatmeal

If you've ever enjoyed baklava—sweet, nutty dessert bars found at many Greek restaurants—you're going to love this simple recipe for overnight Baklava Oatmeal. Baked with cinnamon topped with a sweet baklava streusel and a drizzle of honey, this healthful oatmeal is a delicious breakfast to wake up to any morning.

INGREDIENTS | SERVES 4

Nonstick olive oil cooking spray

4 cups water

1 cup steel-cut oats

1 teaspoon cinnamon

½ cup walnuts, crushed

½ teaspoon cinnamon

1 teaspoon sugar

½ teaspoon water

4 tablespoons honey

About Steel-Cut Oats

Steel-cut oats are the whole-grain, inner parts of the oat kernel that have been cut into pieces. They generally take longer to cook than traditional rolled oats, so preparing them in the slow cooker is the perfect way to bake them for breakfast!

1. Spray the bottom of a small (1½- to 3-quart) slow cooker with nonstick olive oil cooking spray.

2. Place 4 cups water, oats, and cinnamon in slow cooker. Stir until combined.

3. Cover and cook on low overnight, for 7–8 hours.

4. Just before serving, place walnuts in a large skillet over medium heat. Sprinkle with cinnamon, sugar, and ½ teaspoon water. Cook just until the sugar begins to bubble and the walnuts turn a light, toasted golden brown color.

5. Spoon walnut mixture over hot bowls of oatmeal.

6. Drizzle with honey before serving.

PER SERVING: Calories: 242 | Fat: 11g | Protein: 5g | Sodium: 2.5mg | Fiber: 3.5g | Carbohydrates: 34g | Sugar: 19g

Fig and Cherry Oatmeal

*By placing the ingredients in the slow cooker before bed,
you will wake up to a hot, hearty, and fruity bowl of oatmeal.*

INGREDIENTS | SERVES 2

1 teaspoon olive oil
1 cup steel-cut oats
1 cup dried figs
1 cup dried cherries
½ vanilla bean, scraped
⅛ teaspoon cloves
½ teaspoon cinnamon
4 cups water
½ cup whole milk

1. Grease a 1½-quart slow cooker with olive oil.

2. Place oats, figs, cherries, vanilla bean pulp, cloves, cinnamon, water, and milk in slow cooker.

3. Cover and cook on low for 8–9 hours.

4. Serve hot.

PER SERVING: Calories: 446 | Fat: 8g | Protein: 10.5g | Sodium: 36mg | Fiber: 13g | Carbohydrates: 90g | Sugar: 49g

Tomato, Oregano, and Goat Cheese Breakfast Casserole

Tomatoes and oregano pair elegantly with goat cheese to create a luscious casserole that will work just as well on a midweek morning as it will for a breakfast party.

INGREDIENTS | SERVES 4

8 large eggs

1 cup whole milk

1 teaspoon kosher salt

1 teaspoon freshly ground black pepper

2 cups cherry tomatoes, halved

¼ cup chopped fresh oregano

1 (4-ounce) log goat cheese, chopped

1 teaspoon olive oil

Super Herb

Oregano is considered to be a "super herb" by the USDA! It has 3–20 times more antioxidants than any other herb. And it's even more powerful than blueberries when it comes to antioxidant health properties. So, add 2 tablespoons of oregano to your daily meal plan, and reap the potential rewards!

1. Whisk eggs, milk, salt, and pepper together in a medium bowl. Stir in the tomatoes, oregano, and goat cheese and mix well again.

2. Grease a 4- to 5-quart slow cooker with olive oil.

3. Pour egg mixture into slow cooker and cook on low for 4–6 hours or on high for 2–3 hours. The casserole is done when a knife inserted into the center comes out clean.

4. Serve immediately.

PER SERVING: Calories: 340 | Fat: 23g | Protein: 24g | Sodium: 857mg | Fiber: 2g | Carbohydrates: 10g | Sugar: 7g

Ricotta and Parmesan Pancake

A savory slow-cooked pancake filled with ricotta is guaranteed to make breakfast, brunch, or dinner a celebratory meal. To make this even more festive, top the pancake with a salad full of gorgeous, multi-hued cherry tomatoes.

INGREDIENTS | SERVES 4

¾ cup all-purpose flour
1 tablespoon baking powder
2 large eggs
⅔ cup whole milk
½ teaspoon kosher salt
½ teaspoon freshly ground black pepper
1 cup ricotta cheese
½ cup Parmesan cheese
1 teaspoon olive oil

Make Ricotta Yourself

Did you know that you can make rich, homemade, fresh ricotta with very little effort? Simply bring a gallon of milk to a light boil. When the mixture boils, stir constantly while adding ¼ cup of lemon juice and 1 teaspoon of salt. Stir for 3 minutes until the mixture has curdled. Let the ricotta drain for 1 hour through a layer of cheesecloth, and keep refrigerated for up to 2 days. It's the perfect way to use milk that's nearing its expiration date!

1. Whisk together the flour, baking powder, eggs, and milk in a medium bowl. Season with salt and pepper.

2. Add the ricotta and Parmesan to the egg mixture and stir well.

3. Grease a 4- to 5-quart slow cooker with olive oil.

4. Pour the ricotta mixture into the slow cooker and cook on high for 2–3 hours. The pancake is done when a knife in the center comes out clean.

5. Cut into wedges and serve immediately.

PER SERVING: Calories: 279 | Fat: 14g | Protein: 15g | Sodium: 807mg | Fiber: 1g | Carbohydrates: 23g | Sugar: 2.5g

Leek and Feta Frittata with Dill

The classic combination of leeks and dill paired with tangy feta is irresistible.
Note: The recipe doesn't call for much salt, because the feta imparts its own salty flavor to the eggs.

INGREDIENTS | SERVES 4

8 large eggs

½ teaspoon kosher salt

½ teaspoon freshly ground black pepper

1 tablespoon plus 1 teaspoon olive oil, divided

3 leeks (white and pale green parts only), sliced into ½" pieces

2 teaspoons lemon juice

¾ cup feta

2 teaspoons chopped fresh dill

1. In a large bowl, whisk the eggs together and season with salt and pepper. Set aside.

2. In medium skillet, heat 1 tablespoon of olive oil over medium heat until it shimmers, about 1 minute. Add the leeks and sauté for 5 minutes or until softened. Add the lemon juice and sauté for another minute.

3. Add the leeks to the egg mixture and stir well. Stir in the feta and dill.

4. Grease a 4- to 5-quart slow cooker with remaining olive oil.

5. Pour frittata mixture into the slow cooker and cook on low for 4–6 hours or on high for 2–3 hours. The frittata is cooked through when a knife in the center comes out clean. Serve immediately.

PER SERVING: Calories: 303 | Fat: 21g | Protein: 17g | Sodium: 762mg | Fiber: 1g | Carbohydrates: 12g | Sugar: 4.5g

Tri-Colored Pepper and Mozzarella Frittata

*This vibrantly hued dish is as gorgeous to look at as it is delicious to eat.
And given something as pretty as this, children won't mind eating their vegetables!*

INGREDIENTS | SERVES 4

8 large eggs
1 teaspoon kosher salt
1 teaspoon freshly ground black pepper
½ cup diced red bell pepper
½ cup diced yellow bell pepper
½ cup diced orange bell pepper
1 cup shredded mozzarella
½ teaspoon cayenne
1 teaspoon olive oil

Color for Health

Red, yellow, and orange peppers get their good looks, as well as some of their most noteworthy health effects, from plant pigments called carotenoids. These pigments act like sunscreen, protecting the ripening peppers from sun damage. As it turns out, these pigments have a similar safeguarding effect on us. Like other antioxidants, carotenoids help boost immunity and fight cancer and heart disease.

1. Whisk the eggs, salt, and pepper in a medium bowl. Add the bell peppers, mozzarella, and cayenne to the egg mixture.

2. Grease the inside of a 4- to 5-quart slow cooker with olive oil.

3. Pour the egg and bell pepper mixture into the slow cooker and cook on low for 4–6 hours or on high for 2–3 hours. The frittata is done when a knife inserted into the center comes out clean.

4. Serve immediately.

PER SERVING: Calories: 257 | Fat: 18g | Protein: 19g | Sodium: 847mg | Fiber: 1g | Carbohydrates: 5g | Sugar: 3g

Strawberry Pancake with Roasted Blueberry-Mint Sauce

Roasting blueberries brings out their natural sugar, and their wonderful sweetness combines perfectly with strawberries. The mint brings all the fruit together in a wonderfully fresh flavor combination. Lemon slices would make a perfect addition to the plate.

INGREDIENTS | SERVES 4

¾ cup all-purpose flour

1 tablespoon baking powder

1 tablespoon sugar, divided

2 large eggs

⅔ cup whole milk

1 cup diced fresh (or frozen and thawed) strawberries

1 tablespoon plus 1 teaspoon olive oil, divided

1½ cups whole fresh (or frozen and thawed) blueberries

1 tablespoon chopped fresh mint

1. Whisk together the flour, baking powder, sugar, eggs, and milk in a medium bowl. Add the strawberries and stir well to combine.

2. Grease the inside of a 4- to 5-quart slow cooker with 1 teaspoon of olive oil. Pour the pancake batter inside the slow cooker and cook on high for 1½–2 hours.

3. Preheat oven to 350°F. Place the blueberries in a small (7" × 11"), rimmed baking pan with 1 tablespoon of olive oil. Bake for 20–25 minutes or until blueberries implode. Remove from oven, pour blueberries into a small bowl, and stir in mint.

4. Cut the pancake into wedges and serve with blueberry sauce.

5. Serve immediately.

PER SERVING: Calories: 248 | Fat: 9g | Protein: 7.5g | Sodium: 420mg | Fiber: 3g | Carbohydrates: 35g | Sugar: 13g

Savory French Toast with Herb Purée

French toast is traditionally sweet, but in the Mediterranean, savory food is popular for breakfast. This breakfast not only fills you up; it's healthy and beautiful too.

INGREDIENTS | SERVES 4

6 large eggs

3½ cups whole milk

1½ teaspoons kosher salt, divided

2 teaspoons freshly ground black pepper, divided

3 tablespoons plus 1 teaspoon olive oil, divided

1 (16-ounce) loaf of day-old Italian bread, cut into 2" cubes

½ cup flat-leaf parsley

2 tablespoons fresh thyme

1 tablespoon lemon juice

Herb Purée

The herb purée is a delicious and versatile condiment to keep on hand for many meal add-ins. Add it to cooked pasta, serve it with grilled chicken or beef, or spread it on crusty bread for a simple and flavorful appetizer. Add ¼ cup Parmesan cheese to give it an added depth of flavor. The herb purée will keep for 3 days in the refrigerator.

1. Whisk together the eggs, milk, 1 teaspoon salt, and 1½ teaspoons pepper. Grease the inside of a 4- to 5-quart slow cooker with a teaspoon of olive oil. Place the bread in the bottom of the slow cooker and pour the egg mixture over it. Cook on low for 4–6 hours or on high for 2–3 hours.

2. Place the parsley, thyme, 3 tablespoons of olive oil, ½ teaspoon salt, ½ teaspoon pepper, and lemon juice in a blender. Process until smooth. Reserve.

3. Serve French toast immediately with herb purée.

PER SERVING: Calories: 670 | Fat: 28g | Protein: 29g | Sodium: 1,810mg | Fiber: 3g | Carbohydrates: 75g | Sugar: 15g

Rosemary and Pancetta Polenta

Instead of oatmeal in the morning, why not try some hearty polenta with fresh rosemary and Parmesan, served with crispy pancetta? You will start your morning with a spring in your step.

INGREDIENTS | SERVES 4

2 cups polenta (not quick cooking) or corn meal

7 cups hot water

2 tablespoons olive oil

1½ teaspoons kosher salt

1 teaspoon freshly ground black pepper

2 teaspoons chopped fresh rosemary

1 cup shredded Parmesan cheese

6 pieces pancetta, diced into 1" pieces

1. Whisk together the polenta, hot water, olive oil, salt, pepper, and rosemary in a 4- to 5-quart slow cooker. Stir well. Gently whisk in Parmesan.

2. Cook on low for 3–4 hours or on high for 2 hours. The mixture should be smooth and without any clumps.

3. Preheat oven to 400°F.

4. Line a baking sheet with parchment. Place pancetta on parchment paper and bake for 5–10 minutes or until crispy. Drain on paper towels.

5. Serve polenta garnished with crispy pancetta.

PER SERVING: Calories: 616 | Fat: 34g | Protein: 19g | Sodium: 1,575mg | Fiber: 3g | Carbohydrates: 56g | Sugar: 1g

Panzanella Strata

Panzanella is a traditional Tuscan salad that is a popular way to use tomatoes when the garden is overflowing with them. Celebrate the flavors of summer in this casserole loaded with tomatoes, basil, and onion.

INGREDIENTS | SERVES 4

8 large eggs

2 cups skim milk

1 teaspoon kosher salt

1 teaspoon freshly ground black pepper

½ cup finely diced red onion

1 teaspoon olive oil

1 day-old baguette, cut into 1" cubes

1½ cups cherry tomatoes, halved

½ cup chopped fresh basil

1. In a large bowl, whisk together the eggs and milk. Stir in salt, pepper, and onion.

2. Grease a 4- to 5-quart slow cooker with olive oil.

3. Combine the baguette cubes and tomatoes in the slow cooker.

4. Pour the egg mixture over the tomatoes and bread.

5. Cook on low for 4 hours and serve the strata topped with fresh basil.

PER SERVING: Calories: 224 | Fat: 12g | Protein: 17g | Sodium: 787mg | Fiber: 1g | Carbohydrates: 11g | Sugar: 9g

Egg, Tomato, and Pesto Breakfast Bruschetta

One of the joys of eating Mediterranean-style is that there are beautiful vegetables at every meal, including breakfast.

INGREDIENTS | SERVES 4

1½ teaspoons plus 1 tablespoon olive oil, divided

8 large eggs

1 teaspoon kosher salt

1 teaspoon freshly ground black pepper

1 large tomato, diced into ½" pieces

1 teaspoon coarse sea salt, crushed

½ loaf of Italian or French bread, cut into 4 slices

¼ cup pesto

1 roasted red pepper, diced

½ cup shredded mozzarella cheese

1. Grease a 4- to 5-quart slow cooker with 1½ teaspoons olive oil. In a large bowl, whisk eggs, kosher salt, and pepper together until frothy. Pour into slow cooker and cook on low for 1 hour. Break eggs apart and cook on low for an additional hour.

2. Place tomato pieces on a plate and season with sea salt. Let sit for 15 minutes and blot dry with towel.

3. While tomatoes are resting, preheat a grill. Brush bread slices with remaining olive oil. Grill for 3 minutes. Flip and grill for 3 more minutes. Spread pesto on each slice of grilled bread.

4. Stir tomatoes, peppers, and mozzarella into cooked eggs in the slow cooker. Divide egg mixture between grilled bread slices.

5. Serve immediately.

PER SERVING: Calories: 464 | Fat: 34g | Protein: 20g | Sodium: 1,564mg | Fiber: 2g | Carbohydrates: 20g | Sugar: 3g

Rye-Pumpernickel Strata with Bleu and Goat Cheese

Savory breakfast is traditional in the Mediterranean.
This dish is perfect to serve at brunch as well.

INGREDIENTS | SERVES 6

3 (1½-inch) slices seedless rye bread

3 (1½-inch) slices pumpernickel bread

1½ teaspoons olive oil

8 large eggs

¼ cup skim milk

½ teaspoon fresh-cracked black pepper

½ cup fresh spinach, chopped

¼ small red onion, peeled and diced

¼ cup plain low-fat Greek yogurt

2 ounces bleu cheese, crumbled

2 ounces goat cheese, crumbled

1. Preheat oven to 200°F. Tear the bread into large pieces. Place bread on a large (12" × 17") rimmed cookie sheet. Bake for 10–15 minutes or until bread is dry and feels "day-old."

2. Grease a 4- to 5-quart slow cooker with the oil. Place bread in slow cooker. In a large bowl, whisk eggs, milk, and black pepper together until frothy. Add spinach, onion, yogurt, and cheeses. Whisk well. Pour egg mixture over bread in the slow cooker.

3. Cover and cook on low for 4 hours, or until internal temperature is 170°F. Turn off heat and uncover strata.

4. Let sit for 30 minutes and serve.

PER SERVING: Calories: 273 | Fat: 14g | Protein: 17g | Sodium: 449mg | Fiber: 1g | Carbohydrates: 18g | Sugar: 2.5g

Breakfast Risotto

Serve this as you would cooked oatmeal: topped with additional brown sugar, raisins or other dried fruit, and milk.

INGREDIENTS | SERVES 6

Nonstick olive oil cooking spray
¼ cup butter, melted
1½ cups Arborio rice
3 small apples, peeled, cored, and sliced
1½ teaspoons ground cinnamon
⅛ teaspoon freshly ground nutmeg
⅛ teaspoon ground cloves
⅛ teaspoon kosher salt
⅓ cup packed light brown sugar
1 cup apple juice
3 cups whole milk

1. Spray the inside of a 4- to 5-quart slow cooker with cooking spray. Add butter and rice to the slow cooker; stir to coat the rice in the butter.

2. Add the remaining ingredients and stir to combine. Cover and cook on low for 6–7 hours or on high for 2–3 hours until the rice is cooked through and is firm, but not mushy.

3. Serve immediately.

PER SERVING: Calories: 419 | Fat: 12g | Protein: 7g | Sodium: 108mg | Fiber: 2.5g | Carbohydrates: 71g | Sugar: 29g

Almond and Dried Cherry Granola

Using the slow cooker virtually eliminates any chance of overcooking or burning the granola.

INGREDIENTS | SERVES 24

5 cups old-fashioned rolled oats
1 cup slivered almonds
¼ cup mild honey
¼ cup canola oil
1 teaspoon vanilla
½ cup dried tart cherries
¼ cup unsweetened flaked coconut
½ cup sunflower seeds

1. Place the oats and almonds in a 4- to 5-quart slow cooker. Drizzle with honey, oil, and vanilla. Stir the mixture to distribute the syrup evenly. Cook on high, uncovered, for 1½ hours, stirring every 15–20 minutes.

2. Add the cherries, coconut, and sunflower seeds. Reduce heat to low. Cook for 4 hours, uncovered, stirring every 20 minutes.

3. Allow the granola to cool fully, and then store it in an airtight container for up to 1 month.

PER SERVING: Calories: 140 | Fat: 7g | Protein: 4g | Sodium: 2mg | Fiber: 2.5g | Carbohydrates: 16g | Sugar: 4g

Overnight Marinara Poached Eggs

You can make dinner and dessert in your slow cooker, but did you know you can poach eggs, too? Serve this unusual breakfast with slices of Italian or French bread to soak up the delicious sauce.

INGREDIENTS | SERVES 6

2 tablespoons olive oil

1 (28-ounce) can fire-roasted diced tomatoes

1 (15-ounce) can crushed tomatoes

2 cloves garlic, crushed

1½ tablespoons sugar

¾ teaspoon kosher salt

6 large eggs

½ cup fresh basil, roughly chopped

¼ cup shredded Parmesan cheese

Flavor Without Adding More Fat

Though you can make this recipe with a plain olive oil, try swapping in a rosemary, garlic, or spicy-flavored olive oil for even more flavor and not an ounce of extra fat!

1. Drizzle the olive oil across the bottom of a 6-quart slow cooker.

2. Pour the diced tomatoes, crushed tomatoes, garlic, sugar, and salt into the slow cooker. Stir with a wooden spoon to mix.

3. Cover the slow cooker and set to low. Allow sauce to cook overnight.

4. In the morning, remove the cover of the slow cooker and use a wooden spoon to make 6 wells in the sauce. Crack each egg and gently pour into one of the wells you've created in the sauce.

5. Cover and set slow cooker to high. Cook for 15–20 minutes for soft cooked eggs, or 20–25 minutes to cook the yolks through.

6. Use a ladle to scoop the eggs and sauce into individual bowls. Top with basil and cheese.

7. Serve immediately.

PER SERVING: Calories: 169 | Fat: 10g | Protein: 9g | Sodium: 689mg | Fiber: 2g | Carbohydrates: 12g | Sugar: 8g

Overnight Spiced Cranberry Quinoa

This delicious hot cereal with the classic Mediterranean flavors of lemon, nutmeg, and cloves is chock-full of protein! You'll love the way this cereal cooks up sweet and creamy, with a burst of tart cranberries in every bite.

INGREDIENTS | SERVES 4

1 cup uncooked quinoa
2 cups unsweetened almond milk
1 tablespoon pumpkin pie spice
½ teaspoon vanilla
Juice and zest of 1 lemon
2 tablespoons agave or pure maple syrup
½ cup fresh cranberries

1. In a medium bowl, rinse quinoa in water. Drain.

2. Place quinoa in a small (1½- to 3-quart) slow cooker with almond milk, pumpkin pie spice, vanilla, lemon juice and zest, syrup, and cranberries.

3. Cover and cook for 1½–2 hours. If the cereal begins to get overly thick and clumpy, add an extra 2–3 tablespoons of almond milk or water to the slow cooker.

4. Once the quinoa has expanded in size and is tender, use a fork to fluff the cereal.

5. Spoon into a bowl and enjoy!

PER SERVING: Calories: 267 | Fat: 5g | Protein: 10g | Sodium: 66mg | Fiber: 5g | Carbohydrates: 47g | Sugar: 14g

Eureka Egg White Omelet

In Greek, the word eureka! is used to celebrate a discovery. (It means "I have found!")
After enjoying this healthful, flavorful egg white omelet, you'll want to shout "Eureka!"
and pat yourself on the back for finding such a delicious, simple breakfast dish!

INGREDIENTS | SERVES 4

Nonstick olive oil cooking spray

3 cups mushrooms

4 cups fresh spinach

1 (16-ounce) carton egg whites or 12 egg whites (from large eggs)

1 clove garlic, chopped

1 tablespoon dried onions

¾ teaspoon kosher salt

½ teaspoon ground black pepper

½ teaspoon red pepper flakes

⅓ cup shredded Parmesan cheese, divided

Eat Egg Whites and Save on Calories

One omega-3 enriched egg generally has 71 calories, but enjoy the egg white and you're consuming just 17 calories per egg. That's a savings of more than 50 calories by using egg whites only!

1. Spray the bottom of a small (1½- to 3-quart) slow cooker with nonstick olive oil cooking spray.

2. Layer the mushrooms and spinach in the bottom of the slow cooker.

3. In a small bowl, whisk together egg whites, garlic, onions, salt, pepper, red pepper flakes, and ¼ cup Parmesan cheese. Pour over the mushrooms and spinach.

4. Sprinkle remaining cheese over the egg mixture.

5. Cover the slow cooker and cook on low for 5–6 hours.

6. Remove from slow cooker, slice, and serve.

PER SERVING: Calories: 144 | Fat: 5g | Protein: 21g | Sodium: 935mg | Fiber: 1g | Carbohydrates: 5g | Sugar: 2g

Hard-Cooked Eggs with Olive Oil Drizzle

Hard-cooked eggs are a perfect high-protein snack, rich in nutrients. But making them can be tricky. They can cook too long or not long enough, they might crack in the pan if they're boiled too quickly, or they can be hard to peel. Cooking eggs in the slow cooker resolves all of these issues, yielding perfect results every time.

INGREDIENTS | SERVES 12

12 large eggs

1½ teaspoons salt, divided

2 tablespoons white vinegar

3 tablespoons olive oil, divided

1 teaspoon Italian seasoning

½ teaspoon cayenne pepper

1. Place eggs, 1 teaspoon salt, vinegar, and 1 tablespoon oil in a 4- to 5-quart slow cooker. Cover eggs with water. Cover and cook on high for 2½ hours. Turn slow cooker off and allow water to cool completely before removing eggs.

2. In a small bowl, whisk together remaining olive oil, Italian seasoning, cayenne pepper, and remaining salt. Set aside.

3. Shell eggs. Slice in half. Drizzle with olive oil mixture. Serve and enjoy.

PER SERVING: Calories: 101 | Fat: 8g | Protein: 6g | Sodium: 364mg | Fiber: 0g | Carbohydrates: 0g | Sugar: 0g

Breads and Rolls

Parmesan Olive Focaccia

Whole-wheat focaccia cooks up dense and delicious when made in the slow cooker. The dough is surprisingly simple to make. Then you can set it and forget it until it's hot and ready to devour!

INGREDIENTS | SERVES 9

Nonstick olive oil cooking spray
2 cups white whole-wheat flour
1 cup white all-purpose flour
1 packet dry yeast
1 teaspoon dried rosemary
¾ teaspoon sea salt
1 cup warm water (approximately 80°F)
¼ cup Kalamata or Spanish olives, sliced
¼ cup Parmesan cheese, shredded

Why Kalamata Olives?

Kalamata olives are one of the gems of Mediterranean cooking. They are large, purple-black olives, generally packed in vinegar, so they're full of flavor. A natural source of vitamin E, they're also a healthful addition to a well-balanced diet.

1. Spray the bottom of a large (6- to 6½-quart) slow cooker with nonstick olive oil cooking spray.

2. In a large bowl, stir together the flours, yeast, rosemary, salt, and water until well combined in a soft dough.

3. Cover with a clean towel and allow dough to sit in a warm, dry place for 60 minutes.

4. Place dough in the unheated slow cooker. Press down with your fingers to spread the dough to the edges of the slow cooker and make small holes in the top of the dough.

5. Sprinkle olives and cheese over dough.

6. Cover and allow to rise for 30 more minutes before turning slow cooker on to low.

7. After 30 minutes on low, turn slow cooker to high and allow bread to cook 1½–2 hours, or until golden brown.

8. Turn bread out onto a serving platter and slice into 9 pieces.

PER SERVING: Calories: 222 | Fat: 8g | Protein: 7g | Sodium: 299mg | Fiber: 4g | Carbohydrates: 31g | Sugar: 0g

Manzanillo and Kalamata Rolls

You can replace the Manzanillo and Kalamata olives with any other combination of olives that appeals to you.

INGREDIENTS | SERVES 6

2 teaspoons sugar

1 tablespoon active dry yeast

½ cup warm water (approximately 80°F)

½ cup whole milk

1 large egg

2 tablespoons plus 1 teaspoon olive oil, divided

1½ teaspoons kosher salt

1 teaspoon freshly ground black pepper

3¼ cups all-purpose flour, divided

¼ cup Manzanillo olives, chopped

¼ cup Kalamata olives, roughly chopped

1. In a small bowl, combine the sugar and yeast. Add the warm water and let sit for 5 minutes in a warm place until the yeast foams.

2. In a large bowl, mix together the milk, egg, 2 tablespoons olive oil, salt, and pepper. Add in 3 cups flour and the yeast mixture and stir well. Stir in olives.

3. Sprinkle remaining flour on work surface and knead dough for 5–10 minutes until smooth. Cut dough into 12 squares, and gently roll into balls.

4. Place a large piece of parchment in a 6-quart slow cooker. Make sure that it's large enough to come up the sides. Grease the paper with remaining olive oil. Place rolls onto parchment. If there isn't room for all of the rolls in the slow cooker, freeze the remaining rolls for future use.

5. Cover slow cooker and cook rolls on low for 1 hour to let rolls rise. Turn heat on high and cook rolls for 1 hour.

6. Preheat broiler. Use parchment to remove rolls from slow cooker. Place rolls on a baking sheet and discard parchment. Place rolls under broiler until golden brown, about 2–5 minutes.

PER SERVING: Calories: 170 | Fat: 4g | Protein: 5g | Sodium: 330mg | Fiber: 1g | Carbohydrates: 28g | Sugar: 1g

Windowsill Herb Dinner Rolls

You can keep herbs growing all year long with the right kitchen light. These herbs are some of the most popular to grow on a kitchen windowsill—and they're delicious in slow cooker rolls.

INGREDIENTS | SERVES 6

1 tablespoon yeast

2 teaspoons sugar

1½ cups warm water (approximately 80°F)

3½ cups all-purpose flour, divided

3 teaspoons sea salt, crushed in mortar and pestle

2 tablespoons chopped flat-leaf or curly parsley

2 tablespoons chopped fresh basil

2 teaspoons chopped fresh thyme

2 teaspoons chopped fresh dill

1 teaspoon olive oil

2 tablespoons unsalted butter, melted

Growing Herbs from the Produce Aisle

If you buy fresh herbs in the grocery store, you can induce root growth and then plant them! Make a fresh cut at the bottom of the stems, remove lower leaves, and place cuttings in a glass of water. Within 2 weeks the stems will have rooted and are ready to be planted. You can do this with basil, oregano, mint, thyme, and many other herbs.

1. Mix together the yeast and sugar in a small bowl. Add the warm water and let sit for 5 minutes until the mixture is foamy.

2. Combine 3 cups of flour and sea salt in a large bowl. Add the yeast mixture and stir well. Stir in the parsley, basil, thyme, and dill.

3. Sprinkle remaining flour on a flat work surface and knead the dough for 5–10 minutes or until smooth.

4. Cut dough into 6 sections. Roll each into a ball.

5. Place a large piece of parchment in a 6-quart slow cooker. Make sure that it's large enough to come up the sides. Grease the paper with olive oil. Place rolls onto parchment. If there isn't room for all of the rolls in the slow cooker, freeze the remaining rolls for future use.

6. Cover slow cooker and cook rolls on low for 1 hour.

7. Turn heat on high and cook for an additional 1–1½ hours, or until rolls are set and no longer sticky to the touch.

8. Preheat broiler. Remove rolls from the slow cooker and place on a rimmed baking sheet. Brush rolls with melted butter and broil until brown, 2–5 minutes.

PER SERVING: Calories: 234 | Fat: 4g | Protein: 6g | Sodium: 887mg | Fiber: 1.5g | Carbohydrates: 43g | Sugar: 1g

Sun-Dried Tomato and Fennel Focaccia

Sun-dried tomatoes and fennel combined together make a fantastic bread.

INGREDIENTS | SERVES 4

1 fennel bulb, trimmed and sliced into ½" rounds

¼ cup white wine

1½ teaspoons kosher salt, divided

1 teaspoon freshly ground black pepper

2½ teaspoons active dry yeast

1 teaspoon sugar

1 cup warm water (approximately 80°F)

3¼ cups all-purpose flour, divided

½ cup oil-packed sun-dried tomatoes, chopped

2 tablespoons olive oil, divided

2 teaspoons sea salt, crushed in mortar and pestle

Make Your Own Dried Tomatoes

Making "sun-dried" tomatoes in your kitchen is incredibly simple. Simply slice plum tomatoes in half lengthwise and season with salt and pepper. Bake them in a 200°F oven for 3 hours and voila! For a fraction of the cost, you can indulge in the wonderful sweet flavor of dried tomatoes. Toss them with olive oil before serving on pasta or bread. Leftovers can be frozen for up to 3 months.

1. Place fennel rounds and white wine in a small saucepan. Season with ½ teaspoon kosher salt and black pepper. Cook over low heat for 5–7 minutes or until softened. Remove from heat and let cool.

2. Combine yeast and sugar in a small bowl and stir well. Add the warm water and let sit for 5 minutes until mixture is foamy. Add the yeast mixture to 3 cups flour, 1 teaspoon salt, sun-dried tomatoes, and fennel mixture. Mix well.

3. Sprinkle remaining flour on a flat surface and knead dough for 8–10 minutes until smooth. Cover with a damp towel and let rest for 15 minutes.

4. Grease the inside of a 4- to 5-quart slow cooker with 2 teaspoons olive oil, making sure to go up the sides. Place dough in slow cooker and stretch out so that it's touching all sides. Turn heat on low and cook for 30 minutes.

5. Turn heat on high and remove lid. Quickly poke ½-inch holes all over the focaccia. Brush with remaining olive oil and sprinkle with sea salt. Cook for 1½–2 hours, or until browned.

6. Serve warm or at room temperature.

PER SERVING: Calories: 477 | Fat: 8g | Protein: 12g | Sodium: 2,100mg | Fiber: 5g | Carbohydrates: 85g | Sugar: 2g

Red Pepper, Shallot, and Roasted Garlic Focaccia

By quickly sautéing the pepper, shallot, and garlic together, you will infuse the focaccia with aromatic flavors for an out-of-this-world flatbread.

INGREDIENTS | SERVES 4

½ red bell pepper, diced

1 shallot, diced

1 tablespoon roasted garlic

3 tablespoons olive oil, divided

1½ teaspoons kosher salt, divided

1 teaspoon freshly ground black pepper, divided

2½ teaspoons active dry yeast

1 teaspoon sugar

1 cup warm water (approximately 80°F)

3¼ cups all-purpose flour, divided

2 teaspoons sea salt

How to Make Roasted Garlic

You can easily make your own roasted garlic in the oven. Simply cover a small baking sheet with aluminum foil and place 2–4 whole (unpeeled) heads of garlic on the pan. Drizzle 2 tablespoons of olive oil over the garlic and bake at 350°F for about 45 minutes. Allow to cool for 5–10 minutes, then gently squeeze garlic cloves out of the "paper" surrounding them. Alternately you could place the same ingredients in a 1½- to 2½-quart slow cooker. Cover and cook on high for 2 hours. Store roasted garlic cloves in the fridge for up to 2 weeks.

1. In a medium skillet, sauté the red pepper, shallot, and garlic together with 1 tablespoon olive oil, ½ teaspoon kosher salt, and ½ teaspoon ground black pepper. Cook over medium heat until red pepper has softened, about 5–7 minutes. Remove from heat and let cool.

2. Combine yeast and sugar in a small bowl. Stir well. Add the warm water and let sit for 5 minutes until the mixture becomes foamy.

3. Combine yeast mixture with 3 cups of flour, red pepper mixture, and remaining kosher salt and black pepper. Sprinkle remaining flour on a flat work surface and knead the dough until it becomes a smooth ball, about 10 minutes. Cover with a damp cloth and let rest for 15 minutes.

4. Grease a 4- to 5-quart slow cooker with 2 teaspoons olive oil, making sure to go up the sides. Place dough in slow cooker and stretch out so that it's touching all sides. Turn heat on low and cook for 30 minutes.

5. Turn heat on high and remove lid. Quickly poke ½-inch holes all over the focaccia with fingertips. Brush with remaining olive oil and sprinkle with sea salt. Cook on high for 1½–2 hours, or until the focaccia is firm.

6. Serve warm or at room temperature.

PER SERVING: Calories: 486 | Fat: 11g | Protein: 12g | Sodium: 2,070mg | Fiber: 4g | Carbohydrates: 83g | Sugar: 2g

Herbed Focaccia with Arugula and Shaved Parmesan

Focaccia filled with herbs and topped with peppery arugula and salty Parmesan is the perfect accompaniment to a meal or as an appetizer on its own.

INGREDIENTS | SERVES 4

2½ teaspoons active dry yeast
1 teaspoon sugar
1 cup warm water (approximately 80°F)
3¼ cups all-purpose flour, divided
1 teaspoon kosher salt
1 teaspoon freshly ground black pepper
1 teaspoon dried basil
1 teaspoon oregano
2 tablespoons olive oil, divided
1 tablespoon chopped fresh rosemary
2 teaspoons sea salt
1 cup arugula
1 cup shredded Parmesan cheese

1. Combine yeast and sugar in a small bowl. Stir well. Add the warm water and let sit for 5 minutes until mixture is foamy.

2. Combine yeast mixture with 3 cups flour, kosher salt, pepper, basil, and oregano in a large bowl. Sprinkle remaining flour on a flat work surface and knead the dough until it becomes a smooth ball, about 10 minutes. Cover with a damp cloth and let rest for 15 minutes.

3. Grease a 4- to 5-quart slow cooker with 2 teaspoons olive oil, making sure to go up the sides. Place dough in slow cooker and stretch out so that it's touching all sides. Turn heat on low and cook for 30 minutes.

4. Turn heat on high and remove lid. Quickly poke ½-inch holes all over the focaccia with fingertips. Brush with remaining olive oil and sprinkle with rosemary and sea salt. Let cook for 1½–2 hours, or until focaccia is firm.

5. Remove bread from slow cooker and cut into quarters. Top quarters with arugula and cheese.

6. Serve warm or at room temperature.

PER SERVING: Calories: 555 | Fat: 15g | Protein: 21g | Sodium: 2,223mg | Fiber: 4g | Carbohydrates: 81g | Sugar: 1g

Brown and Orange Bread

This bread is delicious as toast or with almost any kind of soup.
And it's amazing with any type of slow-cooked beans.

INGREDIENTS | SERVES 20

½ cup rye flour

½ cup all-purpose flour

½ cup cornmeal

1 tablespoon sugar

½ teaspoon baking powder

½ teaspoon baking soda

½ teaspoon cinnamon

½ cup sweetened dried cranberries

1 tablespoon dried orange peel

½ teaspoon ground ginger

1 cup fat-free buttermilk

⅓ cup molasses

1 teaspoon olive oil

Hot water, as needed

Don't Throw Those Peels Away!

Dried orange peel may seem like an exotic ingredient, but it's simple and inexpensive to make at home. Just buy pesticide-free oranges and remove the peels. With a sharp knife remove the pith (the white part of the peel) until you see the bright orange part of the peel. Then, cut the peel into short strips and bake in a 200°F oven until the strips start to curl, about 20–30 minutes. Store in a clean, airtight container in the refrigerator.

1. In a medium bowl, whisk together the flours, cornmeal, sugar, baking powder, baking soda, cinnamon, cranberries, orange peel, and ginger. Set the mixture aside.

2. In another bowl, stir together the buttermilk and molasses. Pour into the dry mixture and stir until combined.

3. Grease a 6-cup metal bowl with olive oil and pour the batter into the bowl. Use aluminum foil to cover bowl. Tightly wrap aluminum foil to keep moisture from escaping. Place bamboo skewers or an empty can on the bottom of a 6-quart slow cooker as a rack for the bowl—you want air to be able to circulate around the bread. Pour 2 inches of hot water into slow cooker. Cook on low for 4–5 hours or until a toothpick inserted into the bread comes out clean.

4. Let bread cool for 5 minutes in bowl, and then invert on a wire rack. Let bread cool for 15 minutes before serving.

PER SERVING: Calories: 69g | Fat: 0.5g | Protein: 1g | Sodium: 51mg | Fiber: 1g | Carbohydrates: 15g | Sugar: 7g

Fresh Apple Bread

This bread makes a wonderful breakfast or dessert.

INGREDIENTS | SERVES 8

1 cup granulated sugar

½ cup plus ½ teaspoon olive oil, divided

2 large eggs

1½ teaspoons vanilla

1½ tablespoons buttermilk

½ teaspoon kosher salt

2 Granny Smith apples, peeled, cored, and diced

1 cup chopped pecans

2 cups all-purpose flour

1 teaspoon baking soda

1 teaspoon cinnamon

3 tablespoons packed light brown sugar

1. Combine the granulated sugar and ½ cup olive oil together in a small bowl.

2. In a large bowl, whisk the eggs together with the vanilla, buttermilk, and salt. Stir in the sugar mixture along with the apples and pecans.

3. Sift the flour and baking soda together and then add to the apple mixture.

4. Grease a loaf pan with remaining olive oil and dust it with flour. Fill prepared pan half full. Sprinkle with cinnamon and brown sugar. Cover the pan with aluminum foil and place on a trivet in a 4- to 5-quart oval slow cooker. Pour 1 inch of water around the trivet.

5. Cover the slow cooker and turn to high; cook for 2–3 hours. The bread is done when a toothpick inserted into the center of the bread comes out clean.

PER SERVING: Calories: 488 | Fat: 25g | Protein: 6g | Sodium: 327mg | Fiber: 3g | Carbohydrates: 61g | Sugar: 35g

Feta and Spinach Dinner Rolls

These rolls are savory and cheesy and would be delicious on their own or as part of an antipasto platter.

INGREDIENTS | SERVES 8

2 teaspoons sugar

2¼ teaspoons active dry yeast

1½ cups warm water (approximately 80°F)

3½ cups all-purpose flour, divided

½ teaspoon kosher salt

½ teaspoon freshly ground black pepper

½ cup chopped cooked spinach

½ cup crumbled feta

1 tablespoon olive oil, divided

1. In a small bowl, mix together the sugar and yeast. Add the water and let sit for 5 minutes until mixture is foamy.

2. In a large bowl, mix 3 cups flour, salt, and pepper together. Add the yeast mixture, spinach, and feta and stir well.

3. Sprinkle remaining flour on a flat work surface and knead the dough for 5–10 minutes or until smooth.

4. Cut a piece of parchment paper large enough to cover the inside of a 4- to 5-quart slow cooker. Grease the parchment with 1 teaspoon olive oil and place in slow cooker.

5. Divide the dough into 8 pieces. Place the rolls on the parchment paper in the slow cooker. If there isn't enough room for all of the rolls in the slow cooker in one layer, freeze the remaining rolls for future use.

6. Cover slow cooker and cook on low for 1 hour.

7. Turn heat to high and cook for an additional 1–1½ hours or until rolls are set and no longer sticky.

8. Preheat broiler. Place rolls in baking pan and brush rolls with remaining olive oil. Broil until brown, 2–5 minutes.

PER SERVING: Calories: 249 | Fat: 4g | Protein: 8g | Sodium: 262mg | Fiber: 2g | Carbohydrates: 44g | Sugar: 2g

Parmesan Dinner Rolls with Dill Oil

*These dinner rolls get a lively kick from sharp Parmesan and tangy dill.
They would be wonderful with soup or for small sandwiches.*

INGREDIENTS | SERVES 8

2 teaspoons sugar

2¼ teaspoons active dry yeast

1½ cups warm water (approximately 80°F)

3½ cups all-purpose flour, divided

½ teaspoon kosher salt

½ cup shredded Parmesan cheese, divided

1 tablespoon olive oil, divided

2 teaspoons dried dill

1. In a small bowl, mix together the sugar and yeast. Add the water and let sit for 5 minutes until mixture is foamy.

2. In a large bowl, mix together 3 cups flour and salt. Add the yeast mixture and half the cheese to the flour.

3. Sprinkle remaining flour on a flat work surface and knead the dough for 5–10 minutes or until smooth.

4. Cut a piece of parchment paper large enough to cover the inside of a 4- to 5-quart slow cooker. Grease the parchment with 1 teaspoon olive oil and place in slow cooker.

5. Divide the dough into 8 pieces. Place the rolls on the parchment paper in the slow cooker. If there isn't enough room for all of the rolls in the slow cooker in one layer, freeze the remaining rolls for future use.

6. Cover slow cooker and cook on low for 1 hour.

7. Turn heat to high and cook for an additional 1–1½ hours or until rolls are set and no longer sticky.

8. Preheat broiler. In a small bowl, mix together the dill and remaining olive oil. Place rolls in baking pan and brush rolls with the dill olive oil mixture. Sprinkle with remaining cheese. Broil until brown, 2–5 minutes.

PER SERVING: Calories: 262 | Fat: 5g | Protein: 10g | Sodium: 318mg | Fiber: 2g | Carbohydrates: 43g | Sugar: 1g

Rosemary Sea Salt Bread

This bread is lively and savory, and would be delicious with soup.

INGREDIENTS | SERVES 8

1 teaspoon sugar

2¼ teaspoons dry active yeast

1¼ cups warm water

3½ cups all-purpose flour, divided

½ teaspoon kosher salt

½ teaspoon white pepper

2 tablespoons chopped fresh rosemary, divided

¼ cup olive oil, divided

1½ teaspoons sea salt

1. Mix together the sugar and yeast in a small bowl. Add the water and let sit for 5–10 minutes or until foamy.

2. In a large bowl, mix 3 cups flour, kosher salt, pepper, and half of the rosemary together. Add the yeast mixture and 2½ tablespoons olive oil; stir well.

3. Sprinkle remaining flour on a flat work surface and knead the dough for 5–10 minutes or until smooth.

4. Grease a large bowl with 2 teaspoons olive oil.

5. Place the dough in the bowl, and roll it around so that it's completely covered in oil. Place a clean dish towel over the bowl, and let rise in a warm area for 1 hour.

6. Punch the dough down and let rise again for another 20 minutes.

7. Cut a piece of parchment paper large enough to cover the inside of a 6-quart or larger oval slow cooker. Grease the parchment with 1 teaspoon olive oil and place in slow cooker. Place dough on top of parchment paper. Sprinkle with sea salt.

8. Cover and cook on high for 2 hours.

9. Preheat broiler. Place bread on a baking sheet and drizzle with remaining olive oil. Broil until browned, about 3–5 minutes. Place bread on wire rack and let cool completely before serving.

PER SERVING: Calories: 265 | Fat: 7g | Protein: 6g | Sodium: 592mg | Fiber: 2g | Carbohydrates: 42g | Sugar: 1g

Almond and Cherry Bread

Toast a piece of this bread for breakfast or even dessert!

INGREDIENTS | SERVES 8

½ cup sugar

½ cup applesauce

1 tablespoon plus 1 teaspoon olive oil, divided

2 large eggs

1½ tablespoons milk

1 teaspoon cinnamon

1½ cups pitted and chopped fresh cherries

1 cup sliced almonds

2 cups plus 1 tablespoon all-purpose flour, divided

½ teaspoon kosher salt

1 teaspoon baking soda

1. In a small bowl, mix together sugar, applesauce, and 1 tablespoon olive oil.

2. Beat eggs in a large bowl. Add milk and cinnamon to eggs and whisk well. Stir in cherries, almonds, and applesauce mixture. Mix well to incorporate.

3. Sift 2 cups flour, salt, and baking soda into a large bowl. Add the cherry and almond mixture to the flour.

4. Grease and flour an 8½" × 4½" loaf pan with remaining olive oil and flour. Pour batter half to three-quarters full. Discard any remaining batter. Loosely cover the loaf pan with foil. Place the loaf pan on a trivet in a 6-quart or larger oval slow cooker, and pour water around the base of the trivet.

5. Cover and cook on high for 2–3 hours, or until a toothpick inserted into the middle comes out clean. Remove bread from slow cooker and cool on a wire rack.

PER SERVING: Calories: 299 | Fat: 10g | Protein: 8g | Sodium: 324mg | Fiber: 3g | Carbohydrates: 46g | Sugar: 18g

Family Date Bread

This bread would be perfect with regular butter or apple butter for breakfast.

INGREDIENTS | SERVES 8

8 ounces dried dates, chopped

1 cup boiling water

2 tablespoons butter

1 cup sugar

2 tablespoons plus 1 teaspoon olive oil, divided

1 large egg

½ teaspoon vanilla

½ teaspoon kosher salt

1 cup chopped raisins

1 cup chopped walnuts

3 cups plus 1 teaspoon all-purpose flour, divided

2 teaspoons baking soda

4 teaspoons baking powder

1. Place the dates in a medium bowl and cover with boiling water. Let stand until softened, approximately 5–7 minutes. Set aside.

2. Cream together butter, sugar, and 2 tablespoons olive oil.

3. In a medium bowl, whisk egg, vanilla, and salt. Add dates and soaking liquid to the egg mixture. Stir in butter mixture; mix well to incorporate. Add raisins and walnuts and stir well again.

4. Sift 3 cups flour, baking soda, and baking powder together in a large bowl. Stir in the date mixture.

5. Grease and flour an 8½" × 4½" loaf pan with remaining olive oil and flour. Fill the loaf pan half to three-quarters full and loosely cover with foil. Place the pan on a trivet in a 6-quart or larger oval slow cooker, and pour water around the base of the trivet.

6. Cover and cook on high for 2–3 hours. The bread is done when a toothpick inserted into the middle comes out clean.

PER SERVING: Calories: 569 | Fat: 17g | Protein: 9g | Sodium: 720mg | Fiber: 5g | Carbohydrates: 99g | Sugar: 54g

Pineapple Banana Bread

This bread is lovely served on a cold winter afternoon along with a cup of tea.

INGREDIENTS | SERVES 8

3 cups plus 1 teaspoon all-purpose flour, divided

¼ cup sugar

½ teaspoon baking soda

1½ teaspoons baking powder

1 large egg

1 (8-ounce) can diced pineapple with juice

¼ cup plus 1 teaspoon olive oil, divided

½ teaspoon kosher salt

1 large banana, peeled and chopped

1. In a large bowl, sift together 3 cups flour, sugar, baking soda, and baking powder.

2. In a medium bowl, beat the egg. Add the pineapple with juice, ¼ cup olive oil, salt, and banana. Stir well to combine.

3. Add the egg mixture to the flour mixture and stir well.

4. Grease and flour an 8½" × 4½" loaf pan with remaining olive oil and flour. Fill the pan half to three-quarters full and loosely cover the pan with foil. Place the pan on a trivet in a 6-quart or larger oval slow cooker, and pour water around the base of the trivet.

5. Cover and cook on high for 2–3 hours, or until a toothpick inserted into the middle comes out clean.

PER SERVING: Calories: 300 | Fat: 8g | Protein: 6g | Sodium: 327mg | Fiber: 2g | Carbohydrates: 50g | Sugar: 11g

Holiday Gift Cake

The mayonnaise is a secret ingredient in this cake that's studded with beautiful dried fruits.

INGREDIENTS | SERVES 8

⅔ cup mayonnaise

⅔ cup sugar

⅔ cup water

1 teaspoon vanilla

½ cup chopped walnuts

⅓ cup chopped raisins

⅓ cup chopped candied cherries

⅓ cup chopped dates

⅓ cup chopped dried pineapple

1⅓ cups plus 1 teaspoon all-purpose flour, divided

2 teaspoons baking soda

2 teaspoons cinnamon

2 teaspoons nutmeg

1 teaspoon olive oil

Why Sift Flour?

As flour sits, it settles into the bag or jar. Sifting it allows the flour to loosen up and measure more accurately. It may seem like an extra step in baking, but it's a good habit to develop to ensure that finished dishes come out the way they should.

1. In a medium bowl, combine the mayonnaise and sugar. Add the water, vanilla, walnuts, raisins, cherries, dates, and pineapple.

2. In a separate bowl, sift 1⅓ cups flour with the baking soda. Stir in cinnamon and nutmeg and mix well.

3. Add the flour mixture to the fruit mixture.

4. Grease and flour an 8½" × 4½" loaf pan with olive oil and remaining flour. Fill the pan half to three-quarters full and loosely cover the dish with foil. Place the pan on a trivet in a 6-quart or larger oval slow cooker, and pour water around the base of the trivet.

5. Cover and cook on high for 2–3 hours, or until a toothpick inserted into the center comes out clean.

PER SERVING: Calories: 379 | Fat: 20g | Protein: 4g | Sodium: 421mg | Fiber: 2.5g | Carbohydrates: 47g | Sugar: 27g

Orange Raisin Bread

This bread is filled with citrus flavor, and is hearty enough to serve with meat and game.

INGREDIENTS | SERVES 8

1 orange

¾ cup chopped raisins

½ cup boiling water

2 tablespoons unsalted butter, softened

1 cup sugar

1 teaspoon baking soda

1 teaspoon vanilla

2 cups plus 1 teaspoon all-purpose flour, divided

1 teaspoon baking powder

⅛ teaspoon kosher salt

1 large egg

1 teaspoon olive oil

1. Grate the orange peel into a medium bowl. Make sure to only get the orange part of the skin, not the white pith. Cut the orange in half and juice over a separate small bowl. Discard the remaining flesh of the orange. Add the raisins to the peel and grind into a light paste using a mortar and pestle, or dice extremely finely.

2. Add the boiling water to the juice and add to the orange peel mixture. Stir in butter, sugar, baking soda, and vanilla, and let cool slightly.

3. In a medium bowl, sift 2 cups flour, baking powder, and salt together.

4. Beat the egg in a small bowl and add it to the cooled orange mixture. Combine the flour mixture with the orange mixture.

5. Grease and flour an 8½" × 4½" loaf pan with olive oil and remaining flour. Fill the loaf pan half to three-quarters full, and loosely cover the dish with foil. Place the loaf pan on a trivet or rack in a 6-quart or larger oval slow cooker, and pour water around the base of the trivet.

6. Cover and cook on high for 2–3 hours, or until a toothpick inserted into the center comes out clean.

PER SERVING: Calories: 302 | Fat: 4g | Protein: 5g | Sodium: 267mg | Fiber: 2g | Carbohydrates: 62g | Sugar: 34g

Pecan Rhubarb Bread

To make sour milk, add 1 tablespoon of white vinegar or lemon juice to ¾ cup and 3 tablespoons of milk. Prepare ahead and let stand fifteen minutes before starting the recipe.

INGREDIENTS | SERVES 8

1 large egg
1½ cups diced rhubarb
½ cup chopped pecans
1½ cups packed dark brown sugar
⅔ cup plus 1 teaspoon olive oil, divided
1 cup sour milk
1 teaspoon kosher salt
1 teaspoon baking soda
1 teaspoon vanilla
2½ cups plus 1 teaspoon all-purpose flour, divided
½ cup granulated sugar
1 tablespoon unsalted butter

1. Whisk the egg in a large bowl. Add the rhubarb, pecans, brown sugar, ⅔ cup olive oil, sour milk, salt, baking soda, vanilla, and 2½ cups flour.

2. Grease and flour an 8½" × 4½" loaf pan with remaining olive oil and flour. Fill the loaf pan half to three-quarters full.

3. In a small bowl, cream together the granulated sugar and butter.

4. Using 2 teaspoons, distribute the sugar/butter blend over the dough.

5. Loosely cover the pan with foil, and place on a trivet in a 6-quart or larger oval slow cooker. Pour water around the base of the trivet.

6. Cover and cook on high for 2–3 hours, or until a toothpick inserted into the middle of the bread comes out clean.

PER SERVING: Calories: 611 | Fat: 27g | Protein: 7g | Sodium: 487mg | Fiber: 2g | Carbohydrates: 86g | Sugar: 54g

Chocolaty Banana Bread

This bread will make breakfast into a treat for everyone!

INGREDIENTS | SERVES 8

¼ cup unsalted butter, softened

⅔ cup sugar

1 large egg, lightly beaten

1 large ripe banana, mashed

1⅓ cups plus 1 teaspoon all-purpose flour, divided

½ teaspoon kosher salt

¾ teaspoon baking soda

¼ cup chopped walnuts

½ cup dark chocolate chips

¼ cup chopped maraschino cherries

1 teaspoon olive oil

1. In a large bowl, cream butter and sugar. Stir in egg and banana.

2. Sift together 1⅓ cups flour, salt, and baking soda, and add to the egg mixture. Fold in the walnuts, chocolate chips, and cherries.

3. Grease and flour an 8½" × 4½" loaf pan with olive oil and 1 teaspoon flour. Fill a loaf pan half to three-quarters full and loosely cover the pan with foil. Place the pan on a trivet in a 6-quart or larger oval slow cooker, and pour water around the base of the trivet.

4. Cover and heat on high for 2–3 hours, or until a toothpick inserted into the middle comes out clean.

PER SERVING: Calories: 299 | Fat: 13g | Protein: 4g | Sodium: 267mg | Fiber: 2g | Carbohydrates: 44g | Sugar: 25g

Pumpkin Pie Bread

This bread will fill the entire house with the aroma of pumpkin and spices.

INGREDIENTS | SERVES 8

1¾ cups plus 1 teaspoon flour, divided

1 teaspoon baking soda

¾ teaspoon kosher salt

½ teaspoon nutmeg

½ teaspoon cinnamon

⅛ teaspoon mace

2 large eggs

1 cup cooked or canned pumpkin

1½ cups sugar

½ cup vegetable oil

1 teaspoon vanilla

1 teaspoon olive oil

1. Sift 1¾ cups flour and baking soda together in a large bowl. Add salt, nutmeg, cinnamon, and mace.

2. Beat the eggs in a large bowl and stir in pumpkin, sugar, vegetable oil, and vanilla. Add flour mixture and mix well.

3. Grease and flour an 8½" × 4½" loaf pan with olive oil and 1 teaspoon flour. Fill the pan half to three-quarters full and loosely cover with foil. Place the pan on a trivet in a 6-quart or larger oval slow cooker, and pour water around the base of the trivet.

4. Cover and heat on high for 2–3 hours or until a toothpick in the center comes out clean.

PER SERVING: Calories: 403 | Fat: 16g | Protein: 5g | Sodium: 398mg | Fiber: 2g | Carbohydrates: 61g | Sugar: 39g

CHAPTER 4

Appetizers and Dips

Cinnamon and Sugar Peanuts

This is a festive treat that can be packaged in cellophane bags and given as party favors or gifts.

INGREDIENTS | YIELDS 12 OUNCES

12 ounces unsalted, roasted peanuts

½ tablespoon ground cinnamon

⅓ cup sugar

1 tablespoon melted butter

1. Place the peanuts in a 4-quart slow cooker.

2. Add the cinnamon and sugar and drizzle with butter. Stir to combine.

3. Cook on low, uncovered, for 2–3 hours, stirring occasionally.

4. Spread the peanut mixture onto a cookie sheet or parchment paper and cool until dry.

PER SERVING (1 OUNCE): Calories: 200 | Fat: 15g | Protein: 7g | Sodium: 0mg | Fiber: 2g | Carbohydrates: 12g | Sugar: 7g

Parmesan Artichoke Dip

For a more savory dip, reduce the amount of mayonnaise to 2 cups and stir in 2 cups of room-temperature sour cream immediately before serving. For fewer servings, cut the recipe in half and reduce the cooking time.

INGREDIENTS | SERVES 24

2 (12-ounce) jars marinated artichoke hearts

4 cups mayonnaise

2 (8-ounce) packages cream cheese, cubed

12 ounces (3 cups) freshly grated Parmesan cheese

4 cloves garlic, peeled and minced

1 teaspoon dried dill

½ teaspoon freshly ground black pepper

Spinach Parmesan Dip

Instead of using artichokes, you can use fresh or frozen spinach (drained of all liquids). For a heartier dip, add 1 pound fresh lump crabmeat and ½ teaspoon Old Bay Seasoning.

1. Drain and chop the artichoke hearts. Add to a 2½-quart slow cooker along with the mayonnaise, cream cheese, Parmesan cheese, garlic, dill, and pepper. Stir to combine. Cover and cook on low for 1 hour; uncover and stir well.

2. Re-cover and cook on low for an additional 1–1½ hours or until the cheese is melted completely and the dip is heated through.

3. Serve immediately, or reduce the heat setting of the slow cooker to warm.

PER SERVING: Calories: 398 | Fat: 39g | Protein: 7.5g | Sodium: 523mg | Fiber: 2g | Carbohydrates: 6g | Sugar: 1g

Shrimp and Artichoke Dip

This unusual dip is delicious with sesame pretzels or pita chips.

INGREDIENTS | SERVES 20

8 ounces reduced-fat cream cheese

½ cup reduced-fat sour cream

½ cup diced green onion

1 tablespoon Worcestershire sauce

1½ teaspoons Chesapeake Bay seasoning

12 ounces frozen artichoke hearts, defrosted

8 ounces peeled salad shrimp

Cooking with Cream Cheese

While reduced-fat cream cheese can be successfully cooked, fat-free cream cheese separates when heated. Do not use fat-free cream cheese unless it is specifically called for. In addition, always use brick cream cheese. Whipped or spreadable cream cheese has additives to make it spread easily that cause it to separate during cooking.

1. Place the cream cheese, sour cream, green onion, Worcestershire sauce, and Chesapeake Bay seasoning in a food processor. Pulse until smooth and well blended. Add the artichoke hearts and pulse twice.

2. Scrape into a medium bowl. Add the shrimp and stir to evenly distribute.

3. Scrape into a 2-quart slow cooker. Cook on low for 40 minutes. Stir before serving.

PER SERVING: Calories: 60 | Fat: 5g | Protein: 4g | Sodium: 79mg | Fiber: 1g | Carbohydrates: 3g | Sugar: 1g

Balsamic Almonds

These sweet and sour almonds are a great addition to a cheese platter or appetizer plate.

INGREDIENTS | SERVES 15

2 cups whole almonds

½ cup packed dark brown sugar

½ cup balsamic vinegar

½ teaspoon kosher salt

Healthy Almonds

Botanically speaking, almonds are a seed, not a nut. They are an excellent source of vitamin E and have high levels of monounsaturated fat, one of the two "good" fats responsible for lowering LDL cholesterol.

1. Place all ingredients into a 4- to 5-quart slow cooker. Cook uncovered on high for 4 hours, stirring every 15 minutes or until all the liquid has evaporated. The almonds will have a syrupy coating.

2. Line two cookie sheets with parchment paper. Pour the almonds in a single layer on the baking sheets to cool completely.

3. Store in an airtight container in the pantry for up to 2 weeks.

PER SERVING: Calories: 108 | Fat: 6g | Protein: 3g | Sodium: 82mg | Fiber: 1.5g | Carbohydrates: 11g | Sugar: 9g

Black and White Bean Dip

Cannellini beans make this dip incredibly creamy.

INGREDIENTS | SERVES 25

1 teaspoon canola oil

1 habanero pepper, seeded and minced

1 small onion, peeled and diced

3 cloves garlic, minced

½ teaspoon hot paprika

¼ teaspoon cumin

¼ cup reduced-fat sour cream

2 tablespoons lime juice

1 (15-ounce) can black beans, drained and rinsed

1 (15-ounce) can cannellini beans, drained and rinsed

1. Heat the oil in a nonstick skillet. Sauté the habanero, onion, and garlic until soft and fragrant, about 2–3 minutes. Pour into a medium-sized bowl.

2. Add paprika, cumin, sour cream, lime juice, and beans to the bowl. Mash the mixture with a potato masher until the dip looks creamy but with some black and white beans still distinct.

3. Scrape into a 1½- to 2-quart slow cooker. Cook on low for 2 hours. Stir before serving.

PER SERVING: Calories: 78 | Fat: 1g | Protein: 5g | Sodium: 54mg | Fiber: 4g | Carbohydrates: 14g | Sugar: 2g

Paprika

Hungarian paprika comes in two aptly named varieties: sweet and hot. The spice is used to flavor and, in some cases, color dishes. Spanish paprika is also known as smoked paprika and adds a smoky, spicy note to food.

Baba Ganoush

Serve this with pita bread and fresh vegetables.

INGREDIENTS | SERVES 12

1 (1-pound) eggplant
2 tablespoons tahini
2 tablespoons lemon juice
2 cloves garlic

Tahini Tips

Tahini is a paste made from ground sesame seeds. The most common type of tahini uses seeds that have been toasted before they are ground, but "raw" tahini is also available. The two can be used interchangeably in most recipes, but occasionally a recipe will specify one or the other. Look for tahini near the peanut butter, in the health food section, or with the specialty foods in most grocery stores.

1. Pierce the eggplant with a fork. Cook on high in a 4- to 5-quart slow cooker for 2 hours.

2. Allow to cool. Peel off the skin. Slice in half and remove the seeds. Discard the skin and seeds.

3. Place the pulp in a food processor and add the remaining ingredients. Pulse until smooth.

PER SERVING: Calories: 25 | Fat: 1.5g | Protein: 1g | Sodium: 4mg | Fiber: 1.5g | Carbohydrates: 3g | Sugar: 1g

Hummus

Serve this Middle Eastern spread with pita bread, vegetables, or falafel.

INGREDIENTS | SERVES 20

1 pound dried chickpeas
Water, as needed
3 tablespoons tahini
3 tablespoons lemon juice
3 cloves garlic
¼ teaspoon kosher salt

Easy Snacking

Keeping hummus and fresh vegetables around makes healthy snacking easy. Cut carrots, celery, and radishes into snack-friendly sizes. Place them in a bowl with a tightly fitting lid. Fill the bowl two-thirds with water, then cover with the lid. The vegetables will keep crisp in the refrigerator up to 1 week.

1. Place the chickpeas in a 4- to 5-quart slow cooker and cover with water. Soak overnight. The next day, cook on low for 8 hours. Drain, reserving the liquid.

2. Place the chickpeas, tahini, lemon juice, garlic, and salt in a food processor. Pulse until smooth, adding the reserved liquid as needed to achieve the desired texture.

PER SERVING: Calories: 51 | Fat: 2g | Protein: 2.5g | Sodium: 34mg | Fiber: 2g | Carbohydrates: 7g | Sugar: 1g

Sun-Dried Tomato and Pesto Dip

Tart, rich sun-dried tomatoes are the perfect partner for a fresh-tasting pesto in this creamy dip.

INGREDIENTS | SERVES 20

2 cloves garlic

1 tablespoon reduced-fat mayonnaise

¾ ounce fresh basil

1 teaspoon toasted pine nuts

¼ teaspoon ground white pepper

¼ cup julienne-cut dry (not oil-packed) sun-dried tomatoes

8 ounces reduced-fat cream cheese or Neufchâtel, at room temperature

How to Toast Pine Nuts

Preheat the oven to 350°F. Place the pine nuts on a cookie sheet or cake pan. Roast for 5–8 minutes in the oven. Pine nuts will be slightly browned and fragrant when fully toasted. Cool before using.

1. Place the garlic, mayonnaise, basil, pine nuts, and pepper in a food processor. Pulse until a fairly smooth paste forms. Add the sun-dried tomatoes and pulse 4–5 times.

2. Add the cream cheese and pulse until smooth.

3. Scrape into a 2-quart slow cooker. Cook on low for 1 hour. Stir before serving.

PER SERVING: Calories: 45 | Fat: 4g | Protein: 1g | Sodium: 40mg | Fiber: 0g | Carbohydrates: 1g | Sugar: 1g

Mixed Seafood Dip

Many stores carry frozen bags of cooked seafood with a mix of shrimp, scallops, squid, and/or clams. Defrost overnight in the refrigerator before using.

INGREDIENTS | SERVES 12

8 ounces reduced-fat cream cheese

½ cup reduced-fat sour cream

½ cup diced green onion

⅔ cup minced cooked mixed seafood

1 tablespoon tarragon vinegar

1 tablespoon minced parsley

1 teaspoon dried chopped onion

⅛ teaspoon celery seed

1. In a medium bowl, stir together all ingredients. Scrape into a 2-quart slow cooker. Cook on low for 1 hour or until heated through.

2. Stir before serving.

PER SERVING: Calories: 29 | Fat: 1.5g | Protein: 3g | Sodium: 25mg | Fiber: 0g | Carbohydrates: 1g | Sugar: 0g

Eggplant Caponata

Serve this on small slices of Italian bread as an appetizer or use as a filling in sandwiches or wraps.

INGREDIENTS | SERVES 8

2 (1-pound) eggplants

1 teaspoon olive oil

1 medium red onion, peeled and diced

4 cloves garlic, minced

1 stalk celery, diced

2 medium tomatoes, diced

2 tablespoons nonpareil capers

2 tablespoons toasted pine nuts

1 teaspoon red pepper flakes

¼ cup red wine vinegar

Little Dipper

Slice a baguette into ⅛"-thick slices. Brush lightly with olive oil and sprinkle with dried tarragon and rosemary. Bake at 350°F for 10 minutes or until crisp.

1. Pierce the eggplants with a fork. Cook on high in a 4- to 5-quart slow cooker for 2 hours.

2. Allow to cool. Peel off the skin. Slice each in half and remove the seeds. Discard the skin and seeds.

3. Place the pulp in a food processor. Pulse until smooth. Set aside.

4. Heat the oil in a nonstick skillet. Sauté the onion, garlic, and celery until the onion is soft, about 5–7 minutes. Add the eggplant and tomatoes. Sauté 3 minutes.

5. Return to the slow cooker and add the capers, pine nuts, red pepper flakes, and vinegar. Stir. Cook on low for 30 minutes. Stir prior to serving.

PER SERVING: Calories: 54 | Fat: 1.5g | Protein: 2g | Sodium: 73mg | Fiber: 5g | Carbohydrates: 10g | Sugar: 4g

Fig and Ginger Spread

This rich-tasting spread is great swirled into Greek yogurt or spread on a whole-wheat English muffin.

INGREDIENTS | SERVES 25

2 pounds fresh figs

2 tablespoons minced fresh ginger

2 tablespoons lime juice

½ cup water

¾ cup sugar

1. Clean each fig thoroughly. Slice and remove stems from each fig. Place all ingredients in a 2-quart slow cooker. Stir. Cook on low for 2–3 hours. Remove the lid and cook an additional 2–3 hours until the mixture is thickened.

2. Pour into airtight containers and refrigerate up to 6 weeks.

PER SERVING: Calories: 50 | Fat: 0g | Protein: 0g | Sodium: 1mg | Fiber: 1g | Carbohydrates: 13g | Sugar: 11g

Fresh Herb Dip with Eggplant

*This herby eggplant dip is filled with a fresh and smoky flavor
that is as delicious with pita chips as it is with crudités.*

INGREDIENTS | SERVES 12

1 (1-pound) eggplant

1 clove garlic, diced

1 small onion, peeled and chopped

1 teaspoon cumin

½ teaspoon hot smoked paprika

1 (14½-ounce) can diced tomatoes

½ cup chopped flat-leaf parsley

2 tablespoons chopped cilantro

¼ cup olive oil

A Delicious Secret Weapon

If you don't have hot smoked paprika in your spice drawer, you should. It adds a wonderful deep flavor that is perfect with potatoes, eggs, sauces, soups, stews, meats, and sauces.

1. Trim and cube eggplant into 1-inch pieces. Place eggplant in slow cooker with garlic, onion, cumin, smoked paprika, and tomatoes.

2. Cover and cook on low heat for 6–8 hours. Turn heat off and remove cover. Let sit for ½ hour to cool.

3. Place eggplant mixture in food processor fitted with a metal blade. Add parsley, cilantro, and olive oil. Process to desired consistency.

4. Serve at room temperature or chill for 2 hours.

PER SERVING: Calories: 59 | Fat: 5g | Protein: 1g | Sodium: 51mg | Fiber: 2g | Carbohydrates: 4g | Sugar: 2g

Stuffed Grape Leaves

*Grape leaves are the perfect party food. These neat little packages
are filled with herbs and rice and topped with salty crumbled feta.*

INGREDIENTS | SERVES 8

1 cup basmati rice

½ teaspoon kosher salt

1 leek (pale green and white parts only), finely minced

¼ bunch fresh oregano, chopped

¼ bunch fresh dill, chopped

½ teaspoon freshly ground black pepper

1 small jar grape leaves

2 teaspoons olive oil

8 cups Roasted Chicken Broth (see recipe in Chapter 11)

2 ounces feta cheese

A Blank Canvas

You can make stuffed grape leaves to suit your taste with just a few simple variables. You can make them with ground meat, more vegetables, and different herbs and broths. Replace the chicken broth with Savory Vegetable Stock (see recipe in Chapter 11) for a vegetarian version. Play with ingredients until you find your signature recipe!

1. Parboil rice by bringing a small pot of water to a boil with the salt. Add the rice and cook for 10 minutes. Drain.

2. Combine rice with the leek, oregano, dill, and pepper in a medium bowl. Set aside.

3. Drain, rinse, and separate the grape leaves, placing them on a paper-towel-lined baking sheet.

4. Grease a 4- to 5-quart slow cooker with olive oil.

5. To assemble: Lay out a grape leaf shiny-side down and place a tablespoon of the rice mixture in the center. Fold one end over the other and seal tightly.

6. Stack stuffed grape leaves in slow cooker. Add broth and cover. Cook on low for 6–8 hours or until rice is cooked.

7. Serve grape leaves with crumbled feta on top.

PER SERVING: Calories: 238 | Fat: 7g | Protein: 9g |
Sodium: 2,075mg | Fiber: 0.5g | Carbohydrates: 35g | Sugar: 1g

Mushrooms Stuffed with Creamy Crab

*Mushrooms stuffed with crab, tomatoes, and shallots
make a light and flavorful appetizer.*

INGREDIENTS | SERVES 12

2 teaspoons plus 1 tablespoon olive oil, divided

3 shallots, peeled and diced

2½ pounds button mushrooms

½ cup grape tomatoes, diced

2 teaspoons sherry vinegar

10 ounces crabmeat

1 egg white

½ teaspoon kosher salt

1 teaspoon freshly ground black pepper

1 tablespoon chopped fresh thyme

1. Grease a 4- to 5-quart slow cooker with 2 teaspoons olive oil.

2. Heat remaining oil in a sauté pan over medium heat. Sauté shallots until softened, about 3 minutes.

3. Clean the mushrooms and remove the stems from the caps. Set caps aside.

4. Finely chop the stems and place them in a medium bowl. Stir in shallots, tomatoes, vinegar, crabmeat, egg white, salt, pepper, and thyme.

5. Stuff the mushroom caps with the crab mixture and place in slow cooker. Cook on high for 2 hours.

PER SERVING: Calories: 51 | Fat: 2g | Protein: 5g | Sodium: 138mg | Fiber: 0.5g | Carbohydrates: 2g | Sugar: 1g

Curried Chicken Meatballs with Tomatoes

*Curried chicken meatballs with vegetables are a succulent
appetizer that's sure to please everyone.*

INGREDIENTS | SERVES 4

2 teaspoons plus 1 tablespoon olive oil,
divided

2 slices toasted Italian bread

1 pound ground chicken

2 large eggs

1 small red onion, finely diced

1 small carrot, peeled and finely diced

1 teaspoon curry powder

½ teaspoon paprika

¼ bunch flat-leaf parsley, chopped

½ teaspoon kosher salt

½ teaspoon freshly ground black pepper

1 (28-ounce) can crushed tomatoes

1. Grease a 4- to 5-quart slow cooker with 2 teaspoons olive oil.

2. Soak the bread in water for 20 minutes, or until bread has absorbed all of the moisture, and squeeze out by hand. Roughly chop the bread. In a large bowl, combine bread, chicken, eggs, onion, carrot, curry powder, paprika, parsley, salt, and pepper.

3. Form into 16 small meatballs. Heat remaining olive oil in a large skillet over medium heat until it shimmers, about 1 minute. Add meatballs and brown on all sides, about 8 minutes. Place meatballs in slow cooker and add tomatoes.

4. Cook on low for 6 hours.

PER SERVING: Calories: 416 | Fat: 25g | Protein: 26g | Sodium: 809mg | Fiber: 3g | Carbohydrates: 20g | Sugar: 7g

Roasted Garlic on Herbed Crostini

Slow roasting garlic brings out its natural sweetness. And serving the garlic with lemony ricotta on toasted baguette makes it irresistible.

INGREDIENTS | SERVES 4

4 bulbs unpeeled garlic

2 teaspoons plus 1 tablespoon olive oil, divided

½ teaspoon kosher salt

½ teaspoon freshly ground black pepper

1 cup low-fat ricotta

2 teaspoons lemon juice

¼ bunch flat-leaf parsley, chopped

1 French baguette

1. Cut the bottom off of each bulb of garlic. Wrap aluminum foil around each bulb, leaving part of the bottom exposed and the top open. Divide 2 teaspoons of olive oil between the bulbs and season with salt and pepper. Fold aluminum foil over the top of the garlic.

2. Place garlic in the bottom of a 4- to 5-quart slow cooker. Cover and cook on low for 4 hours. When garlic is done, it will have the consistency of a baked potato. Remove from slow cooker.

3. In a small bowl, combine the ricotta, lemon juice, and parsley and stir well. Slice the baguette thinly on the bias into 16 slices. Brush bread slices with the remaining oil and place on a baking sheet. Bake until lightly browned, about 5–8 minutes.

4. Divide ricotta mixture between toasted baguette slices. Divide roasted garlic between crostini.

PER SERVING: Calories: 360 | Fat: 12g | Protein: 16g | Sodium: 743mg | Fiber: 2g | Carbohydrates: 48g | Sugar: 2g

Curried Chicken Dip

*Slow-cooked curried chicken dip is a fantastic addition to any party,
or even as a special weekend appetizer. Serve this dip with pita chips and crudités.*

INGREDIENTS | SERVES 6

1 tablespoon olive oil

1 pound boneless, skinless chicken breast, diced in ½" pieces

½ teaspoon kosher salt

1 teaspoon freshly ground black pepper

1 large carrot, peeled and diced

1 large red onion, peeled and diced

1 shallot, peeled and diced

1 garlic clove, minced

2 tablespoons curry powder

¼ teaspoon red pepper flakes

½ cup Roasted Chicken Broth (see recipe in Chapter 11)

½ cup chopped fresh spinach leaves

½ cup low-fat Greek yogurt

2 teaspoons lemon juice

1. Heat olive oil in a large skillet over medium heat. Add chicken to pan and season with salt and pepper. Sauté over medium heat for 2 minutes.

2. Add the carrot, onion, and shallot and cook for 5–7 minutes until softened. Add garlic, curry powder, and red pepper flakes and cook for 1 minute, stirring well. Place the chicken mixture in a 4- to 5-quart slow cooker with the chicken broth. Heat on low for 3½ hours.

3. Add the spinach, yogurt, and lemon juice and stir well. Cook for an additional hour.

PER SERVING: Calories: 155 | Fat: 5g | Protein: 18g | Sodium: 398mg | Fiber: 2g | Carbohydrates: 9g | Sugar: 4g

Curry: Beautiful and Healthy

One of the main ingredients in curry is turmeric, and not only does it add a lovely golden color to the spice mixture; it also adds an unexpected health benefit. Turmeric's active compound, curcumin, prevents sharp spikes in blood sugar. It's also an anti-inflammatory agent.

Spicy Olive Oil Dip

This warm marinated dip will make you feel like you're eating at an authentic Italian restaurant. This recipe is perfect for parties, because you can prep it in a small slow cooker, set it to warm, and have it ready to serve with rustic bread as guests walk through the door.

INGREDIENTS | SERVES 8

1 cup extra-virgin olive oil

1 garlic clove, chopped

½ teaspoon crushed red pepper flakes

1 teaspoon Italian seasoning

¼ teaspoon sea salt

¼ cup balsamic vinegar

½ teaspoon freshly ground black pepper

1. Place olive oil, garlic, red pepper flakes, Italian seasoning, and sea salt in a small 1-quart slow cooker. Cover and cook on low for 1–2 hours, just until the oil gets very warm.

2. Serve olive oil on a plate, drizzled with balsamic vinegar and sprinkled with freshly ground pepper.

PER SERVING: Calories: 246 | Fat: 27g | Protein: 0g | Sodium: 76mg | Fiber: 0g | Carbohydrates: 1.5g | Sugar: 1g

Caramelized Onion Dip

Caramelized onions make this dip irresistible. It's creamy with a great depth of flavor, which means that this appetizer is going to be the star at any gathering you attend.

INGREDIENTS | MAKES 2 CUPS

⅔ cup Caramelized Onions (see recipe in Chapter 13)

8 ounces reduced-fat cream cheese

8 ounces reduced-fat or fat-free sour cream

2 teaspoons dry white wine

2 teaspoons sherry vinegar

1 teaspoon sea salt, crushed in mortar and pestle

½ teaspoon ground white pepper

⅛ teaspoon all-purpose flour

1. Place all ingredients into a 1½- to 2-quart slow cooker. Stir well.

2. Heat on low for 2 hours. Whisk before serving.

PER SERVING (2 TABLESPOONS): Calories: 140 | Fat: 12g | Protein: 2.5g | Sodium: 396mg | Fiber: 0.5g | Carbohydrates: 4g | Sugar: 1.5g

Strawberry-Mango Chutney

This chutney is the perfect accompaniment to grilled pork or chicken.
It also makes a lovely sandwich spread or dip.

INGREDIENTS | SERVES 6

3 cups fresh or thawed frozen strawberries, chopped

1½ cups fresh mango, diced

2 tablespoons minced onion

¼ cup balsamic vinegar

2 cloves garlic, minced

3 tablespoons lime juice

⅓ cup packed dark brown sugar

1. Put all ingredients into a 4- to 5-quart slow cooker. Stir. Turn to high and cook for 3 hours until soft.

2. Uncover and continue to cook on high for 1 hour.

PER SERVING: Calories: 110 | Fat: 0g | Protein: 1g | Sodium: 9mg | Fiber: 2g | Carbohydrates: 27g | Sugar: 23g

A Marriage of Flavor

The flavor combinations for chutneys are boundless. Apple and summer savory, green tomatoes and shallots, mango and mint are all delicious possibilities. And even though hot peppers aren't traditional in the Mediterranean diet, they can be a delicious add-in to a fruit chutney.

Sweet and Salty Nuts

These nuts are incredibly addictive. Put a batch of them in a bowl during your next cocktail party and watch them magically disappear!

INGREDIENTS | MAKES 2 CUPS

1 cup shelled walnuts
1 cup almonds
½ cup packed dark brown sugar
½ teaspoon kosher salt
½ teaspoon cumin
¼ teaspoon cinnamon
¼ teaspoon cloves
¼ teaspoon nutmeg
1 egg white (from 1 large egg)
2 tablespoons water
1 teaspoon sea salt, crushed

1. Make sure there aren't any loose skins attached to nuts and place them in a 4- to 5-quart slow cooker.

2. Mix the brown sugar, kosher salt, cumin, cinnamon, cloves, and nutmeg in a small bowl.

3. In a medium bowl, beat the egg white and water until frothy.

4. Sprinkle the egg mixture over the nuts. Stir the nuts well and add the spice mixture. Stir well again.

5. Cover and cook on low for 3–4 hours. Stir the mixture to break it up. While still hot, add the sea salt.

PER SERVING (¼ CUP): Calories: 218 | Fat: 15g | Protein: 5g | Sodium: 453mg | Fiber: 2.5g | Carbohydrates: 18g | Sugar: 14g

Spicy Walnuts

Pecans would be delicious in this recipe too.

INGREDIENTS | MAKES 4 CUPS

¼ cup olive oil
½ teaspoon onion powder
½ teaspoon kosher salt
½ teaspoon curry powder
½ teaspoon freshly ground black pepper
¼ teaspoon garlic powder
¼ teaspoon ground ginger
1 pound shelled walnuts

1. In a large bowl, whisk together the olive oil, onion powder, salt, curry, pepper, garlic powder, and ginger.

2. Add walnuts and stir well to coat with the seasoned oil.

3. Place walnut mixture in a 4- to 5-quart slow cooker. Cover and cook on low for 3–4 hours, stirring once halfway through. Serve hot or at room temperature.

PER SERVING (¼ CUP): Calories: 213 | Fat: 21g | Protein: 4g | Sodium: 74mg | Fiber: 2g | Carbohydrates: 4g | Sugar: 1g

CHAPTER 5

Chicken and Other Poultry

Poached Chicken Breasts

Choose a good dry wine that you enjoy for this dish. To make the finish even more impressive, let butter come to room temperature and mix in chopped herbs like dill and parsley to make a compound butter. Top each breast with the compound butter before serving.

INGREDIENTS | SERVES 6

1 leek, sliced

1 shallot, diced

2 cloves garlic, minced

1 large carrot, peeled and diced

1 stalk celery, diced

1½ pounds boneless, skinless chicken breasts

¼ cup dry white wine

1 cup Roasted Chicken Broth (see recipe in Chapter 11)

¼ cup olive oil

1. Spray a 4- to 5-quart slow cooker with nonstick olive oil cooking spray.

2. Place all of the ingredients in the cooker.

3. Cover and cook on low for 7–8 hours.

4. Serve each breast with some of the cooking liquid and a drizzle of olive oil.

PER SERVING: Calories: 252 | Fat: 13g | Protein: 25g | Sodium: 322mg | Fiber: 1g | Carbohydrates: 7g | Sugar: 2g

Rosemary Chicken with Potatoes

This simple rustic dish will make you feel like you're dining in a bistro in Paris.

INGREDIENTS | SERVES 6

1 tablespoon olive oil

2 pounds boneless, skinless chicken thighs

½ teaspoon kosher salt

½ teaspoon freshly ground black pepper

6 small red potatoes, halved

1 leek (white and pale green parts only), sliced into 1" pieces

6 sprigs rosemary, divided

1 garlic clove, minced

½ cup Roasted Chicken Broth (see recipe in Chapter 11)

¼ cup capers

1. Heat the olive oil in a large skillet over medium heat until hot but not smoking. Add chicken, and season with salt and pepper. Cook for 5 minutes on one side and flip. Cook for an additional 5 minutes.

2. Place the potatoes and leek into a 4- to 5-quart slow cooker. Top with 5 sprigs of rosemary and garlic.

3. Place chicken thighs on the rosemary. Pour broth over chicken and potatoes.

4. Cover and cook on high for 3–4 hours or until the juices run clear from the chicken. Sprinkle with capers just before serving, and garnish with remaining rosemary.

PER SERVING: Calories: 336 | Fat: 9g | Protein: 33g | Sodium: 595mg | Fiber: 3g | Carbohydrates: 30g | Sugar: 2g

Sage Ricotta Chicken Breasts

*For a different flavor, you could substitute one tablespoon
of fresh chopped thyme for the sage.*

INGREDIENTS | SERVES 4

6 fresh sage leaves, chopped

½ cup part-skim ricotta cheese

4 (4-ounce) boneless, skinless chicken breasts

½ teaspoon kosher salt

½ teaspoon freshly ground black pepper

1 tablespoon olive oil

½ cup white wine

¾ cup chicken broth

¼ cup niçoise olives, pitted and chopped

1. Combine sage and ricotta in a small bowl.

2. Gently slice a slit into a chicken breast to form a pocket. Stuff 2 tablespoons of filling into the chicken. Tie with kitchen twine and trim ends. Repeat with the rest of the chicken and cheese.

3. Season the chicken breasts with salt and pepper. Heat olive oil in a large skillet until it's hot but not smoking. Place chicken in the skillet and sear on one side, about 3 minutes. Flip and brown on the second side, about 3 minutes. Gently place chicken in a 4- to 5-quart slow cooker. Pour wine and chicken broth into the slow cooker.

4. Cook on low for 6–8 hours.

5. Cut twine from chicken breasts and sprinkle with olives.

PER SERVING: Calories: 168 | Fat: 7g | Protein: 19g | Sodium: 489mg | Fiber: 0g | Carbohydrates: 3g | Sugar: 0g

Sweet and Tangy Duck

*Duck is an incredibly versatile protein, and it tastes delicious
with layered flavored combinations like this one.*

INGREDIENTS | SERVES 6

1 (3-pound) duckling, skin removed

1 tablespoon olive oil

½ teaspoon kosher salt

½ teaspoon freshly ground black pepper

½ teaspoon red pepper flakes

2 cloves garlic, minced

1 medium Granny Smith apple, peeled, cored, and cut into 1" pieces

1 medium pear, peeled, cored, and cut into 1" pieces

1 tablespoon lemon juice

1 large red onion, peeled and chopped

1 large carrot, peeled and chopped

1 stalk celery, chopped

½ cup dry red wine

¼ cup honey

¼ cup cider vinegar

1 cup Roasted Chicken Broth (see recipe in Chapter 11)

1. Remove any extraneous fat from the duck. Cut into serving-size portions.

2. Heat olive oil in a large skillet or Dutch oven until hot but not smoking. Add the duck and season with salt, pepper, and red pepper flakes. Cook for 3 minutes on one side. Add garlic to the pan, flip the duck, and cook for 1 minute.

3. While duck is browning, place apple and pear pieces in a bowl of cold water with lemon juice to keep from browning while prepping the vegetables.

4. Place onion, carrot, and celery in the bottom of a 4- to 5-quart slow cooker. Drain the apple and pear, and top vegetables with the duck and apple and pear mixture.

5. In a small bowl, whisk the wine, honey, vinegar, and broth together. Pour over the duck. Cover and cook on high for 3–4 hours.

PER SERVING: Calories: 422 | Fat: 12g | Protein: 46 | Sodium: 516mg | Fiber: 2g | Carbohydrates: 26g | Sugar: 19g

Classic Chicken Parmesan

*This chicken Parmesan recipe creates an incredible aroma while it's cooking—
be prepared for hungry people clamoring for dinner!*

INGREDIENTS | SERVES 6

1 large egg

½ cup bread crumbs

½ teaspoon dried basil

½ teaspoon dried oregano

6 (4-ounce) boneless, skinless chicken breast halves

1 tablespoon olive oil

1¾ cups Long-Cooking Traditional Tomato Sauce (see recipe in Chapter 10)

½ cup shredded mozzarella cheese

2 tablespoons grated Parmesan cheese

¼ cup chopped fresh parsley

1. In a shallow dish, whisk the egg until foamy. In another shallow dish, combine the bread crumbs, basil, and oregano. Dip the chicken in the egg, then into the bread crumb mixture to coat.

2. Heat olive oil in a large skillet until hot but not smoking. Add the chicken and brown for 3 minutes. Flip, and cook for an additional 3 minutes.

3. Place the chicken in a 4- to 5-quart slow cooker. Cover with tomato sauce. Cook on high for 3–4 hours.

4. Sprinkle with cheeses, turn heat to low, and cook for 10 minutes. Remove from slow cooker and garnish with parsley.

PER SERVING: Calories: 278 | Fat: 11g | Protein: 32g | Sodium: 732mg | Fiber: 1.5g | Carbohydrates: 11g | Sugar: 4g

Lemony Roast Chicken

Come home from a day of work or play to an incredibly moist roast chicken!

INGREDIENTS | SERVES 6

1 (3½- to 4-pound) frying chicken

1 teaspoon kosher salt

1 teaspoon freshly ground black pepper

1 clove garlic, crushed

3 tablespoons olive oil

2 lemons, quartered

½ cup Roasted Chicken Broth (see recipe in Chapter 11)

Two Recipes in One!

Once you're done with dinner, place the chicken bones back in the slow cooker. Cover with water, and add in some celery, onion, carrots, dill, and parsley. Cook on low for 10 hours, and you have chicken stock!

1. Rinse chicken inside and out and pat dry. Rub with salt, pepper, and garlic. Brush with olive oil.

2. Place lemon quarters in the bottom of a 4- to 5-quart slow cooker. Top with the chicken. Pour the broth over the chicken.

3. Cover and cook on high for 1 hour. Reduce heat to low and cook for 5–6 hours.

4. Insert a meat thermometer into the thickest part of the thigh. The chicken is done when it registers 165°F.

PER SERVING: Calories: 608 | Fat: 20g | Protein: 96g | Sodium: 825mg | Fiber: 1g | Carbohydrates: 3g | Sugar: 0.5g

Cornish Game Hens

If you have trouble finding Cornish game hens in your local supermarket,
try a specialty market or butcher.

INGREDIENTS | SERVES 2

2 (1½-pound) game hens

1 teaspoon kosher salt, divided

1 teaspoon freshly ground black pepper, divided

2 scallions, finely diced

2 fresh mint leaves, chopped

¼ cup coarse cornmeal

2 tablespoons olive oil, divided

½ cup White Wine Vegetable Stock (see recipe in Chapter 11)

1. Wash the hens inside and out. Pat dry. Season the inside of each with half of the salt and pepper.

2. Combine scallions, mint, and cornmeal in a small bowl. Place 2 tablespoons of the cornmeal mixture in the cavity of each hen. Pull loose skin over the cavity and secure with kitchen string.

3. Heat 1 tablespoon of olive oil in a large skillet over medium heat until hot but not smoking. Season the hens with remaining salt and pepper. Place hens in the pan and cook for 5 minutes. Flip and brown for 5 minutes more.

4. Grease inside of a 4- to 5-quart slow cooker with 2 teaspoons olive oil. Use remaining olive oil to brush on the hens.

5. Place hens in the slow cooker and pour in stock. Cover and cook on high for 4–5 hours. The stuffing temperature should read 165°F with an instant-read thermometer.

PER SERVING: Calories: 991 | Fat: 34g | Protein: 145g | Sodium: 1,837mg | Fiber: 1g | Carbohydrates: 16g | Sugar: 1g

Mediterranean Chicken Casserole

Raisins may seem like an odd ingredient to add to a main dish, but they provide a slightly sweet flavor that beautifully complements the tomatoes and spices.

INGREDIENTS | SERVES 4

1 medium butternut squash, peeled and cut into 2" cubes

1 medium bell pepper, seeded and diced

1 (14½-ounce) can diced tomatoes, undrained

4 (4-ounce) boneless, skinless chicken breast halves, cut into bite-sized pieces

½ cup mild salsa

¼ cup raisins

¼ teaspoon ground cinnamon

¼ teaspoon ground cumin

2 cups cooked white rice

¼ cup chopped fresh parsley

1. Add squash and bell pepper to the bottom of a greased 4- to 5-quart slow cooker. Mix tomatoes, chicken, salsa, raisins, cinnamon, and cumin together and pour on top of squash and peppers.

2. Cover and cook on low for 6 hours or on high for 3 hours until squash is fork tender.

3. Remove chicken and vegetables from slow cooker with slotted spoon. Serve over cooked rice. Ladle remaining sauce from slow cooker over the vegetables. Garnish with parsley.

PER SERVING: Calories: 317 | Fat: 3g | Protein: 28.5g | Sodium: 474mg | Fiber: 3g | Carbohydrates: 43g | Sugar: 10g

Chicken Pesto Polenta

This recipe uses precooked polenta that is cut and layered in a casserole lasagna-style. You can make your own polenta and chill it or buy prepared polenta in tube form from the grocery store.

INGREDIENTS | SERVES 6

4 (4-ounce) boneless, skinless chicken breasts, cut into bite-sized pieces

1 cup prepared pesto, divided

1 medium onion, peeled and finely diced

4 cloves garlic, minced

1½ teaspoons dried Italian seasoning

1 (16-ounce) tube prepared polenta, cut into ½" slices

2 cups chopped fresh spinach

1 (14½-ounce) can diced tomatoes

1 (8-ounce) bag shredded low-fat Italian cheese blend

1. In a large bowl, combine chicken pieces with pesto, onion, garlic, and Italian seasoning.

2. In a greased 4- to 5-quart slow cooker, layer half of chicken mixture, half the polenta, half the spinach, and half the tomatoes. Continue to layer, ending with tomatoes. Cover and cook on low for 4–6 hours or on high for 2–3 hours.

3. Top with cheese. Cover and continue to cook for 45 minutes to an hour until cheese has melted.

PER SERVING: Calories: 535 | Fat: 16g | Protein: 32g | Sodium: 429mg | Fiber: 4g | Carbohydrates: 65g | Sugar: 4g

Make Your Own Pesto

Instead of using prepared pesto you can easily make your own: In a high-powered blender or food processor add 2 cups fresh basil leaves, ½ cup extra-virgin olive oil, ½ cup Parmesan cheese, ½ cup pine nuts, 3 garlic cloves, and salt and pepper to taste. Blend on high for a few minutes until mixture is creamy.

Rotisserie-Style Chicken

Here is a delicious alternative to buying rotisserie chicken in your grocery store. This flavorful roast chicken is incredibly easy to make in your slow cooker. For a fast weekend meal, cook the chicken in the afternoon in the slow cooker and serve for dinner. Go out and play; dinner will be waiting for you.

INGREDIENTS | SERVES 6

1 (4-pound) whole chicken
1½ teaspoons kosher salt
2 teaspoons paprika
½ teaspoon onion powder
½ teaspoon dried thyme
½ teaspoon dried basil
½ teaspoon ground white pepper
½ teaspoon ground cayenne pepper
½ teaspoon ground black pepper
½ teaspoon garlic powder
2 tablespoons olive oil

Gravy

If you would like to make a gravy to go with the chicken, follow these directions: After removing the cooked chicken, turn slow cooker on high. Whisk ⅓ cup flour into the cooking juices. Add salt and pepper to taste and cook for 10–15 minutes, whisking occasionally, until sauce has thickened. Spoon gravy over chicken.

1. Rinse chicken in cold water and pat dry with a paper towel.

2. In a small bowl, mix together salt, paprika, onion powder, thyme, basil, white pepper, cayenne pepper, black pepper, and garlic powder.

3. Rub spice mixture over entire chicken. Rub part of the spice mixture underneath the skin, making sure to leave the skin intact.

4. Place the spice-rubbed chicken in a greased 6-quart slow cooker. Drizzle olive oil evenly over the chicken. Cook on high for 3–3½ hours or on low for 4–5 hours.

5. Remove chicken carefully from the slow cooker and place on a large plate or serving platter.

PER SERVING: Calories: 400 | Fat: 14g | Protein: 64g | Sodium: 820mg | Fiber: 0.5g | Carbohydrates: 1g | Sugar: 0g

Tuscan Chicken and White Beans

Hearty white beans with warm Tuscan spices and tomatoes make this super easy slow-cooked chicken special enough for company! Serve this dish over rice or pasta if you like.

INGREDIENTS | SERVES 4

3 large (6-ounce) boneless, skinless chicken breasts

1 (15½-ounce) can white beans, drained and rinsed

1 (14½-ounce) can diced tomatoes with juice

1 (4-ounce) can mushrooms, drained

¼ cup Spanish olives stuffed with pimientos, sliced in half

2 teaspoons onion powder

1 teaspoon garlic powder

1 teaspoon basil

1 teaspoon oregano

1 teaspoon ground black pepper

½ teaspoon kosher salt

2 teaspoons olive oil

1. Cut chicken breasts into large chunks and place in a greased 4- to 5-quart slow cooker.

2. Add beans, tomatoes (including the juice), mushrooms, and olives. Add onion powder, garlic powder, basil, oregano, pepper, and salt.

3. Mix all ingredients together in the slow cooker. Drizzle olive oil over the top of the chicken and vegetables.

4. Cook on high for 3½–4 hours or on low for 6 hours.

PER SERVING: Calories: 304 | Fat: 7.5g | Protein: 35g | Sodium: 1,109mg | Fiber: 8g | Carbohydrates: 23g | Sugar: 5g

White Beans

White beans, which are also called navy beans, Boston beans, or Yankee beans, are small, lightly colored beans that are very mild in taste and work well in a variety of recipes. If you don't have white beans available, cannellini beans or northern beans, which are slightly larger, are excellent substitutes.

Chicken in Lemon Sauce

This recipe is for a one-pot meal. By completing a simple step at the end of the cooking time, you have meat, potatoes, vegetables, and sauce all ready to serve and eat.

INGREDIENTS | SERVES 4

1 (16-ounce) bag frozen cut green beans, thawed

1 small onion, peeled and cut into thin wedges

4 (4-ounce) boneless, skinless chicken breast halves

4 medium potatoes, peeled and cut in quarters

2 cloves garlic, peeled and minced

¼ teaspoon freshly ground black pepper

1 cup chicken broth

4 ounces cream cheese, cut into cubes

1 teaspoon freshly grated lemon peel

1. Place green beans and onion in the slow cooker. Arrange the chicken and potatoes over the vegetables. Sprinkle with the garlic and pepper. Pour broth over all. Cover and cook on low for 5 or more hours or until chicken is cooked through and moist.

2. Evenly divide the chicken, potatoes, and vegetables between 4 serving plates or onto a serving platter; cover to keep warm.

3. To make the sauce, add the cream cheese cubes and grated lemon peel to the broth in the slow cooker. Stir until cheese melts into the sauce. Pour the sauce over the chicken, potatoes, and vegetables.

PER SERVING: Calories: 439 | Fat: 14g | Protein: 32g | Sodium: 502mg | Fiber: 8g | Carbohydrates: 47g | Sugar: 8g

Roast Chicken with Lemon and Artichokes

This is an elegant twist on a simple roast chicken. Marinated artichoke hearts add a hint of zest while fresh lemons give the dish a bright flavor reminiscent of summer.

INGREDIENTS | SERVES 4

1 small onion, peeled and quartered

1 large carrot, peeled and sliced

1 large lemon

3 cloves garlic

1 (4-pound) whole chicken

½ teaspoon kosher salt

½ teaspoon freshly ground black pepper

2 tablespoons olive oil

1 (6-ounce) jar marinated artichoke hearts

Make a Quick Lemon Sauce

Make a sauce using the liquids from the cooked chicken by straining them into a saucepan. Whisk in 2 tablespoons of flour and cook on low heat until thickened. The resulting sauce will have a fragrant aroma of lemon, artichokes, and garlic. Serve over rice or pasta with green beans or a salad.

1. Grease a large 6-quart slow cooker with nonstick cooking spray.

2. Place the onion and carrot in the slow cooker. Cut the lemon in half. Place half of the lemon, along with the garlic cloves, into the cavity of the chicken.

3. Cut the remainder of the lemon into 4–5 large slices.

4. Place the chicken on top of the onion and carrots. Place lemon slices on top of the chicken. Sprinkle salt and pepper over the chicken. Drizzle olive oil over chicken. Cook on low for 6–8 hours, or on high for 3–4 hours.

5. One hour before serving, place artichokes (discarding the oil) over the top of the chicken in slow cooker.

PER SERVING: Calories: 630 | Fat: 20g | Protein: 97g | Sodium: 692mg | Fiber: 3g | Carbohydrates: 8g | Sugar: 2g

Spicy Olive Chicken

This recipe creates a delicious sauce underneath the roasted chicken.
The pan juices will add flavor to the sauce.

INGREDIENTS | SERVES 4

1 (3-pound) whole chicken, cut into 8 pieces

1 teaspoon kosher salt

½ teaspoon ground black pepper

4 tablespoons unsalted butter

⅔ cup chopped sweet onion

2 tablespoons capers, drained and rinsed

24 green olives, pitted

½ cup chicken broth

½ cup dry white wine

1 teaspoon prepared Dijon mustard

½ teaspoon hot sauce

2 cups cooked white rice

¼ cup fresh chopped parsley

Capers

Capers are flavorful unopened buds from the *Capparis spinosa* bush. They can be packed in salt or brine. Try to find the smallest—they seem to have more flavor than the big ones do. Capers are great on their own or incorporated into sauces. They are also good in salads and as a garnish on many dishes that would otherwise be dull.

1. Sprinkle the chicken pieces with salt and pepper and then brown them in the butter in a large skillet over medium-high heat for about 3 minutes on each side. Remove chicken from skillet and place in a greased 4- to 5-quart slow cooker.

2. Sauté the onion in the same skillet for an additional 3–5 minutes. Add onion to slow cooker, along with capers and olives.

3. In a small bowl, whisk together the broth, wine, and mustard. Pour over chicken in the slow cooker. Add hot sauce. Cover and cook on high for 3–3½ hours or on low for 5½–6 hours.

4. When ready to serve, place chicken over rice. Ladle sauce and olives over each serving. Garnish with parsley.

PER SERVING: Calories: 703 | Fat: 25g | Protein: 75g | Sodium: 1,373mg | Fiber: 2g | Carbohydrates: 34g | Sugar: 1.5g

Sun-Dried Tomato and Feta Stuffed Chicken

*Three Greek-inspired ingredients give these lovely chicken rolls
an attractive appearance and exceptional flavor.*

INGREDIENTS | SERVES 4

4 (4-ounce) boneless, skinless chicken breasts

½ cup chopped oil-packed sun-dried tomatoes

⅓ cup crumbled feta cheese

¼ cup chopped pitted Kalamata olives

1½ cups fresh baby spinach leaves

2 tablespoons olive oil

½ teaspoon kosher salt

½ teaspoon freshly ground black pepper

Sun-Dried Tomatoes

Sun-dried tomatoes are tomatoes that have been dried in the sun to remove moisture content. They have a distinct sweet, yet savory flavor. Most grocery stores carry them in the produce section. They are often preserved in oil, but can also be found dry. If not packed in oil, the tomatoes will need to be reconstituted in water before use.

1. Flatten chicken breasts on a wooden cutting board with the flat side of a meat mallet, to ½-inch thick. Set chicken breasts aside.

2. In a small bowl, mix together the tomatoes, cheese, and olives.

3. Place 3–4 spinach leaves in the middle of each flattened chicken breast. Place 2–3 tablespoons of the tomato filling on top the spinach leaves.

4. Fold one side of the flattened chicken breast over the filling and continue to roll into a cylinder; secure with 2–3 toothpicks per chicken breast. Place the chicken rolls seam-side down in a greased 4- to 5-quart slow cooker.

5. Drizzle olive oil evenly over the top of the chicken rolls and sprinkle the chicken with salt and pepper. Cook on high for 3 hours or on low for 6 hours.

PER SERVING: Calories: 248 | Fat: 12.5g | Protein: 27g | Sodium: 715mg | Fiber: 1g | Carbohydrates: 7g | Sugar: 3g

Chicken Piccata

Serve over mashed potatoes or pasta.

INGREDIENTS | SERVES 4

2 large (6-ounce) boneless, skinless chicken breasts, cut horizontally into very thin slices

1 cup all-purpose flour

1 tablespoon olive oil

¼ cup lemon juice

3 tablespoons nonpareil capers

¾ cup chicken stock

¼ teaspoon freshly ground black pepper

Dredge Details

Dredging is a process in which food is dragged through dry ingredients like cornstarch or bread crumbs to coat it. Dredging can be a one-step process, but if a thicker crust or coating is desired the food is dredged in flour once, dipped in egg or milk, then dredged through flour, cornmeal, or bread crumbs again. In slow cooking, dredging often has a dual purpose of coating the meat and thickening the sauce.

1. Dredge both sides of the chicken breast slices in the flour. Discard leftover flour.

2. Heat olive oil in a nonstick pan over medium-high heat. Quickly sear the chicken on both sides to brown, approximately 1 minute per side.

3. Place the chicken, lemon juice, capers, stock, and pepper into a greased 4- to 5-quart slow cooker.

4. Cook on high for 2–3 hours or on low for 4–6 hours until the chicken is cooked through and the sauce has thickened.

PER SERVING: Calories: 260 | Fat: 6.5g | Protein: 22g | Sodium: 356mg | Fiber: 1g | Carbohydrates: 27g | Sugar: 1g

Pesto Chicken

Pesto has such a unique nutty flavor from pine nuts and basil that it takes plain old chicken and makes it fabulous. This chicken also presents beautifully for a company dinner.

INGREDIENTS | SERVES 4

2 pounds boneless, skinless chicken thighs

4 medium red potatoes, peeled and diced

1 pint cherry tomatoes

½ cup prepared pesto

½ teaspoon ground black pepper

½ teaspoon kosher salt

Place all ingredients in a greased 4- to 5-quart slow cooker. Cook on high for 3–4 hours or on low for 6–8 hours until chicken is tender.

PER SERVING: Calories: 296 | Fat: 5g | Protein: 26g | Sodium: 407mg | Fiber: 4.5g | Carbohydrates: 34g | Sugar: 4g

Chicken Ragu

Serve this over linguine with a sprinkle of Parmesan.

INGREDIENTS | SERVES 6

1 pound boneless skinless chicken breasts, finely chopped

3 shallots, finely minced

4 cups marinara sauce

2 teaspoons crushed rosemary

2 cloves garlic, minced

½ teaspoon freshly ground pepper

½ teaspoon oregano

Place all ingredients into a 4- to 5-quart slow cooker. Stir. Cook on low for 4–6 hours. Stir before serving.

PER SERVING: Calories: 247 | Fat: 6.5g | Protein: 19g | Sodium: 771mg | Fiber: 5g | Carbohydrates: 27g | Sugar: 16g

Chicken Meatball Sun-Dried Tomato Sauce

Sun-dried tomatoes make this sauce taste rich without adding fat.

INGREDIENTS | SERVES 6

1 pound ground chicken

½ cup bread crumbs

1 large egg

2 cloves garlic, minced

1 shallot, minced

1 (28-ounce) can crushed tomatoes

½ cup julienne-cut dry (not oil-packed) sun-dried tomatoes

1 medium onion, peeled and minced

1 tablespoon minced fresh basil

The Scoop on Sun-Dried Tomatoes

Despite losing moisture as they are dried, sun-dried tomatoes retain all of the nutritional benefits of fresh tomatoes, making them a good source of vitamin C and lycopene. Their flavor is more concentrated than fresh tomatoes.

1. Preheat the oven to 375°F. Line two baking sheets with parchment paper.

2. In a large bowl, use your hands to mix the chicken, bread crumbs, egg, garlic, and shallot. Form into 1" balls. Place on the baking sheets and bake for 15 minutes or until cooked through.

3. Pour the crushed tomatoes into a 4- to 5-quart slow cooker. Add the sun-dried tomatoes, onion, and basil. Stir. Add the meatballs and stir to coat with sauce. Cook on low for 6 hours.

PER SERVING: Calories: 253 | Fat: 13g | Protein: 17g | Sodium: 236mg | Fiber: 3g | Carbohydrates: 17g | Sugar: 7g

Tarragon Chicken

The tarragon infuses the chicken with flavor without added fat.

INGREDIENTS | SERVES 4

2 (8-ounce) split chicken breasts
2 cups loosely packed fresh tarragon
1 medium onion, peeled and sliced
¼ teaspoon kosher salt
¼ teaspoon freshly ground black pepper

1. Place the chicken in a 4- to 5-quart slow cooker. Top with remaining ingredients. Cook on low for 7–8 hours.

2. Remove the chicken from the slow cooker. Peel off the skin and remove bones from chicken. Discard skin and bones. Discard the tarragon and onion. Place chicken on a serving platter and slice thinly.

PER SERVING: Calories: 139 | Fat: 3g | Protein: 24g | Sodium: 278mg | Fiber: 0.5g | Carbohydrates: 3g | Sugar: 1g

Chicken with Figs

This recipe was inspired by traditional Moroccan tagines, a type of savory slow-cooked stew. Try it with whole-grain couscous or quinoa.

INGREDIENTS | SERVES 8

½ pound boneless, skinless chicken thighs

¾ pound boneless, skinless chicken breasts

¾ cup dried figs

1 medium sweet potato, peeled and diced

1 medium onion, peeled and chopped

3 cloves garlic, minced

2 teaspoons cumin

1 teaspoon coriander

½ teaspoon cayenne pepper

½ teaspoon ground ginger

½ teaspoon turmeric

½ teaspoon ground orange peel

½ teaspoon freshly ground black pepper

2¾ cups Roasted Chicken Broth (see recipe in Chapter 11)

¼ cup orange juice

1. Cube the chicken. Quickly sauté the chicken in a dry nonstick skillet until it starts to turn white. Drain off any excess grease.

2. Place the chicken and remaining ingredients into a 4- to 5-quart slow cooker. Stir. Cook for 6 hours on low. Stir before serving.

PER SERVING: Calories: 179 | Fat: 4g | Protein: 17g | Sodium: 445mg | Fiber: 2g | Carbohydrates: 19g | Sugar: 9g

Chicken Fricassee

Chicken Fricassee is a dish that is easily adapted for personal taste.
Fennel, mushrooms, or parsnips can be used with great success.

INGREDIENTS | SERVES 6

2 cups sliced red cabbage

2 large carrots, peeled and cut into coin-sized pieces

2 stalks celery, diced

1 medium onion, peeled and sliced

3 (8-ounce) bone-in chicken breasts

¾ cup chicken stock

2 teaspoons paprika

2 teaspoons dried thyme

2 teaspoons dried parsley

1. Place the cabbage, carrots, celery, and onion on the bottom of an oval 4- to 5-quart slow cooker.

2. Place the chicken skin-side up on top of the vegetables. Pour the stock over the chicken and sprinkle it evenly with the spices. Pat the spices onto the chicken skin.

3. Cook on low 6 hours or until the chicken is cooked through. Remove the skin and bones prior to serving.

PER SERVING: Calories: 167 | Fat: 3.5g | Protein: 25.5g | Sodium: 206mg | Fiber: 2g | Carbohydrates: 7g | Sugar: 3.5g

Chicken Saltimbocca

Saltimbocca can refer to a number of ham- or prosciutto-wrapped meat dishes.
In this version, the mild chicken takes on the strong flavors of the capers and prosciutto.

INGREDIENTS | SERVES 6

6 boneless, skinless chicken breast tenderloins (about ¾ pound)

6 paper-thin slices prosciutto

2¼ cups Roasted Chicken Broth (see recipe in Chapter 11)

4 tablespoons capote capers

½ cup minced fresh sage

1. Wrap each tenderloin in prosciutto. Secure with a toothpick if necessary. Place them in a single layer in an oval 4- to 5-quart slow cooker.

2. Pour the broth over the chicken. Sprinkle with the capers and sage. Cook on low for 5 hours or until the chicken is fully cooked. Discard the cooking liquid prior to serving.

PER SERVING: Calories: 136 | Fat: 5.5g | Protein: 16g | Sodium: 808mg | Fiber: 0g | Carbohydrates: 5g | Sugar: 0g

Balsamic Chicken and Spinach

Serve this with rice pilaf.

INGREDIENTS | SERVES 4

¾ pound boneless, skinless chicken breasts, cut into strips

¼ cup balsamic vinegar

4 cloves garlic, minced

1 tablespoon minced fresh oregano

1 tablespoon minced fresh Italian parsley

½ teaspoon freshly ground black pepper

5 ounces baby spinach

1. Place the chicken, vinegar, garlic, and spices into a 4- to 5-quart slow cooker. Stir. Cover and cook on low for 6 hours.

2. Add the baby spinach and cover again. Cook until it starts to wilt, about 15 minutes. Stir before serving.

PER SERVING: Calories: 123 | Fat: 2g | Protein: 19g | Sodium: 129mg | Fiber: 1g | Carbohydrates: 5g | Sugar: 2.5g

Slow-Roasted Chicken with Potatoes, Parsnips, and Onions

Chicken made in the slow cooker is very tender. The onions add a lot of flavor with no added fat needed.

INGREDIENTS | SERVES 6

4 medium onions, peeled and sliced

1 (6-pound) roasting chicken

6 large red potatoes, peeled and quartered

4 medium parsnips, peeled and diced

1 teaspoon kosher salt

1 teaspoon ground black pepper

A Snippet about Parsnips

Parsnips have a mild flavor and a texture that is well suited to extended cooking times. Always peel off the bitter skin before cooking. If parsnips are not available, carrots are an acceptable substitute.

1. Cover the bottom of a 6- to 6½-quart oval slow cooker with half of the onions.

2. Place the chicken, breast-side up, on top of the onions.

3. Cover the chicken with the remaining onions.

4. Arrange the potatoes and parsnips around the chicken and sprinkle with salt and pepper.

5. Cover and cook on low for 8 hours or until the chicken has an internal temperature of 165°F as measured using a food thermometer. Discard the chicken skin before serving.

PER SERVING: Calories: 840 | Fat: 14.5g | Protein: 104g | Sodium: 796mg | Fiber: 9g | Carbohydrates: 70g | Sugar: 9g

Citrusy and Sticky Honey Wings

Making wings in the slow cooker is simple, and the cooker serves double duty as a warmer during an event or party. Once the wings are done, switch the setting to warm so that the wings will stay hot and sticky, but not continue to cook. Perfection!

INGREDIENTS | SERVES 10

3 pounds chicken wings, tips removed

¼ cup honey

¼ cup orange juice

1 tablespoon lime juice

1 teaspoon sea salt, crushed in a mortar and pestle

1 teaspoon freshly ground black pepper

¼ teaspoon garlic powder

¼ teaspoon onion powder

1. Place the wings into a 4- to 5-quart slow cooker.

2. In a small bowl, whisk the honey, orange juice, lime juice, salt, pepper, garlic powder, and onion powder. Pour over the wings. Toss to coat with sauce.

3. Cook for 6–7 hours on low. Stir before serving.

PER SERVING: Calories: 328 | Fat: 21g | Protein: 24g | Sodium: 334mg | Fiber: 0g | Carbohydrates: 8g | Sugar: 7.5g

Italian Chicken Meatloaf

Plenty of herbs and spices fill this slow-cooked meatloaf with tons of flavor.

INGREDIENTS | SERVES 6

6 slices toasted Italian bread

½ cup skim milk

2 teaspoons olive oil

3 shallots, diced

2 cloves garlic, finely minced

1 pound ground chicken

2 large eggs

1 teaspoon dried basil

1 teaspoon dried oregano

½ teaspoon ground thyme

½ teaspoon hot smoked paprika

½ teaspoon freshly ground black pepper

½ teaspoon kosher salt

1. Soak bread in milk for 1 minute, then squeeze dry. Roughly chop the bread and place in a large bowl.

2. Grease slow cooker with the olive oil.

3. Mix remaining ingredients with the bread. Place meat mixture in slow cooker and pat out so that it's an even thickness. Cook on low for 4–6 hours. Use a meat thermometer to make sure internal temperature is 170°F. Let sit for 15 minutes and serve.

PER SERVING: Calories: 313 | Fat: 15g | Protein: 20g | Sodium: 495mg | Fiber: 1.5g | Carbohydrates: 23g | Sugar: 3.5g

A Meat Thermometer Is Your Best Friend

It's extremely important to cook poultry to the proper temperature. And in order to do that, an instant-read meat thermometer is a vital kitchen tool. For a meal like this one, make sure that the thermometer is in the thickest part of the meat. However, if you were checking the temperature of a roast chicken for example, you would place the thermometer in the inner thigh near the breast, but not touching the bone.

Turkey Cutlets with Red Onion Sauce

Turkey cutlets are 1" slices of uncooked turkey breast that can be purchased from many large grocery stores in the poultry section. Cutlets are a great way to prepare turkey for dinner without having to cook the whole bird.

INGREDIENTS | SERVES 4

1¼ pounds turkey cutlets

Salt and pepper, to taste

2 tablespoons olive oil

1 large red onion, peeled and thinly sliced

⅓ cup sweetened rice vinegar

Make It Chicken

If your family prefers the flavor of chicken to turkey, simply use 3–4 boneless chicken breasts instead of turkey cutlets.

1. Season turkey cutlets with salt and pepper and place in a greased 2½-quart slow cooker.

2. In a small bowl, mix together olive oil, red onion, and sweetened rice vinegar. Pour over the turkey cutlets. Cook on high for 3–4 hours or on low for 6–8 hours until turkey is cooked through.

PER SERVING: Calories: 232 | Fat: 9g | Protein: 31g | Sodium: 87mg | Fiber: 1g | Carbohydrates: 3.5g | Sugar: 1.5g

Five-Ingredient Greek Chicken

If you've got these five things in your cupboard, you've got a gorgeously slow-cooked meal waiting to feed you and your family. It's the perfect meal to serve with crusty French bread on a cold, rainy night.

INGREDIENTS | SERVES 6

6 (5-ounce) bone-in chicken thighs, skinned

½ cup Kalamata olives

1 (6½-ounce) jar artichokes in olive oil, undrained

1 pint cherry tomatoes

¼ cup chopped parsley

1. Place chicken, olives, artichokes and artichoke oil, and cherry tomatoes in a 4- to 5-quart slow cooker.

2. Cover and cook on low for 4–6 hours. Serve in large bowls garnished with parsley.

PER SERVING: Calories: 231 | Fat: 5g | Protein: 29g | Sodium: 153mg | Fiber: 2.5g | Carbohydrates: 8g | Sugar: 1.5g

CHAPTER 6

Beef

Rouladen

Rouladen is a German dish that has many variations; this one is simply delicious! Round steaks are traditionally low in ribbons of fat, making them slightly tougher than more expensive cuts of meat, but the slow cooking method here produces a tender, melt-in-your-mouth final bite.

INGREDIENTS | SERVES 4

¼ cup red wine

1 cup water

4 very thin round steaks (about ¾ pound total)

2 tablespoons grainy German-style mustard

1 tablespoon lean bacon crumbles

4 dill pickle spears

Roulade Rules

Roulade, the generic term for steak wrapped around a savory filling, works best with steaks that are approximately ⅛" thick, 8–10" long, and 5" wide. Look for them in the meat section labeled as "rolling steaks," or ask the butcher to specially cut some. They are a great way to enjoy red meat in small portions.

1. Pour the wine and water into the bottom of an oval 4- to 5-quart slow cooker.

2. Place the steaks on a platter. Spread ½ tablespoon mustard on each steak and sprinkle with one-quarter of the bacon crumbles. Place one of the pickle spears on one end of each steak. Roll pickle end of steak until it looks like a spiral, with the pickle in the middle. Place on a skillet seam-side down. Cook over medium-high heat for 1 minute, then use tongs to flip the steaks carefully and cook the other side for 1 minute.

3. Place each roll in a single layer in the water-wine mixture. Cook on low for 1 hour. Remove the rolls, discarding the cooking liquid.

PER SERVING: Calories: 233 | Fat: 12.5g | Protein: 20g | Sodium: 367mg | Fiber: 0.5g | Carbohydrates: 6g | Sugar: 5g

Warmly Spiced Beef

Traditionally made with lamb, this lean-beef version is lower in fat but full of flavor. Serve it over rice.

INGREDIENTS | SERVES 6

1 pound cubed bottom round

1 medium onion, peeled and diced

4 cloves garlic, minced

2 tablespoons cumin

2 tablespoons coriander

1 tablespoon turmeric

2 teaspoons cardamom

2 teaspoons minced fresh ginger

2 teaspoons freshly ground black pepper

2 teaspoons chili powder

1 (28-ounce) can crushed tomatoes

1 cup fat-free Greek yogurt

1. Spray a 4- to 5-quart slow cooker with nonstick olive oil cooking spray.

2. In a nonstick skillet over medium-high heat, sauté the beef, onion, and garlic until just browned. Drain off any excess fat. Place into prepared slow cooker.

3. Add the spices and crushed tomatoes. Cook on low for 8 hours. Stir in the yogurt prior to serving.

PER SERVING: Calories: 197 | Fat: 8g | Protein: 19g | Sodium: 80mg | Fiber: 4g | Carbohydrates: 13.5g | Sugar: 6g

Skinny French Dip Beef for Sandwiches

The long cooking time makes lean meat fork tender, perfect for stuffing into crusty bread for sandwiches. If you're watching your carb intake, try serving this delicious beef over mashed cauliflower.

INGREDIENTS | SERVES 8

2 pounds lean bottom round roast

1 large Vidalia or Walla Walla onion, peeled and sliced

2 cloves garlic, sliced

3 tablespoons soy sauce

1 tablespoon minced fresh thyme

1 teaspoon minced fresh rosemary

1 teaspoon freshly ground black pepper

1. Slice the beef into rounds, removing excess fat. Place into a 4- to 5-quart slow cooker. Add the remaining ingredients.

2. Cook 10 hours on low or until the meat is falling apart. Shred with a fork.

PER SERVING: Calories: 156 | Fat: 5g | Protein: 25.5g | Sodium: 404mg | Fiber: 0.5g | Carbohydrates: 3g | Sugar: 1g

Dijon Beef Roast

Dijon mustard gives this roast a delicious tangy flavor. This recipe is perfect for roast beef sandwiches, or you can serve it alongside steamed greens for a flavorful Sunday evening dinner.

INGREDIENTS | SERVES 6

1 large onion, peeled and thickly sliced

1 (4-pound) beef round roast

3 tablespoons Dijon mustard

½ teaspoon kosher salt

½ teaspoon ground black pepper

1 tablespoon olive oil

½ cup beef broth

Internal Temperatures for Beef

Beef must reach a specific internal temperature, depending on your preference: medium rare, 145°F; medium, 160°F; and well done, 170°F. Use a probe thermometer to determine the internal temperature before you shut off the slow cooker.

1. Spray a 4- to 5-quart slow cooker with nonstick olive oil cooking spray.

2. Place the onion slices in the prepared slow cooker.

3. Rub the beef roast with the mustard. Place on top of sliced onion.

4. Sprinkle salt and pepper on top of beef roast and drizzle with olive oil and broth.

5. Cover and cook on high for 2½–3 hours or on low for 5–6 hours. Cooking time will vary depending on your preference of doneness (either rare/medium or well done). For a rarer roast, check the internal temperature (should be around 145°F) after cooking for 1½ hours on high or 3 hours on low. Serve roast with the cooked onion and au jus drizzled on top.

PER SERVING: Calories: 496 | Fat: 24g | Protein: 64g | Sodium: 512mg | Fiber: 1g | Carbohydrates: 3g | Sugar: 1g

Meatloaf-Stuffed Green Peppers

This recipe is slightly different from traditional stuffed pepper recipes because it doesn't contain rice or potatoes to supplement the meat mixture. This is a great main dish option for a low-carb dinner.

INGREDIENTS | SERVES 4

1 slice sturdy bread, torn into very small pieces

¼ cup 2% milk

1 pound ground beef

½ teaspoon kosher salt

½ teaspoon ground black pepper

1½ teaspoons dried onion

1 large egg

4 large green peppers

1. Spray a 4- to 5-quart slow cooker with nonstick olive oil cooking spray.

2. In a large bowl, mix together the bread and milk. Set aside for 5 minutes.

3. Add ground beef, salt, pepper, dried onion, and egg to the softened bread. Mix together well.

4. Carefully remove the tops, seeds, and membranes of the peppers. Fill each pepper with ¼ of the meatloaf mixture.

5. Place the stuffed peppers in the prepared slow cooker. Add ⅓ cup water around the bottom of the stuffed peppers.

6. Cook on high for 3–4 hours or on low for 6–8 hours until green peppers are softened.

PER SERVING: Calories: 281 | Fat: 13g | Protein: 27g | Sodium: 449mg | Fiber: 3g | Carbohydrates: 13g | Sugar: 5g

Ground Beef Ragout

Ragout is a term that generally refers to a slow-cooked stew with a variety of vegetables that can be made with or without meat. Ground beef is used in this version for a very economical main dish. Serve over cooked rice or prepared polenta.

INGREDIENTS | SERVES 4

1 pound ground beef

2 medium onions, peeled and finely chopped

1 large green pepper, diced with seeds removed

1 tablespoon olive oil

1 (14½-ounce) can Italian-style stewed tomatoes

3 medium carrots, peeled and cut into ½" slices

½ cup beef broth

½ teaspoon kosher salt

½ teaspoon ground black pepper

1 medium zucchini, halved lengthwise and cut into ½" slices

Not a Fan of Zucchini?

Instead of using zucchini, use yellow squash, precooked potatoes or sweet potatoes, parsnips, or even mushrooms. Use whatever vegetables you have on hand!

1. Brown ground beef in a skillet over medium heat, discard grease, and spoon ground beef into a greased 4- to 5-quart slow cooker.

2. In the same pan, sauté onions and green pepper in olive oil for several minutes until softened. Add onions and green pepper to slow cooker.

3. Add tomatoes, carrots, broth, salt, and pepper to the slow cooker. Stir to combine all ingredients.

4. Cook for 4 hours on high or 8 hours on low.

5. In the last hour of cooking, stir in zucchini and allow to cook until fork tender.

PER SERVING: Calories: 304 | Fat: 15g | Protein: 25g | Sodium: 650mg | Fiber: 4.5g | Carbohydrates: 17g | Sugar: 9g

Red Wine Pot Roast

A little bit of wine goes a long way in flavoring this simple one-crock meal.
Using lean meat creates a light and delicate broth surrounding the vegetables.

INGREDIENTS | SERVES 6

⅓ cup red wine

½ cup water

4 medium red potatoes, peeled and quartered

3 medium carrots, peeled and cut into thirds

2 medium bulbs fennel, quartered

2 medium rutabagas, peeled and quartered

1 medium onion, peeled and sliced

4 cloves garlic, sliced

1½ pounds lean top round roast, excess fat removed

½ teaspoon kosher salt

½ teaspoon freshly ground black pepper

1. Pour the wine and water into a greased 4- to 5-quart slow cooker. Add the potatoes, carrots, fennel, rutabagas, onion, and garlic. Stir.

2. Add the roast. Sprinkle with salt and pepper. Cook on low for 8 hours.

3. Remove and slice the beef. Use a slotted spoon to serve the vegetables. Discard the cooking liquid.

PER SERVING: Calories: 355 | Fat: 5g | Protein: 31g | Sodium: 362mg | Fiber: 9g | Carbohydrates: 44g | Sugar: 11g

Lean Roast with Fennel and Rutabaga

Serve this flavorful roast with roasted potatoes and a crisp green salad.

INGREDIENTS | SERVES 4

2 pounds boneless bottom round roast

½ teaspoon kosher salt

½ teaspoon ground black pepper

1 large Vidalia or other sweet onion, peeled and sliced

1 pound rutabaga, peeled and cubed

2 medium bulbs fennel, sliced

1. Cut any excess fat off the roast. Sprinkle the salt and pepper on all sides of the roast.

2. Heat a nonstick skillet on medium-high heat for 30 seconds. Place the roast in the pan. Quickly sear each side of the roast, approximately 5 seconds per side.

3. Place the roast in a 4- to 5-quart slow cooker. Cover it with the onion, rutabaga, and fennel.

4. Cook on low for 6 hours or until desired doneness.

PER SERVING: Calories: 378 | Fat: 10g | Protein: 53g | Sodium: 511mg | Fiber: 7g | Carbohydrates: 21g | Sugar: 8g

Braciola

Look for steaks that are approximately ⅛" thick, 8"–10" long, and 5" wide to make this Italian roulade.

INGREDIENTS | SERVES 8

½ teaspoon olive oil

½ cup diced onions

2 cloves garlic, minced

1 (32-ounce) can diced tomatoes

8 stalks rapini

8 very thin-cut round steaks (about 1¼ pounds total)

4 teaspoons bread crumbs

4 teaspoons grated Parmesan

1. Heat the oil in a nonstick skillet over medium-high heat. Sauté the onions and garlic until the onions are soft, about 5 minutes. Place in a 6-quart oval slow cooker. Add the tomatoes and stir to combine.

2. Cut the stems off the rapini. Place the steaks flat on a platter horizontally. Sprinkle each steak with ½ teaspoon bread crumbs and ½ teaspoon Parmesan. Place a bunch of rapini leaves on one end of each steak. Roll each steak lengthwise, so that the rapini filling is wrapped tightly. It should look like a spiral. Place in the skillet seam-side down. Cook for 1 minute over medium-high heat, use tongs to flip the steaks carefully, and cook the other side for 1 minute.

3. Place each roll in a single layer on top of the tomato sauce. Cook on low for 1–2 hours or until the steaks are cooked through.

PER SERVING: Calories: 195 | Fat: 6g | Protein: 20g | Sodium: 117mg | Fiber: 5.5g | Carbohydrates: 16g | Sugar: 6g

Portobello Tri-Tip

Lean, often overlooked cuts of beef like the tri-tip are perfect for the slow cooker. The long, moisture-rich environment creates tender meat, despite the lack of fat.

INGREDIENTS | SERVES 12

1 (3-pound) tri-tip roast, excess fat removed

6 large portobello mushroom caps, sliced

1 medium onion, peeled and diced

1 tablespoon steak seasoning

¼ cup beef broth

1 tablespoon Worcestershire sauce

1 tablespoon balsamic vinegar

Make Your Own Steak Seasoning

In a small bowl, stir 2 tablespoons each black pepper, kosher salt, caraway seeds, paprika, granulated garlic, and dehydrated mushrooms. Store in an airtight container. Mix into hamburgers or meatloaf or use as a dry rub on steaks.

1. In a large dry skillet, sear the tri-tip over high heat for about 3 minutes per side. Place in a 6- to 6½-quart slow cooker.

2. Spray a medium nonstick skillet with cooking spray. Sauté mushrooms and onion until the onion is soft but not browned, about 5 minutes. Add to the slow cooker, along with the remaining ingredients.

3. Cook on low for 6–8 hours or until the meat is falling apart and tender.

PER SERVING: Calories: 200 | Fat: 10g | Protein: 24g | Sodium: 387mg | Fiber: 1g | Carbohydrates: 3g | Sugar: 2g

Beef with Root Vegetables

This rustic beef and root vegetable stew is perfect with a glass of dry red wine.

INGREDIENTS | SERVES 6

2 medium parsnips, peeled and chopped into 1" pieces

4 medium carrots, peeled and chopped into 1" pieces

2 medium turnips, peeled and chopped into 1" pieces

2 medium onions, peeled and chopped into 1" pieces

2 large leeks (white and pale green parts only), chopped into 1" pieces

2 stalks celery, chopped into 1" pieces

½ cup all-purpose flour

2 teaspoons freshly ground black pepper

2 pounds chuck roast, cubed into 1" pieces

2 tablespoons olive oil

3 cups Roasted Beef Stock (see recipe in Chapter 11)

½ teaspoon kosher salt

12 peppercorns

1. Layer parsnips, carrots, and turnips on the bottom of a 4- to 5-quart slow cooker. Top with onions, leeks, and celery.

2. Place flour and pepper in a large paper bag. Add meat and shake well to coat. Heat oil in large skillet over medium heat until it shimmers, about 1 minute. Add beef and brown in batches, about 3 minutes per side. Place meat on top of vegetables in slow cooker.

3. Pour stock over beef and add salt and peppercorns.

4. Cover and cook on low for 6–8 hours.

PER SERVING: Calories: 547 | Fat: 35g | Protein: 31g | Sodium: 618mg | Fiber: 4.5g | Carbohydrates: 27g | Sugar: 9g

Lighter Moussaka

Traditionally moussaka uses lamb, but this version utilizes lean beef and baked eggplant instead of fried. (Which makes it healthier and has the added bonus of easier clean up!) Even though there are some changes, you won't notice them—because the dish has the authentic taste of the original.

INGREDIENTS | SERVES 6

2 (1-pound) eggplants, peeled

1½ teaspoons kosher salt

1 teaspoon olive oil

1 large red onion, peeled and diced

2 cloves garlic, minced

1 (28-ounce) can whole tomatoes in purée

½ cup dry red wine

1 tablespoon tomato paste

½ teaspoon cinnamon

½ teaspoon allspice

1 tablespoon chopped fresh oregano

1 tablespoon minced flat-leaf parsley

1 pound 94% lean ground beef

1 cup fat-free evaporated milk

1 tablespoon butter

1 large egg

2 tablespoons all-purpose flour

Eggplant: A Nutritional Powerhouse

Eggplant is low in saturated fat and cholesterol, and it has few calories. In fact, one cup of cooked eggplant has less than 40 calories. Eggplant also contains omega-3 and omega-6 fatty acids, which can promote good brain function and help with heart health and cancer prevention.

1. Slice the eggplants lengthwise vertically into ¼" slices. Place slices in a colander and divide salt between the slices. Let sit for 15 minutes. Rinse well to remove salt and pat dry.

2. Preheat oven to 375°F. Arrange the eggplant slices in a single layer on two parchment paper–lined baking sheets. Bake for 15 minutes and reserve.

3. Heat the oil in a large nonstick skillet over medium-high heat. Sauté the onion and garlic for 1 minute, then add the tomatoes, wine, tomato paste, cinnamon, allspice, oregano, parsley, and ground beef. Break up the tomatoes and beef into small chunks using a potato masher. Reduce heat to medium-low and simmer, stirring occasionally, until the meat is browned and most of the liquid evaporates, about 10 minutes.

4. Ladle half of the tomato and beef mixture onto the bottom of a 4- or 6-quart oval slow cooker. Top with a single layer of eggplant, taking care to leave no gaps between slices. Top with remaining tomato and beef mixture. Top with another layer of eggplant. Cover and cook on high for 3 hours.

5. In a small saucepan, whisk together the evaporated milk, butter, egg, and flour. Bring to a boil over high heat and then reduce the heat to low. Whisk until smooth. Remove from heat.

6. Pour the sauce over the eggplant and cook an additional 1–1½ hours on high.

PER SERVING: Calories: 269 | Fat: 9g | Protein: 25g | Sodium: 710mg | Fiber: 7g | Carbohydrates: 20g | Sugar: 10g

Guilt-Free Meatloaf

*This meatloaf is chock-a-block with vegetables, herbs, and spices,
which makes it a colorful, healthy—and extra delicious—version.*

INGREDIENTS | SERVES 6

4 slices toasted Italian bread

1 medium yellow onion, peeled and chopped

1 medium carrot, peeled and chopped

1 stalk celery, chopped

1 clove garlic, chopped

1 medium shallot, peeled and chopped

¼ bunch fresh parsley, large stems removed

1½ tablespoons fresh thyme leaves

2 large plum tomatoes, diced into ½" pieces

½ cup shredded Parmesan cheese

½ pound lean ground beef

¼ pound lean ground pork

¼ pound lean ground veal

1 large egg, beaten

1 teaspoon fresh-cracked black pepper

½ teaspoon kosher salt

1 teaspoon olive oil

1. Place the toast in a medium bowl. Cover with water and soak for 30 seconds. Squeeze out liquid and set aside.

2. Place onion, carrot, celery, garlic, shallot, parsley, and thyme into a food processor. Pulse 4–5 times until finely chopped. Add tomatoes and pulse twice. Add bread and Parmesan and pulse twice more.

3. Place vegetable mixture in a large bowl with beef, pork, veal, egg, pepper, and salt. Mix well.

4. Grease a 4- to 5-quart slow cooker with olive oil. Place the meatloaf mixture in slow cooker and pat out so that it's an even size. Cover and cook on high for 4 hours, or on low for 6–8 hours. The meatloaf is done when the internal temperature reaches 170°F. Let sit for 30 minutes, then remove from slow cooker. Slice and serve.

PER SERVING: Calories: 294 | Fat: 13g | Protein: 24g | Sodium: 638mg | Fiber: 2g | Carbohydrates: 20g | Sugar: 4.5g

Caramelized Onion Dip (Chapter 4)

Roasted Beets (Chapter 13)

Spiced Tomatoes (Chapter 14)

Breakfast Spanish Tortilla (Chapter 2)

Paella (Chapter 8)

Classic Polenta with Herbs and Parmesan
(Chapter 13)

Overnight Marinara Poached Eggs (Chapter 2)

White Bean Cassoulet (Chapter 14)

Lemony Roast Chicken (Chapter 5)

Savory Cauliflower Custard (Chapter 13)

Fingerling Potatoes with Herb Vinaigrette
(Chapter 9)

Fennel and Caper Sauce (Chapter 10)

Long-Cooking Traditional Tomato Sauce
(Chapter 10)

Parmesan Olive Focaccia (Chapter 3)

Fish Chili with Beans (Chapter 12)

Tomato, Oregano, and Goat Cheese
Breakfast Casserole (Chapter 2)

Pork Tenderloin with Fennel (Chapter 7)

Herbed Focaccia with Arugula and Shaved Parmesan (Chapter 3)

Classic Minestrone (Chapter 13)

Cranberry Bean Paste (Chapter 14)

Savory French Toast with Herb Purée (Chapter 2)

Greek Lemon-Chicken Soup (Chapter 11)

Nomad's Fruit and Nut Dish (Chapter 14)

Spicy Walnuts (Chapter 4)

Short Ribs of Beef with Red Wine

Use your favorite dry red wine in this succulent beef dish.
Serve it on polenta or mashed potatoes to absorb the rich sauce.

INGREDIENTS | SERVES 6

1½ pounds short ribs of beef, excess fat trimmed

1 tablespoon ground cumin

1 teaspoon dried thyme

½ teaspoon onion powder

½ teaspoon garlic powder

1 teaspoon kosher salt

1 teaspoon freshly ground black pepper

1 tablespoon olive oil

2 large red onions, peeled and chopped

12 large plum tomatoes, chopped

1 cup dry red wine

1 quart Red Wine and Tomato Vegetable Stock (see recipe in Chapter 11)

1. Season the ribs with cumin, thyme, onion powder, garlic powder, salt, and pepper.

2. Heat the oil over medium-high heat in a Dutch oven, and sear the ribs on both sides until browned, about 5 minutes per side. Place ribs in slow cooker. Add the onions to the Dutch oven and sauté for 2 minutes, and add the tomatoes and sauté 1 minute more. Add the wine and deglaze the pan. Reduce heat to low and let wine reduce by half, about 10 minutes.

3. Add the stock and bring to a simmer. Pour wine mixture over ribs. Cover and cook on low for 6–8 hours. If you want the sauce to thicken up, remove cover from slow cooker and turn on high for 15 minutes.

PER SERVING: Calories: 325 | Fat: 11g | Protein: 28g | Sodium: 844mg | Fiber: 5.5g | Carbohydrates: 23g | Sugar: 13g

Roast Beef for Two

Couples deserve a good roast dinner just as much as larger families.
So enjoy this one without having to eat leftovers for a week.

INGREDIENTS | SERVES 2

½ teaspoon freshly ground black pepper

½ teaspoon fennel seeds

½ teaspoon crushed rosemary

¼ teaspoon kosher salt

½ teaspoon dried oregano

¾-pound bottom round roast, excess fat removed

¼ cup Caramelized Onions (see recipe in Chapter 13)

¼ cup Roasted Beef Stock (see recipe in Chapter 11)

1 clove garlic, sliced

1. In a small bowl, stir the pepper, fennel seeds, rosemary, salt, and oregano. Rub it onto all sides of the meat. Refrigerate for 15 minutes.

2. Place the roast in a 4- to 5-quart slow cooker. Add the caramelized onions, stock, and garlic. Cook on low for 6 hours, or on high for 3 hours. Remove roast and slice. Serve the slices topped with the caramelized onions. Discard any cooking juices.

PER SERVING: Calories: 235 | Fat: 7g | Protein: 38g | Sodium: 455mg | Fiber: 1g | Carbohydrates: 4g | Sugar: 1g

Meatballs with Mushrooms

Serve these meatballs with skewers or, for a more substantial dish, provide rolls and let your guests make little meatball sandwiches.

INGREDIENTS | SERVES 6

1 pound lean ground beef
1 clove garlic, minced
¼ cup chopped celery
½ cup uncooked rice
½ cup bread crumbs
½ teaspoon sage
½ teaspoon kosher salt
½ teaspoon ground white pepper
3 tablespoons vegetable oil, divided
½ pound mushrooms, minced
1 medium onion, peeled and minced
1 tablespoon all-purpose flour
1 cup water
1 cup tomato sauce

Rice and Slow Cooking

Rice is nice, especially when it's made in a slow cooker. Use converted rice (not instant) and it will come out light and fluffy. You can also add vegetables and spices to the rice for an easy meal.

1. Spray a 4- to 5-quart slow cooker with nonstick olive oil cooking spray. In a large bowl, combine the ground beef, garlic, celery, rice, bread crumbs, sage, salt, and pepper.

2. Form mixture into ¾" balls. Heat 2 tablespoons oil in a large skillet over medium heat. Brown meatballs on all sides and drain on a paper-towel-lined plate. Arrange meatballs in the slow cooker.

3. Heat remaining oil in a skillet over medium-high heat. Sauté the mushrooms and onion until softened, about 5 minutes. Add the flour to the mushroom mixture and stir to thicken. Add the water and tomato sauce and mix until smooth.

4. Pour the tomato and mushroom mixture over meatballs.

5. Cover and cook on low for 3–4 hours.

PER SERVING: Calories: 369 | Fat: 20g | Protein: 20g | Sodium: 533mg | Fiber: 2g | Carbohydrates: 26g | Sugar: 4g

Paprika Meatballs

These can be served with skewers as a finger food or over pasta as a main dish.
They are excellent with fresh angel hair pasta.

INGREDIENTS | SERVES 8

1 pound ground veal

1 pound ground pork

1 clove garlic, minced

¼ pound shredded mozzarella cheese

3 large eggs

1 tablespoon paprika

1 teaspoon kosher salt

1 cup bread crumbs

½ cup milk

2 tablespoons vegetable oil

2 large plum tomatoes, diced

1 cup tomato sauce

Pasta and Slow Cooking

Pasta is a great addition to slow-cooked meals, but it shouldn't be added at the beginning of a slow cooker meal. Add uncooked pasta to the slow cooker about an hour before serving.

1. Spray a 4- to 5-quart slow cooker with nonstick olive oil cooking spray.

2. Combine the veal, pork, garlic, and cheese in a large bowl with the eggs, paprika, salt, bread crumbs, and milk; mix well.

3. Form mixture into ¾" balls. Heat oil in a large skillet over medium heat. Brown meatballs on all sides and drain on a paper-towel-lined plate. Arrange meatballs in the slow cooker.

4. Pour the tomatoes and tomato sauce over the meatballs.

5. Cover and cook on low for 3–4 hours.

PER SERVING: Calories: 410 | Fat: 26g | Protein: 29g | Sodium: 724mg | Fiber: 2g | Carbohydrates: 15g | Sugar: 4.5g

Tangy Burgundy Ribs

You can serve this as a finger food, or with rice as a more substantial dish.
Don't forget to include plenty of napkins!

INGREDIENTS | SERVES 8

½ cup all-purpose flour

¼ teaspoon coarsely ground black pepper

4 pounds lean short ribs, cut into serving-size pieces

2 tablespoons vegetable oil

4 stalks celery, sliced

2 medium onions, peeled and sliced

3 teaspoons prepared mustard

2 tablespoons Worcestershire sauce

1 teaspoon kosher salt

1 cup ketchup

½ cup wine vinegar

1 cup Burgundy wine

1. Spray a 4- to 5-quart slow cooker with nonstick olive oil cooking spray. Mix the flour and pepper in a shallow dish. Toss ribs in flour mixture to lightly coat the ribs.

2. Heat oil in a large skillet over medium heat. Brown ribs 5 minutes per side, then place in slow cooker.

3. Add celery, onions, mustard, Worcestershire sauce, salt, ketchup, and vinegar to the slow cooker.

4. Cover and cook on low for 4–5 hours. Half an hour before the end of cooking, add the wine to the slow cooker.

PER SERVING: Calories: 522 | Fat: 26g | Protein: 44g | Sodium: 858mg | Fiber: 1g | Carbohydrates: 18g | Sugar: 9g

Protect Your Slow Cooker

When the party's over, don't forget to let your slow cookers cool before you fill them with dishwater. If they're still hot when you add the water, they could crack. Once they've cooled and you've added water, you might want to let them soak overnight to loosen any hardened foods.

Burgundy Pepper Beef

*You can serve this with small forks, or provide your guests
with small bowls of warm egg noodles to enjoy with the sauce.*

INGREDIENTS | SERVES 8

½ cup plus 2 tablespoons all-purpose flour, divided

½ teaspoon ground black pepper

2 pounds stew beef, such as blade roast or chuck steak, cut into 1" cubes

2 tablespoons oil

2 medium onions, peeled and quartered

½ pound button mushrooms, halved

1 tablespoon Worcestershire sauce

½ teaspoon kosher salt

1 tablespoon sugar

1 cup water

½ cup vinegar

1 cup Burgundy wine

Be Cool, But Not Too Cool

Don't add icy cold ingredients to a pre-heated slow cooker. Sudden temperature changes can crack the crockery pot. That's a surprise you definitely don't want on the day of your party.

1. Spray a 4- to 5-quart slow cooker with nonstick olive oil cooking spray. Mix ½ cup flour and pepper in a shallow dish. Toss beef cubes in flour mixture to lightly coat.

2. Heat oil in a large skillet over medium heat. Brown beef 3 minutes per side in batches, then place in slow cooker. Keep the oil in the pan.

3. Sauté the onions and mushrooms over medium heat in the pan in the oil used for the beef, until onions are soft, about 8 minutes.

4. Add onion mixture to the slow cooker with Worcestershire sauce, salt, sugar, water, and vinegar. Cover and cook on low for 3–4 hours.

5. One hour before serving, remove 2 tablespoons of sauce from the slow cooker and let it cool in a small bowl briefly before mixing it well with the remaining flour. Stir this into the sauce in the slow cooker, mixing well. Add the wine.

PER SERVING: Calories: 284 | Fat: 11g | Protein: 25g | Sodium: 232mg | Fiber: 1g | Carbohydrates: 13g | Sugar: 3g

Osso Bucco

Osso bucco is an extremely inexpensive yet chic dish to make.
The slow cooker takes a lot of the work out of making this classic dish.

INGREDIENTS | SERVES 12

1 cup all-purpose flour
1 teaspoon freshly ground black pepper
6 pounds veal shanks (12 shanks)
1 tablespoon olive oil
1 tablespoon butter
2 cups chopped onion
8 cloves garlic, minced
2 anchovies
2 tablespoons minced fresh rosemary
2 tablespoons minced fresh thyme
6 cups beef broth

Soaking and the Slow Cooker

If there is food stuck inside your slow cooker's insert, don't be tempted to soak it in the sink overnight. If your slow cooker has an unglazed bottom, it will absorb water, which may lead to cracking. Instead, place the slow cooker on the counter and use a pitcher to fill it with water.

1. In a shallow bowl, mix together the flour and pepper. Dredge the veal shanks in flour. Set aside.

2. Heat the oil in a nonstick skillet over medium-high heat. Brown the veal shanks on all sides, about 5 minutes per side. Drain off all the grease. Drain the veal on paper-towel-lined plates, and then place the shanks in a 6- to 6½-quart slow cooker.

3. Heat the butter in a large skillet over medium-high heat. Sauté the onion, garlic, and anchovies for 3 minutes. Add the rosemary, thyme, and broth. Bring to a boil. Boil for 5–8 minutes or until the mixture starts to reduce. Pour over the veal shanks in the slow cooker. Cook on low for 9 hours.

4. Skim off any fat that has risen to the top. Divide the shanks and drizzle each with ¼ cup of sauce.

PER SERVING: Calories: 334 | Fat: 10g | Protein: 46g | Sodium: 589mg | Fiber: 1g | Carbohydrates: 12g | Sugar: 1g

Sherry Meatballs

When serving these as finger foods, be sure to include small slices of French bread to soak up the rich sauce.

INGREDIENTS | SERVES 8

6 slices bacon

2 medium onions, peeled and diced

2 cloves garlic, minced

1 cup dry bread crumbs

2 pounds ground beef

2 large eggs

1 teaspoon kosher salt

½ teaspoon ground black pepper

½ teaspoon oregano

3 tablespoons butter

1 pound button mushrooms, sliced

2 tablespoons all-purpose flour

½ cup milk

½ cup water

½ cup sherry

Meatball Mayhem

No one wants to spend hours forming meatballs. Instead, use an ice cream scoop. You can even get scoops in different sizes, so you can churn out petite or jumbo meatballs in no time.

1. Spray a 4- to 5-quart slow cooker with nonstick olive oil cooking spray. Heat the bacon in a large skillet over medium heat until browned. Remove the browned slices from the pan to drain, crumble bacon, and set aside; leave bacon fat in the pan.

2. Sauté the onions and garlic in the remaining bacon fat, then remove the onion mixture from the pan and add it to the bread crumbs, ground beef, eggs, salt, pepper, and oregano in a large bowl. Form the meat mixture into ¾" balls.

3. In the same skillet, brown the meatballs in the remaining bacon fat over medium heat; drain. Arrange the meatballs in the slow cooker with the crumbled bacon.

4. Heat butter in a medium skillet over medium heat. Sauté mushrooms in butter for 10 minutes until browned. Stir in the flour and allow the juices to thicken. Slowly stir in the milk and water. Pour the thickened mushroom sauce over the meatballs in the slow cooker.

5. Cover and cook on low for 2–3 hours.

6. Half an hour before serving, add the sherry and stir well to combine.

PER SERVING: Calories: 413 | Fat: 25g | Protein: 28g | Sodium: 606mg | Fiber: 1g | Carbohydrates: 13g | Sugar: 3.5g

CHAPTER 7

Lamb and Pork

Leg of Lamb

To really infuse the meat with flavor, you should marinate the lamb for at least 6 hours or overnight.

INGREDIENTS | SERVES 12

2 (12-ounce) cans pilsner beer

3 bay leaves

¼ bunch flat-leaf parsley, chopped

4 sprigs thyme, chopped

3 sprigs mint, chopped

3 cloves garlic, minced

½ teaspoon kosher salt

½ teaspoon freshly ground black pepper

1 (4-pound) leg of lamb, shank end removed

1 tablespoon olive oil

2 large red onions, peeled and chopped

2 medium carrots, peeled and chopped

2 stalks celery, chopped

1 cup White Wine Vegetable Stock (see recipe in Chapter 11)

1. Combine beer, bay leaves, parsley, thyme, mint, garlic, salt, and pepper in a large bowl. Add lamb and turn to coat. Cover bowl and marinate in the refrigerator overnight.

2. Remove the lamb from the marinade. Heat olive oil in a large skillet over medium heat until hot but not smoking. Sear lamb on all sides (about 3 minutes per side).

3. While the lamb cooks, place onions, carrots, and celery in the bottom of a 4- to 5-quart slow cooker.

4. Place lamb on top of vegetables. Pour stock over the lamb.

5. Cover and cook on low for 6–8 hours.

PER SERVING: Calories: 351 | Fat: 21g | Protein: 28g | Sodium: 244mg | Fiber: 1g | Carbohydrates: 6g | Sugar: 2g

Apricot-Stuffed Pork Tenderloin

If you don't have dried apricots, dried cranberries would be lovely instead.

INGREDIENTS | SERVES 6

6 dried apricots, chopped

1 shallot, peeled and minced

1 clove garlic, minced

½ cup pecans, chopped

3 fresh sage leaves, chopped

1½ pounds pork tenderloin

½ teaspoon kosher salt

½ teaspoon freshly ground black pepper

1 tablespoon plus 1 teaspoon olive oil, divided

Sage: It's Not Just Aromatic

It's healthy, too! Sage is full of vitamin A, calcium, iron, and potassium. Combined with heart-healthy garlic, fruit, and nuts, that makes this recipe a nutritional knockout.

1. Combine the apricots, shallot, garlic, pecans, and sage in a small bowl.

2. Butterfly the tenderloin by making a lengthwise slit down the middle. Be careful not to cut completely through. Lay out the tenderloin like an open book on a work surface.

3. Spread the apricot mixture on the tenderloin, leaving a 1" border around the filling. Gently roll up the loin and tie securely. Season the outside with salt and pepper.

4. Heat 1 tablespoon olive oil in a large skillet over medium heat until hot but not smoking. Place the tenderloin in the pan and brown on all 4 sides, about 5 minutes per side.

   Grease a 4- to 5-quart slow cooker with remaining olive oil. Place pork in slow cooker. Cover and cook on high for 3½–4 hours. The pork is done when an instant-read thermometer registers 145°F–155°F.

PER SERVING: Calories: 236 | Fat: 12g | Protein: 28g | Sodium: 267mg | Fiber: 2g | Carbohydrates: 8g | Sugar: 5g

Garlic Lamb

This recipe works best with lamb chops or lamb shoulder. Avoid the shank, which is often unpalatable for first-time lamb eaters due to its gamey flavor.

INGREDIENTS | SERVES 6

4 tablespoons olive oil

5 pounds lamb, cut into thin strips

5 cloves garlic, minced

6 medium potatoes, peeled and quartered

2 medium onions, peeled and sliced

½ teaspoon kosher salt

½ teaspoon ground black pepper

1 cup water

2 stems fresh thyme

2 bay leaves

2 stems fresh rosemary

½ cup chopped parsley

Tenderizing Meat

Use chemistry to your advantage. Cover your meat with an acidic liquid such as tomato juice, pineapple juice, dry wine, or vinegar, and let it stand for an hour or more before cooking. The acid breaks down collagen, the toughest protein in the meat, making the meat softer.

1. Heat oil in a large skillet over medium heat. Sauté the lamb and garlic until the lamb is browned, about 8 minutes.

2. Arrange the potatoes and onions on the bottom of a 4- to 5-quart slow cooker. Place lamb mixture on top of the vegetables.

3. Add salt, pepper, and water to slow cooker. Tie the thyme, bay leaves, and rosemary together with kitchen twine, and add to the slow cooker.

4. Cover and cook on low for 6–8 hours.

5. Before serving, stir the parsley into the lamb mixture.

PER SERVING: Calories: 997 | Fat: 60g | Protein: 73g | Sodium: 428mg | Fiber: 6g | Carbohydrates: 40g | Sugar: 4g

Pork Tenderloin with Nectarines

Pork combined with the flavor of ripe nectarines makes a lovely sweet and slightly tangy sauce. Serve sliced pork and sauce over cooked pasta, rice, or steamed zucchini strips.

INGREDIENTS | SERVES 4

1¼ pounds pork tenderloin

1 teaspoon kosher salt

½ teaspoon freshly ground black pepper

1 tablespoon olive oil

4 large ripe but firm nectarines, peeled, pitted, and quartered

2 tablespoons white balsamic vinegar

1. Spray a 4- to 5-quart slow cooker with nonstick olive oil cooking spray.

2. Rub pork tenderloin with salt, pepper, and olive oil. Place in the slow cooker.

3. Pour nectarines on top of and around the pork tenderloin. Drizzle balsamic vinegar over the pork and fruit. Cook on high for 3–4 hours or on low for 6–8 hours until pork is very tender.

4. Remove pork from slow cooker and slice before serving.

PER SERVING: Calories: 258 | Fat: 7g | Protein: 31g | Sodium: 665mg | Fiber: 3g | Carbohydrates: 18g | Sugar: 13.5g

Zucchini and Sausage Casserole

Serve this casserole on a bed of mixed greens with a fruit salad on the side.

INGREDIENTS | SERVES 6

1 pound mild pork sausage, casings removed

1¼ cups grated Parmesan cheese

½ teaspoon kosher salt

½ teaspoon freshly ground black pepper

2 teaspoons Greek seasoning, or 1 teaspoon dried mint, ½ teaspoon dried oregano, and ½ teaspoon basil

2 large eggs, beaten

1 cup whole milk

3 medium zucchini, sliced into ½" rounds

1 small onion, peeled and sliced

1. In a large skillet, brown sausage over medium heat for about 10 minutes, until no longer pink. Drain the fat from the skillet and set the sausage aside.

2. Grease a 4- to 5-quart slow cooker with nonstick spray. In a large bowl, whisk together the cheese, salt, pepper, and Greek seasoning. In another bowl, whisk together the eggs and the milk.

3. Place ⅓ of the zucchini over the bottom of the slow cooker. Add ⅓ of the onion over the zucchini. Add ⅓ of the cooked sausage over the onion. Add ⅓ of the milk/egg mixture over the sausage. Lastly add ⅓ of the cheese mixture over everything. Repeat layers two more times, ending with the last of the cheese mixture.

4. Cover, vent lid with a chopstick, and cook on low for 6 hours or on high for 3 hours. Cut into squares to serve.

PER SERVING: Calories: 255 | Fat: 12g | Protein: 29g | Sodium: 600mg | Fiber: 1g | Carbohydrates: 7g | Sugar: 5g

Easy Leg of Lamb

Although lamb can be an expensive cut of meat, you can often find it on sale during the holidays. Stock up on several cuts and freeze them when you find good prices.

INGREDIENTS | SERVES 6

1 (4-pound) bone-in leg of lamb
5 cloves garlic, peeled and cut into spears
2 tablespoons olive oil
1 tablespoon dried rosemary
½ teaspoon kosher salt
½ teaspoon ground black pepper
4 cups low-sodium chicken stock
¼ cup soy sauce

1. Make small incisions evenly over the lamb. Place garlic spears into the slices in the lamb.

2. Rub olive oil, rosemary, salt, and pepper over the lamb. Place lamb into a greased 4- or 6-quart slow cooker.

3. Pour stock and soy sauce around the leg of lamb. Cook on high for 4 hours or on low for 8 hours.

4. Ladle the sauce from the slow cooker over each serving of roast lamb.

PER SERVING: Calories: 507 | Fat: 23g | Protein: 64g | Sodium: 1,100mg | Fiber: 0.5g | Carbohydrates: 5g | Sugar: 1.5g

Lamb with Garlic, Lemon, and Rosemary

You can use the spice rub in this recipe as a marinade by applying it to the leg of lamb several hours (or up to one full day) before cooking. The red wine in this dish can be replaced with chicken or beef stock.

INGREDIENTS | SERVES 4

4 cloves of garlic, crushed
1 tablespoon chopped fresh rosemary
1 tablespoon olive oil
½ teaspoon kosher salt
1 teaspoon ground black pepper
1 (3-pound) leg of lamb
1 large lemon, cut into ¼" slices
½ cup red wine

1. In a small bowl, mix together garlic, rosemary, olive oil, salt, and pepper. Rub this mixture onto the leg of lamb.

2. Place a few lemon slices in the bottom of a greased 4- to 5-quart slow cooker. Place spice-rubbed lamb on top of lemon slices.

3. Add remaining lemon slices on top of lamb. Pour wine around the lamb.

4. Cook on low for 8–10 hours, or on high for 4–6 hours.

PER SERVING: Calories: 733 | Fat: 48g | Protein: 62g | Sodium: 487mg | Fiber: 0g | Carbohydrates: 1.5g | Sugar: 0g

Herbed Lamb Chops

This simple herb rub would make a fun Christmas gift to give to friends or family members who enjoy cooking! Include this recipe with a small jar of the rub.

INGREDIENTS | SERVES 4

1 medium onion, peeled and sliced

1 teaspoon dried oregano

½ teaspoon dried thyme

½ teaspoon garlic powder

¼ teaspoon kosher salt

⅛ teaspoon ground black pepper

2 pounds (about 8) lamb loin chops

1 tablespoon olive oil

1. Place onion on the bottom of a greased 4- to 5-quart slow cooker.

2. In a small bowl, mix together oregano, thyme, garlic powder, salt, and pepper. Rub herb mixture over the lamb chops.

3. Place herb-rubbed lamb chops over the sliced onion. Drizzle olive oil over the lamb chops.

4. Cook on high for 3 hours or on low for 6 hours, until tender.

PER SERVING: Calories: 352 | Fat: 17g | Protein: 46g | Sodium: 291mg | Fiber: 0g | Carbohydrates: 0.5g | Sugar: 0g

Italian Pork with Cannellini Beans

This is an incredibly simple one-dish meal that is packed with flavor.

INGREDIENTS | SERVES 4

1½ pounds pork loin

1 (28-ounce) can crushed tomatoes

1 head roasted garlic

1 medium onion, peeled and minced

2 tablespoons capers

1 (15-ounce) can cannellini beans, drained and rinsed

2 teaspoons Italian seasoning

1. Place the pork loin into a 4- to 5-quart slow cooker. Add the tomatoes, garlic, onion, and capers. Cook on low for 7–8 hours.

2. One hour before serving, add the cannellini beans and Italian seasoning and continue to cook on low for the remaining time.

PER SERVING: Calories: 615 | Fat: 7g | Protein: 62g | Sodium: 239mg | Fiber: 23g | Carbohydrates: 77g | Sugar: 15g

Pork Roast with Prunes

Pork pairs wonderfully with fruit, and this recipe is no exception.
The prunes add richness to the pork that is perfect for autumn.

INGREDIENTS | SERVES 6

1½ pounds lean pork roast, excess fat removed

1 medium onion, peeled and diced

2 cloves garlic, minced

¾ cup pitted prunes

½ cup water

½ teaspoon freshly ground black pepper

¼ teaspoon kosher salt

⅛ teaspoon nutmeg

⅛ teaspoon cinnamon

Place all ingredients into a 4- to 5-quart slow cooker. Cook on low for 8 hours.

PER SERVING: Calories: 202 | Fat: 4g | Protein: 25g | Sodium: 155mg | Fiber: 2g | Carbohydrates: 15g | Sugar: 9g

Picking Prunes

Prunes are dried plums. They are wrinkly and chewy. Because of their somewhat negative association as a fruit that only the elderly enjoy, they are sometimes marketed as "dried plums."

Greek Boneless Leg of Lamb

Lamb does surprisingly well in the slow cooker. It is nearly impossible to overcook lamb, and every bite is meltingly tender.

INGREDIENTS | SERVES 12

4 pounds boneless leg of lamb

1 tablespoon crushed rosemary

1 teaspoon freshly ground black pepper

¼ teaspoon kosher salt

¼ cup lemon juice

¼ cup water

Healthy Cooking with Lamb

Lamb has a reputation as a somewhat fatty meat. However, buying a leaner cut, like the boneless leg where much of the fat and bone has been removed by the butcher, and slicing off any excess at home can eliminate much of the fat. When slow cooking, the fat melts off the meat and accumulates in the bottom of the cooker, where it can easily be discarded after removing the meat.

1. Slice off any visible fat from the lamb and discard. Place in a 4- to 5-quart slow cooker.

2. Add the remaining ingredients on top of the lamb. Cook on low for 8 hours.

3. Remove from the slow cooker. Discard cooking liquid. Remove any remaining visible fat from the lamb. Slice the lamb prior to serving.

PER SERVING: Calories: 313 | Fat: 21g | Protein: 27g | Sodium: 134mg | Fiber: 0g | Carbohydrates: 0g | Sugar: 0g

Pork Tenderloin with Fennel

Slightly sweet fennel accents the pork's natural sweetness.

INGREDIENTS | SERVES 10

4 pounds pork tenderloin, excess fat removed

4 bulbs fennel, cubed

1½ cups Caramelized Onions (see recipe in Chapter 13)

1 teaspoon freshly ground black pepper

½ teaspoon kosher salt

Place the pork into an oval 6- to 6½-quart slow cooker. Top with remaining ingredients. Cook on low for 8 hours.

PER SERVING: Calories: 234 | Fat: 4g | Protein: 38g | Sodium: 262mg | Fiber: 3g | Carbohydrates: 9g | Sugar: 1g

Greek-Style Meatballs and Artichokes

Mediterranean flavors abound in this dish. Serve it with an orzo pilaf.

INGREDIENTS | SERVES 10

2 thin slices white sandwich bread

½ cup 1% milk

2¾ pounds lean ground pork

2 cloves garlic, minced

1 large egg

½ teaspoon lemon zest

¼ teaspoon freshly ground black pepper

16 ounces frozen artichoke hearts, defrosted

3 tablespoons lemon juice

2 cups Roasted Chicken Broth (see recipe in Chapter 11)

¾ cup frozen chopped spinach, defrosted

⅓ cup sliced Greek olives

1 tablespoon minced fresh oregano

1. Preheat the oven to 350°F. Place the bread and milk in a shallow saucepan. Cook over low heat until the milk is absorbed, about 1 minute. Place into a large bowl and add the pork, garlic, egg, zest, and pepper. Mix until all ingredients are evenly distributed. Roll into 1" balls.

2. Line two baking sheets with parchment paper. Place the meatballs in a single layer on the baking sheets. Bake for 15 minutes, and then drain on paper-towel-lined plates.

3. Add the meatballs to a 6- to 6½-quart slow cooker. Add the remaining ingredients.

4. Cook on low for 6–8 hours.

PER SERVING: Calories: 399 | Fat: 28g | Protein: 2g | Sodium: 496mg | Fiber: 2.5g | Carbohydrates: 10g | Sugar: 1.4g

Braised Lamb Shanks

*Serve with polenta to help soak up the delicious and complex sauce
that's created by slow-braising lamb until it's falling off the bone.*

INGREDIENTS | SERVES 6

1 tablespoon olive oil

6 (1-pound) lamb shanks, extra fat trimmed

1 teaspoon kosher salt

1 teaspoon freshly ground black pepper

2 large red onions, peeled and diced into 1" pieces

4 stalks celery, chopped into 1" pieces

3 large carrots, peeled and chopped into 1" pieces

2 teaspoons garlic, minced

½ cup dry red wine

¼ cup crushed tomatoes

2 tablespoons tomato paste

1½ quarts Red Wine and Tomato Vegetable Stock (see recipe in Chapter 11)

2 bay leaves

1 tablespoon chopped fresh rosemary

1. Heat the olive oil in a large roasting pan over medium-high heat. Add the lamb shanks and season with salt and pepper. Sear on both sides, about 5 minutes each.

2. Add the onions, celery, and carrots. Cook for 5–8 minutes or until softened and slightly browned. Add the garlic and cook for 1 minute.

3. Place lamb and vegetables in a 4- to 5-quart slow cooker.

4. Add the wine to roasting pan and scrape up any browned bits. Reduce heat to medium, and let reduce for 3 minutes. Add the tomatoes, paste, stock, bay leaves, and rosemary. Stir well to combine.

5. Pour sauce over lamb and vegetables. Cover slow cooker and turn on low. Cook for 6–8 hours or until lamb is falling off the bone.

PER SERVING: Calories: 718 | Fat: 38g | Protein: 77g | Sodium: 999mg | Fiber: 3g | Carbohydrates: 11g | Sugar: 5g

Lemon and Garlic Lamb

The smell of spring abounds in this lemon and garlic dish.

INGREDIENTS | SERVES 6

5 garlic cloves

½ bunch flat-leaf parsley, chopped, divided

¼ cup lemon juice

5 ounces trimmed lamb loin, cut into 1" cubes

6 medium red potatoes, peeled and quartered

2 large red onions, peeled and quartered

3 tablespoons olive oil

½ teaspoon kosher salt

½ teaspoon freshly ground black pepper

1 cup Red Wine and Tomato Vegetable Stock (see recipe in Chapter 11)

Play with Your Marinade!

Although the springlike flavors of parsley, lemon, and garlic pair wonderfully with lamb, this dish would be equally delicious with cumin and paprika or dried basil and oregano. Make your spice cabinet your playground—open up your bottles of spices and imagine each fragrance with the lamb.

1. Place garlic, half of the parsley, and lemon juice in a food processor fitted with a metal blade. Process until smooth. Place lamb cubes and garlic/lemon mixture in a large resealable plastic bag, and marinate in refrigerator overnight.

2. The next day, place potatoes on the bottom of a 4- to 5-quart slow cooker, and top with onions.

3. Heat olive oil in large skillet over medium heat until it shimmers, about 1 minute. Remove lamb from marinade, season it with salt and pepper, and brown the meat in batches, about 5 minutes per side. Place lamb in slow cooker. Pour the stock over the lamb and vegetables.

4. Cover and cook on low for 6–8 hours.

5. Serve lamb on a large platter, and garnish with remaining parsley.

PER SERVING: Calories: 282 | Fat: 9g | Protein: 9g | Sodium: 234mg | Fiber: 4.5g | Carbohydrates: 40g | Sugar: 4.5g

Caper Pork

Here is your opportunity to use capers in your cooking.
The capers in this recipe give the pork a refreshing zing.

INGREDIENTS | SERVES 4

2 tablespoons olive oil

2 pounds pork loin, cut into serving-size pieces

1 medium onion, peeled and sliced

4 stalks celery, sliced

2 medium carrots, peeled and sliced

3 cloves garlic, minced

1 cup tomato sauce

6 black olives, pitted and quartered

¼ cup dry white wine

1 tablespoon capers

The Right Olives

Just say no to pimiento-stuffed green olives. Go to a Middle Eastern grocery and buy an olive sampler. Try the giant black olives and the small wrinkled ones. There are olives available you didn't know existed. Once you taste them, you'll forsake the pimiento-stuffed versions in jars, and use these in your cooking instead.

1. Spray a 4- to 5-quart slow cooker with nonstick olive oil spray.

2. Heat olive oil in a large skillet over medium-high heat. Sauté pork until lightly browned, about 5 minutes per side. Remove pork from pan and place in prepared slow cooker, leaving the meat juices in the pan.

3. In the same pan, sauté onion, celery, carrots, and garlic over high heat for 5 minutes.

4. Transfer the vegetable mix to the slow cooker. Pour the tomato sauce over the vegetables and pork.

5. Cover and cook on low for 6–8 hours.

6. Half an hour before serving, add the olives, wine, and capers to the slow cooker.

PER SERVING: Calories: 468 | Fat: 22g | Protein: 50g | Sodium: 568mg | Fiber: 3g | Carbohydrates: 11g | Sugar: 6g

Fennel Chops

These chops are very flavorful; all you need is a simple side of white rice or fresh homemade bread.

INGREDIENTS | SERVES 6

2 cloves garlic
½ teaspoon kosher salt
6 (6-ounce) pork chops
2 tablespoons olive oil
1 tablespoon fennel seed
1 cup white wine

1. Spray a 4- to 5-quart slow cooker with nonstick olive oil spray. Crush the garlic and salt into a paste; rub the paste over the chops.

2. Heat olive oil in a large skillet over medium-high heat. Sauté chops until lightly browned, about 5 minutes per side. Put the chops, pan drippings, fennel seed, and white wine in the slow cooker.

3. Cover and cook on low for 3–4 hours.

PER SERVING: Calories: 293 | Fat: 11g | Protein: 36g | Sodium: 298mg | Fiber: 0.5g | Carbohydrates: 2g | Sugar: 0g

Mountain Honey Lamb with Dates

You can buy ghee for this recipe, or make your own. Serve this with warm, fresh pita bread.

INGREDIENTS | SERVES 6

5 tablespoons Ghee (see recipe in Chapter 10), divided
2 pounds lamb, cubed
1 medium onion, peeled and sliced
1 cup pitted and chopped dates
1 teaspoon turmeric
1 teaspoon cinnamon
½ teaspoon kosher salt
2 tablespoons honey
1 cup uncooked rice
2½ cups water
1 teaspoon finely grated lemon zest

1. Spray a 4- to 5-quart slow cooker with nonstick olive oil spray.

2. Heat 3 tablespoons ghee in a large skillet over medium-high heat. Sauté the lamb and onion for about 10 minutes, until the meat is lightly browned. Place lamb and onion mixture in slow cooker.

3. Add dates, turmeric, cinnamon, salt, honey, rice, and water to the slow cooker. Cover and cook on low for 4–5 hours.

4. Half an hour before serving, add the lemon zest and remaining ghee.

PER SERVING: Calories: 553 | Fat: 25g | Protein: 32g | Sodium: 839mg | Fiber: 3g | Carbohydrates: 50g | Sugar: 25g

Ginger Tomato Lamb

You can substitute beef or pork for lamb in this recipe if you wish.
Serve with triangles of fresh pita bread.

INGREDIENTS | SERVES 6

2 tablespoons butter

2 pounds lamb, cubed

1 medium onion, peeled and chopped

1 clove garlic, minced

3 tablespoons all-purpose flour

1½ tablespoons curry powder

2 large tomatoes, chopped

1" fresh gingerroot, peeled and grated

1 teaspoon kosher salt

¼ cup water

1. Spray a 4- to 5-quart slow cooker with nonstick olive oil spray.

2. Heat butter in a large skillet over medium heat. Sauté lamb until slightly browned, about 8 minutes. Transfer the meat to the slow cooker; set aside the pan with the juices.

3. Add the onion and garlic to the pan used for the lamb and sauté over medium heat until the onion is tender, about 10 minutes. Stir in the flour and curry powder. Continue cooking until thickened, about 5 minutes. Add the onion mixture to the slow cooker.

4. Add the tomatoes, ginger, salt, and water to the slow cooker.

5. Cover and cook on low for 4–5 hours.

PER SERVING: Calories: 317 | Fat: 17g | Protein: 30g | Sodium: 532mg | Fiber: 2g | Carbohydrates: 8g | Sugar: 2g

Eastern Lamb Curry

This should be served with rice, preferably basmati rice. Provide condiments, including white raisins, toasted coconut shavings, and roasted cashews or pistachios.

INGREDIENTS | SERVES 6

3 pounds lamb, cubed

1 medium carrot, peeled

1 medium onion, peeled

3 cups water

1 bouquet garni

½ teaspoon kosher salt

5 tablespoons butter, divided

1 medium banana, peeled and sliced

2 tablespoons curry powder

2 tablespoons all-purpose flour

1 medium apple, peeled, cored, and cubed

½ cup chutney

1. Spray a 4- to 5-quart slow cooker with nonstick olive oil spray.

2. Put the lamb in a large stockpot with the carrot, onion, water, bouquet garni, and salt; boil over high heat for 20 minutes.

3. Remove and discard the carrot, onion, and bouquet garni. Skim the surface of the water and discard any debris. Transfer the meat and strained liquid to the slow cooker.

4. Melt 2 tablespoons butter in a medium skillet over low heat. Sauté banana slices in the melted butter until the banana is lightly browned, about 5 minutes. Transfer the banana and pan juices to the slow cooker.

5. In the same skillet, melt the remaining butter over low heat. Add the curry powder and flour and cook, stirring constantly, for 5 minutes. Stir the apple and chutney into the curry mixture. Transfer the curry mixture to the slow cooker.

6. Cover and cook on low for 3–4 hours.

PER SERVING: Calories: 532 | Fat: 30g | Protein: 44g | Sodium: 415mg | Fiber: 2.5g | Carbohydrates: 20g | Sugar: 10g

Royal Meatballs

These flavorful meatballs are prepared with Regal Caper Sauce (see recipe in Chapter 10). Serve them either skewered as an appetizer or with slices of mini-pumpernickel.

INGREDIENTS | SERVES 6

3 tablespoons butter, divided

1 medium onion, peeled and minced

6 medium shallots, peeled and minced

½ pound ground lamb

½ pound ground veal

½ pound ground turkey breast

1 small bunch parsley, finely chopped

12 anchovies, minced

¼ cup chives, finely chopped

1 clove garlic, peeled and minced

½ teaspoon kosher salt

¼ teaspoon freshly ground black pepper

¼ teaspoon nutmeg

⅛ teaspoon cayenne pepper

½ cup water

2 large eggs

3 cups Regal Caper Sauce (see recipe in Chapter 10)

Watch Your Wiring

Before or after cooking, don't put your slow cooker in the refrigerator unless the crockery is removable and can go in alone. Otherwise the electrical components may rust and leave you needing a whole new appliance.

1. Spray a 4- to 5-quart slow cooker with nonstick olive oil spray.

2. Heat 1 tablespoon butter in a medium skillet over medium heat. Sauté onion and shallots until soft, about 8 minutes. Transfer the onion and shallots to a large bowl.

3. Combine ground meats, parsley, anchovies, chives, garlic, salt, black pepper, nutmeg, cayenne pepper, water, and eggs with the onion mixture and mix well. Form into ¾" balls.

4. Heat remaining butter in a large skillet over medium-high heat. Brown the meatballs in batches until browned, about 10 minutes.

5. Arrange the meatballs in the slow cooker and cover with Regal Caper Sauce.

6. Cover and cook on low for 3–4 hours.

PER SERVING: Calories: 412 | Fat: 23g | Protein: 29g | Sodium: 793mg | Fiber: 2g | Carbohydrates: 8g | Sugar: 2g

CHAPTER 8

Fish and Seafood

Paella

Using a slow cooker to make paella really helps to develop the deep and delicious flavors of this popular Spanish dish.

INGREDIENTS | SERVES 6

1½ cups long grain rice

1 (14½-ounce) can chopped tomatoes

2¼ cups Roasted Chicken Broth (see recipe in Chapter 11)

½ teaspoon crushed saffron threads or ½ teaspoon turmeric

½ teaspoon hot smoked paprika

1 tablespoon olive oil

½ pound Andouille sausage, halved and sliced

1 medium red onion, peeled and finely diced

6 (3-ounce) boneless, skinless chicken thighs

1 cup frozen baby peas, thawed

6 large deveined, shelled, and cooked shrimp, frozen

Slow Cooking with Shrimp

When slow cooking with shrimp, resist the temptation to put the shrimp in at the beginning of the recipe. While it takes longer to overcook foods in the slow cooker, delicate shrimp can go from tender to rubbery very quickly. For most recipes, 20 minutes on high is sufficient cooking time for shrimp.

1. In a 4- to 5-quart slow cooker, mix together the rice, tomatoes, broth, saffron, and paprika.

2. In a large skillet or Dutch oven, heat the olive oil over medium heat until hot but not smoking. Add the sausage and onion and cook until sausage is brown and onion is softened. Remove the sausage and onion with a slotted spoon. Add the sausage and onion to the slow cooker, and stir well.

3. In the same skillet or Dutch oven, brown chicken thighs in remaining oil over medium-high heat until golden brown, about 10 minutes.

4. Place chicken on top of the rice mixture. Cover and cook on low for 5–6 hours.

5. Add thawed peas to the mixture and stir well. Top with shrimp and cook for an additional 30 minutes, or until shrimp and peas are cooked through.

PER SERVING: Calories: 448 | Fat: 16g | Protein: 28g | Sodium: 421mg | Fiber: 3g | Carbohydrates: 45g | Sugar: 3g

Ginger-Lime Salmon

The slow cooker does all the work in this recipe, creating a healthy yet impressive dish that requires virtually no hands-on time.

INGREDIENTS | SERVES 12

1 (3-pound) salmon fillet, bones removed

¼ cup minced fresh ginger

¼ cup lime juice

1 medium lime, thinly sliced

1 medium onion, peeled and thinly sliced

1. Place the salmon skin-side down in an oval 6- to 6½-quart slow cooker. Pour the ginger and lime juice over the fish. Arrange the lime and then the onion in single layers over the fish.

2. Cook on low for 3–4 hours or until the fish is fully cooked and flaky. Remove the skin before serving.

PER SERVING: Calories: 192 | Fat: 8g | Protein: 26g | Sodium: 403mg | Fiber: 0g | Carbohydrates: 2g | Sugar: 0.5g

Cracked!

Before each use, check your slow cooker for cracks. Even small cracks in the glaze can allow bacteria to grow in the ceramic insert. If there are cracks, replace the insert or the whole slow cooker.

Shrimp Fra Diavolo

Serve this spicy sauce over hot pasta.

INGREDIENTS | SERVES 4

1 teaspoon olive oil

1 medium onion, peeled and diced

3 cloves garlic, minced

1 teaspoon red pepper flakes

1 (15-ounce) can diced fire-roasted tomatoes

1 tablespoon minced Italian parsley

½ teaspoon freshly ground black pepper

¾ pound medium shrimp, shelled

1. Heat the oil in a nonstick skillet over medium-high heat. Sauté the onion, garlic, and red pepper flakes until the onion is soft and translucent.

2. Add the onion mixture, tomatoes, parsley, and black pepper to a 4- to 5-quart slow cooker. Stir. Cook on low for 2–3 hours.

3. Add the shrimp. Stir and cover and cook on high for 15 minutes or until the shrimp is fully cooked.

PER SERVING: Calories: 134 | Fat: 3g | Protein: 18g | Sodium: 131mg | Fiber: 2g | Carbohydrates: 8g | Sugar: 4g

Tuna Casserole

Tuna casserole doesn't have to be made with a "cream of something" soup.
This healthy version highlights the delicious flavor of the tuna along with vegetables, herbs, and spices.

INGREDIENTS | SERVES 6

2 tablespoons olive oil

2 pounds fresh tuna steak, cubed

½ teaspoon kosher salt

½ teaspoon freshly ground black pepper

2 cloves garlic, minced

1 (14½-ounce) can diced tomatoes

3 pimientos, diced

½ teaspoon cayenne pepper

2 bay leaves

½ cup dry white wine

½ cup Fish Stock (see recipe in Chapter 11)

4 medium potatoes, peeled and diced

2 tablespoons flat-leaf parsley, chopped

1. Heat olive oil in a large skillet over medium heat until hot but not smoking. Add the tuna to the pan, and season with salt and pepper. Cook tuna for 3 minutes and flip. Add the garlic and cook for 1 minute.

2. Remove from heat and stir in tomatoes, pimientos, cayenne, bay leaves, wine, and stock.

3. Place potatoes on the bottom of a 4- to 5-quart slow cooker.

4. Ladle the tuna mixture over the potatoes.

5. Cover and cook on low for 5–6 hours. Remove bay leaves and garnish with parsley before serving.

PER SERVING: Calories: 405 | Fat: 12g | Protein: 38g | Sodium: 364mg | Fiber: 6g | Carbohydrates: 32g | Sugar: 6g

Shrimp Risotto

Shrimp-flavored broth gives this risotto a flavor boost. If you don't want to take the time to make it, substitute 1 cup of additional chicken broth and stir a pinch of crushed saffron threads directly into the slow cooker.

INGREDIENTS | SERVES 6

1 tablespoon olive oil

2 tablespoons butter, melted

2 medium white onions, peeled and diced

2 cups Arborio rice

5 cups chicken broth

1 cup Shrimp-Infused Broth (see sidebar)

½ cup dry white wine

1½ pounds large shrimp, peeled and deveined

½ cup freshly grated Parmesan cheese

3 tablespoons minced fresh flat-leaf parsley

½ teaspoon kosher salt

Shrimp-Infused Broth

Add 1 cup of chicken broth and the shrimp shells from 1½ pounds of shrimp to a saucepan. Bring to a boil over medium-high heat; reduce the heat and maintain a simmer for 15 minutes or until the shells are pink. Strain; crush a pinch of saffron threads and stir it into the broth.

1. Place the oil, butter, and onions in a 4- to 5-quart slow cooker. Stir to coat the onions in the oil. Cover and cook on high for 30 minutes or until the onion is transparent.

2. Stir in the rice; continue to stir for several minutes until the rice turns translucent. Add the chicken broth, shrimp-infused broth, and wine. Stir together well. Cover and cook on high for 2½ hours or until the rice is cooked al dente.

3. Add the shrimp to the slow cooker atop the risotto. Cover and cook on high for 20 minutes or until the shrimp is pink. Stir in the cheese, parsley, and salt. Serve immediately.

PER SERVING: Calories: 524 | Fat: 12g | Protein: 32g | Sodium: 689mg | Fiber: 3g | Carbohydrates: 67g | Sugar: 1.5g

Salmon with Lemon, Capers, and Rosemary

Salmon is very moist and tender when cooked in the slow cooker. This is a great meal for couples or when you just need to cook something small. Serve it with steamed kale and baked potatoes.

INGREDIENTS | SERVES 2

8 ounces salmon
⅓ cup water
2 tablespoons lemon juice
3 thin slices fresh lemon
1 tablespoon nonpareil capers
½ teaspoon minced fresh rosemary

1. Place the salmon on the bottom of a 2½-quart slow cooker. Pour the water and lemon juice over the fish.

2. Arrange lemon slices in a single layer on top of the fish. Sprinkle with capers and rosemary.

3. Cook on low for 2 hours. Discard lemon slices prior to serving.

PER SERVING: Calories: 166 | Fat: 7g | Protein: 22g | Sodium: 180mg | Fiber: 0.5g | Carbohydrates: 2g | Sugar: 0.5g

Fillet of Sole with Grapes and White Wine

Fillet of sole pairs beautifully with grapes and wine, and the crunchy topping with fresh chives makes this dish a winner!

INGREDIENTS | SERVES 4

1 tablespoon olive oil
½ pound seedless grapes, halved
2 medium red onions, peeled and finely sliced
½ cup dry white wine
2 pounds fillet of sole, cut into 4 pieces
½ teaspoon kosher salt
½ teaspoon ground black pepper
¼ cup buttered toast crumbs
2 tablespoons chopped chives

1. Heat oil in a large skillet over low heat. Sauté grapes and onions until the onions are soft, about 5–8 minutes. Add wine, increase heat to medium, and cook until reduced by half, about 5–7 minutes.

2. Place each piece of fish on a separate piece of aluminum foil and season with salt and pepper. Divide wine sauce between each piece of sole. Wrap tightly. Place packets in slow cooker, cover, and cook on low for 3–4 hours. The fish is done when it flakes easily with a fork.

3. Before serving, sprinkle each piece of fish with buttered crumbs and chives.

PER SERVING: Calories: 345 | Fat: 6g | Protein: 44g | Sodium: 530mg | Fiber: 2g | Carbohydrates: 21g | Sugar: 11g

Cioppino

This hearty and delicious seafood stew is best served with crusty sourdough bread to sop up all the juices.

INGREDIENTS | SERVES 8

1 medium onion, peeled and chopped

2 stalks celery, diced

6 cloves garlic, minced

1 (28-ounce) can diced tomatoes

8 ounces clam juice

¾ cup Fish Stock (see recipe in Chapter 11)

1 (6-ounce) can tomato paste

1 teaspoon red pepper flakes

2 tablespoons minced fresh oregano

2 tablespoons minced fresh Italian parsley

1 teaspoon red wine vinegar

10 ounces catfish nuggets

10 ounces large shrimp, peeled and deveined

6 ounces diced cooked clams

6 ounces lump crabmeat

¾ cup diced cooked lobster meat

¼ cup diced green onion

1. Place the onion, celery, garlic, tomatoes, clam juice, stock, tomato paste, red pepper flakes, oregano, parsley, and vinegar in a 4- to 5-quart slow cooker. Stir vigorously. Cook on low for 8 hours.

2. Add the remaining ingredients and cook on high for 30 minutes. Stir prior to serving.

PER SERVING: Calories: 150 | Fat: 2g | Protein: 21g | Sodium: 434mg | Fiber: 2.5g | Carbohydrates: 11g | Sugar: 6g

Better Butter

Set out some delicious herbed or spiced butter next to the bread, potatoes, or vegetables on your table. Blend 2 tablespoons of fresh tarragon, dill weed, or dried rosemary or 2 teaspoons of fresh minced garlic or crushed peppercorns into ¼ pound of softened butter.

Mussels Marinara

Clean mussels just before adding to the slow cooker. If you want the dish to be a little spicier, add more dried red chili flakes. Enjoy the marinara on pasta along with crusty bread and a glass of dry wine.

INGREDIENTS | SERVES 6

1 tablespoon olive oil

2 shallots, peeled and diced

3 cloves garlic, minced

1 (28-ounce) can whole tomatoes

½ teaspoon freshly ground black pepper

1 cup dry red wine

½ cup Fish Stock (see recipe in Chapter 11)

¼ teaspoon dried red pepper flakes

1 teaspoon dried oregano

1 teaspoon hot smoked paprika

1½ dozen mussels

1. Heat olive oil in a large skillet over medium heat until it shimmers, about 1 minute.

2. Add shallots and cook until softened, about 3–5 minutes. Add garlic and cook for 1 minute. Add tomatoes and mash with potato masher to break up tomatoes into chunks. Season with pepper.

3. Place shallot mixture in a 4- to 5-quart slow cooker with wine, stock, red pepper flakes, oregano, and paprika. Cook on low for 4–5 hours.

4. Thoroughly clean the mussels. Discard any that are cracked or open. Turn slow cooker on high and add mussels. Cover and cook for 30 minutes. Serve immediately.

PER SERVING: Calories: 82 | Fat: 2.5g | Protein: 1g | Sodium: 189mg | Fiber: 2g | Carbohydrates: 8g | Sugar: 3g

Lobster Risotto

Using frozen lobster tails makes this risotto even less work, without sacrificing quality.

INGREDIENTS | SERVES 6

2 teaspoons extra-virgin olive oil

1 medium yellow onion, peeled and diced

1 shallot, peeled and diced

3 cloves garlic, minced

1½ cups Arborio rice

¼ cup dry white wine

3¾ cups Roasted Chicken Broth (see recipe in Chapter 11)

1½ pounds frozen lobster tails, thawed

¼ cup chopped parsley

¼ cup chopped spinach

¼ cup grated Parmesan cheese

Hands-Off Risotto!

Slow cookers are wonderful for many things, and making risotto is certainly one of them. With this method, it's possible to make a risotto for dinner without constantly tending it, which is incredibly handy when organizing a dinner party. There's no need to worry about burning the dish, and you're free to prepare the other entrées.

1. Heat the oil in a medium skillet over medium heat; sauté the onion for 2 minutes. Add the shallot, and sauté for 1 minute more. Add the garlic, and sauté for 1 minute.

2. Add the rice and mix well. Pour in the wine and cook, stirring occasionally, until reduced by half, about 10 minutes.

3. Place the rice mixture in a 4- to 5-quart slow cooker. Add the broth all at once, cover, and cook on high for 1½ hours.

4. Add lobster, parsley, and spinach. Stir well. Reduce heat to low and cook for an additional 10 minutes. (If rice seems too dry, add an additional 4 tablespoons of broth.) Stir in cheese. Serve immediately.

PER SERVING: Calories: 387 | Fat: 6g | Protein: 29g | Sodium: 609mg | Fiber: 2g | Carbohydrates: 49g | Sugar: 1g

Herby Steamed Snow Crab Legs

Serve with sautéed spinach and garlic for a colorful presentation.

INGREDIENTS | SERVES 6

6 fresh or frozen snow crab claw clusters, rinsed

1 tablespoon olive oil

1 medium onion, peeled and diced

½ teaspoon sea salt, crushed

½ teaspoon freshly ground black pepper

½ cup white wine (pinot grigio or Sauvignon Blanc)

Juice of 1 lemon

1 cup Fish Stock (see recipe in Chapter 11)

2 tablespoons chopped fresh dill

½ cup chopped flat-leaf parsley

3 bay leaves

1. Place crab legs in a 4- to 5-quart slow cooker.

2. In a medium skillet, heat olive oil over medium heat until it shimmers, about 1 minute. Add the onion and season with salt and pepper. Cook until softened, about 5 minutes. Add wine, lemon juice, and stock.

3. Continue to cook over medium heat, stirring occasionally, until reduced by half, about 10 minutes. Add dill, parsley, and bay leaves.

4. Pour onion/wine mixture over crab legs in slow cooker.

5. Cover and cook on high for 4 hours.

PER SERVING: Calories: 221 | Fat: 4g | Protein: 36g | Sodium: 1,409mg | Fiber: 0.5g | Carbohydrates: 3g | Sugar: 1g

Mediterranean Shrimp Jambalaya

Chicken, chicken sausage, and shrimp cook together in a rich, hearty sauce and create a dinner you'll love to share. Makes enough for a crowd! Serve over Arborio rice or pasta for a delicious dish.

INGREDIENTS | SERVES 8

1 (28-ounce) can diced tomatoes

1 (14½-ounce) can chicken broth

1 small onion, peeled and chopped

3 cloves garlic

1 large bell pepper, seeded and chopped

1 eggplant, chopped

1 pound boneless, skinless chicken breast, cut into bite-sized pieces

12 ounces chicken sausage, sliced

1 teaspoon dried thyme

1 teaspoon oregano

2 tablespoons honey or agave syrup

1½ teaspoons sea salt

½ teaspoon ground white pepper

1½ pounds uncooked large shrimp, peeled and deveined

1. Place tomatoes, broth, onion, garlic, bell pepper, eggplant, chicken, sausage, thyme, oregano, honey, salt, and white pepper in a 6½-quart slow cooker.

2. Cover slow cooker and cook on low for 7–8 hours, or high for 4–5 hours.

3. Stir the shrimp into the sauce. Cover and cook until pink, about 10 minutes. Remove from heat and serve immediately.

PER SERVING: Calories: 340 | Fat: 10g | Protein: 35g | Sodium: 799mg | Fiber: 4g | Carbohydrates: 17g | Sugar: 9g

Buying Canned Tomato Sauce

Canned tomatoes have recently come under fire by health food advocates concerned with the possibility of bisphenol A (BPA)—one of the chemicals used in the can-manufacturing process—leaking into the food. To ensure food safety, look for canned tomatoes labeled BPA-free.

Foil-Pack Lemon Pepper Tilapia

Cooking in the slow cooker isn't just easy; it's versatile! Though soups and stews are nice, here's a delicate way to cook fish. Slow cooking tender tilapia in foil makes for a beautiful final dish that is low in fat and calories, but high in flavor.

INGREDIENTS | SERVES 6

6 (6-ounce) tilapia fillets
3 tablespoons olive oil
1½ teaspoons sea salt
1 teaspoon freshly ground black pepper
2 cloves garlic, chopped
1 lemon, thinly sliced
2 tablespoons chopped fresh Italian parsley

Side Dish Suggestion

This beautiful fish tastes great when paired with marinara and pasta, green beans, or a crisp green salad.

1. Tear six 12" × 12" squares of foil, and place one fillet on each square.

2. Drizzle ½ tablespoon olive oil over each fillet. Sprinkle with salt, pepper, and garlic. Place two slices of lemon on top of each fillet.

3. Gently bring all sides of the foil in and roll down until a packet is created, completely enclosing the fish.

4. Place tilapia in a 4- to 5-quart slow cooker. Cook on high for 2 hours. Test with a fork for doneness: if the fish flakes easily, it's ready to serve. Garnish with parsley.

PER SERVING: Calories: 208 | Fat: 8g | Protein: 31g | Sodium: 604mg | Fiber: 1g | Carbohydrates: 1g | Sugar: 0g

Foil-Pack Slow Cooker Salmon and Tomatoes

Want a flavorful slow-cooked meal but only have two hours until eating time? This simple foil-pack salmon cooks in the slow cooker in 120 minutes and tastes delicious! Better yet, it's packed full of healthy nutrients and is naturally low-calorie.

INGREDIENTS | SERVES 4

4 (5-ounce) salmon fillets

2 tablespoons olive oil

1 shallot, peeled and finely chopped

4 medium tomatoes, diced

2 tablespoons capers

1 medium lemon, sliced into 8 thin slices

2 teaspoons Italian seasoning

1 teaspoon sea salt

1. Tear four 12" × 12" pieces of foil. Place one salmon fillet in the center of each piece of foil.

2. Drizzle olive oil over each piece of salmon. Top each with shallots, tomatoes, capers, and two lemon slices. Sprinkle with Italian seasoning and sea salt.

3. Fold foil over the ingredients, creating a packet that completely encloses the fish.

4. Place foil packs in a 6-quart slow cooker. Cook for 2 hours on high, or until fish flakes easily with a fork.

PER SERVING: Calories: 317 | Fat: 17g | Protein: 33g | Sodium: 989mg | Fiber: 2g | Carbohydrates: 5g | Sugar: 3g

Seven-Ingredient Anchovy Fusilli

This simple pasta is surprisingly rich and so easy to make. It cooks in about 45 minutes, so plan the short cooking time in order to keep your pasta from overcooking.

INGREDIENTS | SERVES 4

1 (16-ounce) box fusilli pasta

4 (15-ounce) cans chicken broth

2 (10-ounce) cans anchovies or clams packed in oil, chopped

¼ cup olive oil

1 clove garlic, finely chopped

¼ cup chopped fresh parsley

1 teaspoon sea salt

1. Place pasta and chicken broth in a 6-quart slow cooker. Cook on high for 30–45 minutes.

2. Stir in anchovies, olive oil, and garlic. Sprinkle with parsley and salt.

3. Remove from heat and serve.

PER SERVING: Calories: 1,014 | Fat: 35g | Protein: 65g | Sodium: 3,354mg | Fiber: 4g | Carbohydrates: 102g | Sugar: 3g

Pasta Swap!

Any medium-sized pasta will work in this recipe. Feel free to use rotini, large macaroni, or rigatoni if you can't find fusilli.

Spicy Mussel Stew

Mussels are easy to come by, but can seem overwhelming if you've never made them before. Cooking them in a spicy stew is an easy way to use mussels, even if this is your first time ever having them in your kitchen.

INGREDIENTS | SERVES 4

2 tablespoons olive oil

2 large shallots, peeled and finely chopped

1 (28-ounce) can diced tomatoes

2 teaspoons dried oregano

1 teaspoon paprika

1 teaspoon red pepper flakes

1½ teaspoons sea salt

3 cups fish stock

2 pounds fresh mussels, cleaned

Prepping Fresh Mussels

Before throwing your mussels into the slow cooker, place them in a bowl of fresh water and allow them to sit. They'll start to "breathe" and naturally clean any sand out of the inside of their shells. Lift the mussels from the water and look for a thin thread. This is the "beard." Grasp the thread with a clean, dry towel and yank it quickly toward the hinged part of the mussel. Dry mussels with a towel before cooking.

1. Heat olive oil in a large skillet over medium-high heat. Add shallots to the pan and cook until softened, about 3 minutes.

2. Transfer cooked shallots to a large (6½-quart) slow cooker. Add tomatoes, oregano, paprika, red pepper flakes, salt, and stock to the slow cooker.

3. Cook on low for 4–5 hours, or on high for 2–3 hours.

4. Forty-five minutes before serving, turn slow cooker to high. Place cleaned mussels in the slow cooker, cover, and allow to cook for 30 minutes more, until the mussels open up.

5. Throw away any mussels that didn't open. Use a ladle to transfer the stew to bowls. Serve immediately.

PER SERVING: Calories: 290 | Fat: 13g | Protein: 30g | Sodium: 1,486mg | Fiber: 0.5g | Carbohydrates: 10g | Sugar: 0g

Skinny Shrimp Alfredo

Traditional rich Alfredo sauce is transformed into a healthy, creamy, delicious sauce made with a cauliflower base instead of tons of cream!

INGREDIENTS | SERVES 4

1 large cauliflower, cored and chopped

6 cups water

1 tablespoon butter

2 cloves garlic, chopped

1 large shallot, peeled and chopped

¼ cup heavy cream

2 cups chicken broth

½ teaspoon kosher salt

½ cup Parmesan cheese, shredded

1 cup sliced mushrooms

1 (16-ounce) package cheese tortellini

½ cup frozen peas

1 pound large shrimp, peeled and deveined

Cooking Pasta in the Slow Cooker

Despite what you may have heard before, it's possible to cook pasta in the slow cooker! However, pasta does not stand up to 6–8 hours of slow cooking. If cooking with pasta, follow recipe directions carefully to keep it from overcooking and turning your entire recipe to mush. Also ensure there's enough liquid in the sauce for the pasta to completely cook, and watch your slow cooker closely once the pasta has been added.

1. Place cauliflower in a 6-quart slow cooker with water. Cover and cook on high for 4–6 hours, or until the cauliflower is cooked through.

2. Melt butter in a small skillet over medium-high heat. Add garlic and shallot to the skillet and cook until softened, about 2–3 minutes. Remove from heat.

3. Drain the cauliflower and put it in a blender with the garlic and shallot mixture, cream, and broth. Purée until smooth.

4. Pour cauliflower sauce back into slow cooker. Stir in salt, cheese, mushrooms, and tortellini. Cook in slow cooker on high for 15–20 minutes, or until the tortellini begins to soften.

5. Add peas and shrimp to slow cooker. Allow to cook for 15–20 minutes more, until the shrimp is pink. Serve immediately.

PER SERVING: Calories: 658 | Fat: 19g | Protein: 42g | Sodium: 1,307mg | Fiber: 7g | Carbohydrates: 70g | Sugar: 6g

CHAPTER 9

Side Dishes

Fresh Artichokes

Preparing artichokes takes some work, but they're good served with an avocado salad and poached salmon.

INGREDIENTS | SERVES 4

2 large fresh artichokes

6 cups hot water

1 lemon

¼ cup butter, melted

¼ teaspoon seasoned salt

1. Rinse the artichokes under cool running water. Use a sharp knife to slice about an inch off the top of each artichoke; cut off the stem near the base. Use kitchen shears to trim about ½ inch off the top of each leaf. Use the knife to cut each artichoke in half vertically. Use a spoon or melon baller to scoop out and discard the fuzzy center, or "choke."

2. Place the artichoke halves in a 2½-quart slow cooker. Pour in the hot water. Cut four thin slices from the center of the lemon and add to the slow cooker; reserve the remaining lemon. Cover and cook on high for 4 hours or until the artichoke hearts are tender when pierced with a knife. Use a slotted spoon to remove the artichoke halves from the slow cooker.

3. To prepare the butter sauce, add the melted butter to a bowl. Add the juice from the reserved portions of the lemon. Stir in seasoned salt.

4. Evenly drizzle the butter sauce over the artichoke halves and serve immediately.

PER SERVING: Calories: 143 | Fat: 11g | Protein: 3g | Sodium: 236mg | Fiber: 4.5g | Carbohydrates: 10g | Sugar: 1g

Fingerling Potatoes with Herb Vinaigrette

Fingerling potatoes are small new potatoes. It's fun to use fingerling potatoes, because often they are small enough that they do not have to be chopped or diced. This dish is also delicious served cold as a potato salad.

INGREDIENTS | SERVES 4

2 pounds red or yellow fingerling potatoes, scrubbed

1 teaspoon kosher salt

¼ cup lemon juice

⅓ cup extra-virgin olive oil

1 small shallot, peeled and minced (about 2 tablespoons)

1½ teaspoons minced fresh thyme leaves

1 tablespoon minced fresh basil leaves

1 tablespoon minced fresh oregano leaves

½ teaspoon Dijon mustard

1 teaspoon sugar

1. Place potatoes in a medium pot and cover with cold water. Bring to a boil and add the kosher salt to the water. Cook potatoes for 6–8 minutes until fork tender.

2. Drain potatoes and place in a greased 4- to 5-quart slow cooker.

3. In a small bowl, whisk together lemon juice, olive oil, shallot, thyme, basil, oregano, mustard, and sugar. Drizzle vinaigrette over potatoes.

4. Cook on low for 4 hours or on high for 2 hours.

5. Serve warm or cold.

PER SERVING: Calories: 326 | Fat: 18g | Protein: 4g | Sodium: 614mg | Fiber: 5g | Carbohydrates: 39g | Sugar: 4g

Sweet and Sour Red Cabbage

Cabbage is often overlooked when it comes to weekly meals, which is unfortunate considering how nutritious it is. The tart apples, sugar, and apple cider vinegar give the cabbage a tangy pickled flavor. Try this recipe as a side to roast pork.

INGREDIENTS | SERVES 6

1 large head red cabbage, sliced

2 medium onions, peeled and chopped

6 small tart apples, peeled, cored, and quartered

2 teaspoons kosher salt

1 cup hot water

1 cup apple juice

⅓ cup sugar

⅔ cup apple cider vinegar

½ teaspoon caraway seeds

6 tablespoons butter, melted

1. Place cabbage, onions, apples, and salt into a greased 4- to 5-quart slow cooker.

2. In a medium bowl, whisk together water, apple juice, sugar, vinegar, and caraway seeds. Pour over the cabbage.

3. Drizzle butter over everything and cover slow cooker. Cook on high for 3–4 hours or on low for 6–8 hours. Stir well before serving.

PER SERVING: Calories: 286 | Fat: 12g | Protein: 3g | Sodium: 820mg | Fiber: 6g | Carbohydrates: 45g | Sugar: 34g

Lemon Garlic Green Beans

*Lemon zest and sliced garlic add a fresh and
bright flavor to these slow-cooked green beans.*

INGREDIENTS | SERVES 4

1½ pounds fresh green beans, trimmed

3 tablespoons olive oil

3 large shallots, peeled and cut into thin
wedges

6 cloves garlic, sliced

1 tablespoon grated lemon zest

½ teaspoon kosher salt

½ teaspoon ground black pepper

½ cup water

1. Place green beans in a greased 4- to 5-quart slow
   cooker. Add remaining ingredients over the top of the
   beans.

2. Cook on high for 4–6 hours, or on low for 8–10 hours.
   If you like your beans crispier, cook them on high and
   check after about 3½ hours or on low and check after
   about 6 hours. Fresh green beans are sturdy enough to
   withstand very long cooking temperatures without
   getting mushy.

PER SERVING: Calories: 167 | Fat: 10g | Protein: 4g |
Sodium: 308mg | Fiber: 4.5g | Carbohydrates: 17g | Sugar: 5g

Rosemary Garlic Mashed Potatoes

*Slow-cooked mashed potatoes are the perfect side for busy holiday cooks. Not only does this dish leave
a burner free for other cooking; there is no need to boil the potatoes before mashing them.*

INGREDIENTS | SERVES 10

3 pounds medium red potatoes,
quartered

4 cloves garlic, minced

¾ cup Roasted Chicken Broth (see recipe
in Chapter 11)

1 tablespoon minced fresh rosemary

¼ cup 1% milk

1 tablespoon butter

⅓ cup reduced-fat sour cream

1. Place the potatoes in a 4- to 5-quart slow cooker. Add
   garlic, broth, and rosemary. Stir. Cover and cook on
   high until potatoes are tender, about 3–4 hours.

2. Pour in milk, butter, and sour cream. Mash with a
   potato masher.

PER SERVING: Calories: 122 | Fat: 2g | Protein: 3.5g |
Sodium: 93mg | Fiber: 2g | Carbohydrates: 23g | Sugar: 2g

Black Bean Confit

The combination of black beans, tomatoes, herbs, and demi-glace makes this side dish a knockout.

INGREDIENTS | SERVES 6

1 cup dried black beans

2 quarts water

1 tablespoon olive oil

2 large onions, peeled and diced

2 stalks celery, diced

2 large carrots, peeled and diced

1 clove garlic, diced

2 shallots, peeled and thinly sliced

1 teaspoon dried thyme

1 teaspoon dried oregano

¼ bunch parsley, chopped

2 dried or fresh bay leaves

1 teaspoon freshly ground black pepper

1 (14½-ounce) can crushed tomatoes

¼ cup Demi-Glace Reduction Sauce (see recipe in Chapter 10)

1 quart Roasted Chicken Broth (see recipe in Chapter 11)

1. Soak the beans in the water overnight; rinse and drain them.

2. Grease a 4- to 5-quart slow cooker with oil. Place all of the ingredients in the slow cooker.

3. Cook on low for 8 hours.

PER SERVING: Calories: 283 | Fat: 5g | Protein: 10g | Sodium: 340mg | Fiber: 8g | Carbohydrates: 37g | Sugar: 6g

Prussian Cabbage

Serve this hot with cold sliced beef and hard sourdough rolls.
Also, provide some scorching horseradish and English mustard on the side.

INGREDIENTS | SERVES 6

1 head red cabbage, finely sliced

3 apples, cored and sliced

4 slices bacon, chopped

½ cup vinegar

2 cups beef broth

½ teaspoon kosher salt

1. Spray a 4- to 5-quart slow cooker with nonstick olive oil spray. Arrange the cabbage, apples, and bacon in the slow cooker.

2. Add the vinegar, beef broth, and salt.

3. Cover and cook on high for 2–3 hours.

PER SERVING: Calories: 154 | Fat: 7g | Protein: 5g | Sodium: 610mg | Fiber: 5g | Carbohydrates: 19g | Sugar: 12g

Jacques' White Beans

These beans are perfect for potlucks and parties! You can complete some parts of this recipe in advance, and save the final assembly until just before you lay out the food and start eating.

INGREDIENTS | SERVES 10

2 pounds white beans

1 ham bone

2 cups water

1 bouquet garni

1 teaspoon kosher salt

3 tablespoons butter

3 medium onions, peeled and diced

1 clove garlic, sliced

¼ cup chopped parsley

1 cup tomato sauce

½ teaspoon ground black pepper

Serving Stations

Have you heard of multitasking? Try "multi-serving" as well. Have slow cookers in three or four serving areas around your party zone, and guests will keep moving around to try all your creations. The more they move around, the more they will chat and enjoy each other.

1. In a large bowl, cover beans with cold water. Soak the beans overnight, then drain.

2. Spray a 4- to 5-quart slow cooker with nonstick olive oil spray. Combine beans, ham bone, 2 cups water, bouquet garni, and salt in the slow cooker.

3. Cover and cook on low for 5–7 hours. Remove the bone and bouquet garni; drain.

4. Heat butter in a large skillet over medium heat. Sauté the onions and garlic until soft.

5. Add the onions, garlic, parsley, tomato sauce, and black pepper to the beans in the slow cooker. Cover and cook for another hour.

PER SERVING: Calories: 353 | Fat: 4g | Protein: 20g | Sodium: 382mg | Fiber: 18g | Carbohydrates: 61g | Sugar: 10g

Spanish Saffron Rice

This fragrant dish goes well with grilled chicken or fish and looks very festive alongside shish kebabs. Use saffron threads instead of powder, if possible.

INGREDIENTS | SERVES 8

2 tablespoons olive oil

1 medium onion, peeled and thinly sliced

4 stalks celery, thinly sliced

3 medium tomatoes, chopped

4 cups water

2 teaspoons kosher salt

¼ teaspoon cayenne pepper

1⅓ cups uncooked quinoa

½ teaspoon saffron threads

1. Spray a 4- to 5-quart slow cooker with nonstick olive oil spray.

2. Heat oil in a medium skillet over medium heat. Sauté the onion and celery until soft. Transfer to the slow cooker.

3. Put the tomatoes, water, salt, and cayenne pepper in the slow cooker.

4. Cover and cook on low for 3–5 hours.

5. Increase heat to high and add quinoa and saffron. Cover slow cooker and allow to cook for 1 hour, or until quinoa is tender.

PER SERVING: Calories: 151 | Fat: 5g | Protein: 5g | Sodium: 613mg | Fiber: 3g | Carbohydrates: 21g | Sugar: 2g

Spicy Fennel and Swiss Chard

This lively and zesty side dish pairs wonderfully with every type of protein, from fish to pork.

INGREDIENTS | SERVES 4

2 large fennel bulbs, trimmed and chopped

1 bundle Swiss chard or kale, trimmed and chopped

½ cup low-sodium chicken broth

2 teaspoons lemon juice

½ teaspoon kosher salt

½ teaspoon freshly ground black pepper

½ teaspoon dried chili flakes

1. Place fennel in a 4- to 5-quart slow cooker and top with Swiss chard or kale. Add remaining ingredients and mix well.

2. Cover and cook on high for 2½–3 hours.

PER SERVING: Calories: 82 | Fat: 1g | Protein: 4g | Sodium: 515mg | Fiber: 5g | Carbohydrates: 16g | Sugar: 0g

Cannellini Beans with Pancetta, Rosemary, and Thyme

These beans are so creamy and decadent, they'll be requested over and over again. You can find pancetta, Italian seasoned and salt-cured pork, at most delicatessens or specialty food stores.

INGREDIENTS | SERVES 10

2 pounds dried cannellini beans
2 cups low-sodium chicken broth
½ teaspoon kosher salt
½ teaspoon ground white pepper
1 tablespoon chopped fresh rosemary
1 tablespoon chopped fresh thyme
4 slices pancetta, chopped

1. Soak the beans in cold water overnight. Drain and rinse.

2. Place the beans, broth, salt, pepper, rosemary, and thyme in a 4- to 5-quart slow cooker. Cover and cook on low for 6–8 hours.

3. Place the pancetta in a medium skillet and cook over low heat, stirring occasionally. When the meat is golden brown, after about 5–8 minutes, drain on paper towels.

4. Serve the beans topped with the crispy pancetta.

PER SERVING: Calories: 364 | Fat: 5g | Protein: 21g | Sodium: 419mg | Fiber: 17g | Carbohydrates: 59g | Sugar: 7g

Herbed Parsnips

When parsnips are slowly cooked, their natural sweetness really shines through. And combined with fresh herbs, they make a wonderfully savory side dish.

INGREDIENTS | SERVES 4

2 pounds parsnips, peeled and chopped
2 tablespoons olive oil
½ teaspoon kosher salt
½ teaspoon freshly ground black pepper
2 teaspoons chopped fresh rosemary
2 teaspoons chopped fresh thyme
1 teaspoon chopped fresh tarragon
¼ cup chopped flat-leaf parsley

1. Place parsnips in a 4- to 5-quart slow cooker and toss with olive oil. Season with salt and pepper.

2. Cover and cook on high for 3 hours. Add rosemary, thyme, and tarragon and cook for 1 more hour.

3. Remove from slow cooker, toss with parsley, and serve.

PER SERVING: Calories: 214 | Fat: 7g | Protein: 3g | Sodium: 317mg | Fiber: 10g | Carbohydrates: 40g | Sugar: 10g

Sherry and Balsamic Eggplant with Tomatoes and Goat Cheese

Combining sherry and balsamic vinegars creates a beautiful depth of flavor in this elegant eggplant dish.

INGREDIENTS | SERVES 4

1 large eggplant, cut into 1" pieces
3 large tomatoes, chopped
2 tablespoons olive oil
1 tablespoon balsamic vinegar
1 tablespoon sherry vinegar
½ teaspoon kosher salt
½ teaspoon freshly ground black pepper
1 tablespoon fresh basil
1 tablespoon fresh oregano
2 tablespoons crumbled goat cheese

1. Place eggplant and tomatoes in a 4- to 5-quart slow cooker with olive oil, and balsamic and sherry vinegar. Season with salt and pepper and stir well.

2. Cover and cook on high for 3 hours.

3. Sprinkle basil, oregano, and goat cheese over eggplant and tomatoes before serving.

PER SERVING: Calories: 185 | Fat: 12g | Protein: 7g | Sodium: 354mg | Fiber: 6g | Carbohydrates: 14g | Sugar: 7g

Vegetable and Chickpea Stew with Lemony Couscous

This delectable side dish marries perfectly with chicken. It could also be a meal itself!

INGREDIENTS | SERVES 4

1 cup cooked chickpeas
2 large carrots, peeled and cut into 1" pieces
1 large onion, peeled and chopped
1 (14½-ounce) can diced tomatoes
¼ cup low-sodium chicken broth
1 teaspoon cumin
1 teaspoon turmeric
1 teaspoon hot smoked paprika
2 cups boiling water
2 teaspoons lemon juice
1 cup couscous
¼ cup chopped flat-leaf parsley

1. Place chickpeas, carrots, onion, and tomatoes in a 4- to 5-quart slow cooker. Add broth, cumin, turmeric, and paprika. Stir well. Cover and cook on high for 3½ hours.

2. Combine boiling water, lemon juice, and couscous in a medium bowl. Cover tightly and let cook for 5 minutes. Stir into the slow cooker.

3. Garnish with parsley before serving.

PER SERVING: Calories: 287 | Fat: 2g | Protein: 11g | Sodium: 249mg | Fiber: 8g | Carbohydrates: 57g | Sugar: 7g

Risotto and Greens

This risotto makes a beautiful side dish for meat, chicken, or pork.

INGREDIENTS | SERVES 4

1 tablespoon plus 1 teaspoon olive oil, divided

1 large red onion, peeled and finely diced

½ teaspoon kosher salt

½ teaspoon ground white pepper

1 cup dry white wine, divided

1 cup Arborio rice

2 (14½-ounce) cans low-sodium chicken broth

2 large leeks (white and pale green parts only), chopped

1 (14½-ounce) can cannellini beans

½ cup shredded Parmesan cheese

1 cup arugula

½ cup flat-leaf parsley, chopped

1. In a large skillet, heat 1 tablespoon olive oil over medium heat. Sauté onion until softened, about 5–8 minutes. Season with salt and pepper. Stir in 1 tablespoon wine and deglaze the pan. Add the rice and cook for 1 minute.

2. Grease a 4- to 5-quart slow cooker with remaining olive oil. Pour rice mixture into slow cooker. Add remaining wine, broth, leeks, and beans.

3. Cover and cook on high for 2 hours. If risotto isn't creamy and cooked through, let it cook for another 30 minutes.

4. Add cheese and arugula and stir well. Serve garnished with parsley.

PER SERVING: Calories: 491 | Fat: 9g | Protein: 15g | Sodium: 632mg | Fiber: 8g | Carbohydrates: 75g | Sugar: 5g

Mashed Cauliflower with Dill and Parmesan

Slow-cooked cauliflower is hearty and creamy. And combined with tangy dill and sharp Parmesan, it makes a succulent side dish.

INGREDIENTS | SERVES 4

1 medium head cauliflower

1 cup low-sodium chicken broth

1 cup water

2 bay leaves

½ teaspoon kosher salt

½ teaspoon ground white pepper

1 tablespoon olive oil

¼ cup shredded Parmesan cheese

1 tablespoon fresh dill, chopped

2 tablespoons chives, for garnish

1. Remove stalk from cauliflower and roughly chop the florets. Place in a 4- to 5-quart slow cooker. Add broth, water, bay leaves, salt, and pepper. Cover and cook on high for 4 hours.

2. Remove cauliflower with a slotted spoon and place in a large bowl. Reserve cooking liquid and discard bay leaves.

3. Mash cauliflower with olive oil, cheese, and dill. If the mixture is too dry, add reserved cooking liquid by the tablespoon until it reaches desired consistency. Garnish with chives and serve immediately.

PER SERVING: Calories: 75 | Fat: 4g | Protein: 4g | Sodium: 413mg | Fiber: 3g | Carbohydrates: 7g | Sugar: 2g

Sherry Vinegar Broccoli

Sherry vinegar and herbs help to elevate broccoli into a side dish that's as good for company as it is on a Wednesday night. Although sherry vinegar can be expensive, you can usually find good-quality vinegar for about nine to twelve dollars a bottle. However, if you'd like to substitute it, you could use red wine vinegar or rice wine vinegar. Balsamic might overwhelm the dish.

INGREDIENTS | SERVES 4

1 large head of broccoli, trimmed and cut into florets

1 small onion, peeled and diced

½ teaspoon kosher salt

½ teaspoon ground white pepper

½ cup low-sodium chicken broth

2 teaspoons sherry vinegar

1 teaspoon lemon juice

2 tablespoons shredded Parmesan cheese

1. Place broccoli and onion in a 4- to 5-quart slow cooker. Season with salt and pepper. Pour broth over vegetables. Cover and cook on high for 1½ hours.

2. Add sherry vinegar and cook for 30 minutes more.

3. Remove broccoli mixture from slow cooker and toss with lemon juice. Sprinkle cheese over broccoli before serving.

PER SERVING: Calories: 80 | Fat: 2g | Protein: 6g | Sodium: 528mg | Fiber: 4g | Carbohydrates: 12g | Sugar: 3g

Endive and Cannellini Beans

Slow-cooked cannellini beans with herbs and vegetables are tossed with endive for a stunning side dish.

INGREDIENTS | SERVES 4

1 pound dried cannellini beans
3 cups low-sodium chicken broth
2 bay leaves
½ teaspoon kosher salt
½ teaspoon freshly ground black pepper
2 large carrots, peeled and chopped
1 large red onion, peeled and chopped
1 (14½-ounce) can diced tomatoes
1 tablespoon chopped fresh rosemary
2 medium heads Belgian endive, thinly sliced
1 tablespoon lemon juice

1. Place beans in a large bowl and cover with cold water. Let sit overnight. Drain and rinse beans.

2. Place beans in a 4- to 5-quart slow cooker. Add broth, bay leaves, salt, pepper, carrots, onion, tomatoes (including juice), and rosemary. Cover and cook on low for 6–8 hours.

3. Stir in endive and lemon juice and discard bay leaves. Serve immediately.

PER SERVING: Calories: 497 | Fat: 3g | Protein: 30g | Sodium: 625mg | Fiber: 24g | Carbohydrates: 90g | Sugar: 18g

Slow Roasted Stuffed Tomatoes

Slow roasting tomatoes brings out their natural sweetness. And when the sweet tomatoes are paired with zesty herbs and cheese, it makes this side dish irresistible.

INGREDIENTS | SERVES 4

1 tablespoon plus 1 teaspoon olive oil, divided
4 large tomatoes, halved
1½ cups panko bread crumbs
¼ cup chopped green olives
2 tablespoons chopped fresh basil
2 tablespoons chopped fresh dill
1 tablespoon chopped fresh oregano
½ teaspoon kosher salt
½ teaspoon ground white pepper
1½ cups shredded Parmesan cheese
½ cup low-sodium chicken broth
¼ cup chopped flat-leaf parsley

Mixing Bowls

Using the right kind of bowl will make mixing easier. Instead of a light bowl with steep sides, use a heavy mixing bowl with sloping sides to mix ingredients. The weight will hold it in place, and the sides will let you slide your spoon around more easily, without keeping your elbow up in the air.

1. Grease the inside of a 4- to 5-quart slow cooker with 1 teaspoon olive oil.

2. Using a spoon, scoop seeds from the tomatoes, leaving a depression for the stuffing.

3. Combine bread crumbs, olives, remaining olive oil, basil, dill, oregano, salt, pepper, and cheese in a medium bowl. Divide the filling between the tomatoes.

4. Place the tomatoes filling-side up in the slow cooker. Pour broth around tomatoes.

5. Cover and cook on high for 1½ hours. Baste with pan juices and cook for an additional 30 minutes.

6. Garnish with parsley before serving.

PER SERVING: Calories: 211 | Fat: 9g | Protein: 8g | Sodium: 496mg | Fiber: 4g | Carbohydrates: 28g | Sugar: 6g

Sweet and Savory Apple and
Brown Sugar Roasted Vegetables

This dish is sweet enough to entice young eaters, and savory enough to please adults.

INGREDIENTS | SERVES 4

1 tablespoon plus 1 teaspoon olive oil, divided

3 large carrots, peeled and chopped into 1" pieces

2 large red potatoes, peeled and chopped into ½" pieces

1 large red onion, peeled and chopped

1 large Delicata squash, seeded and cut into ½" slices

1½ tablespoons packed dark brown sugar

½ teaspoon kosher salt

½ teaspoon ground white pepper

½ cup apple cider or apple juice

1 tablespoon lemon juice

1. Grease the inside of a 4- to 5-quart slow cooker with 1 teaspoon olive oil.

2. Place the carrots, potatoes, onion, and squash in the slow cooker. Stir in remaining olive oil, brown sugar, salt, and pepper.

3. Pour apple cider over the vegetables. Cook on high for 2½–3 hours or until squash is easily pierced with a fork. Toss with lemon juice and serve immediately.

PER SERVING: Calories: 254 | Fat: 5g | Protein: 5g | Sodium: 349mg | Fiber: 6g | Carbohydrates: 49g | Sugar: 15g

Apple Cider Versus Apple Juice

Apple cider is seasonal, and the apples are pressed in the fall. Quite often it's unpasteurized and it has a shorter shelf life than apple juice. Apple cider is less sweet than apple juice, and it has a greater depth of flavor because it's closer to the actual fruit without the pasteurizing process.

Lemony Sweet Potatoes with Pomegranate Seeds

Not only is this dish visually stunning; it's healthy and simple to make.

INGREDIENTS | SERVES 4

1 tablespoon plus 1 teaspoon olive oil, divided

2 large sweet potatoes, peeled and diced into ½" cubes

1½ tablespoons packed light brown sugar

½ teaspoon nutmeg

½ teaspoon cinnamon

1 tablespoon lemon juice

½ cup pomegranate seeds

1 teaspoon sea salt

Removing Pomegranate Seeds Without Staining

Pomegranate seeds are wonderful, but they can stain a wooden chopping board. To avoid that, cut the top off of the pomegranate, quickly cut it into quarters, and drop them into a large bowl filled with water. Work the seeds out in the water, drain, and discard skins.

1. Grease a 4- to 5-quart slow cooker with 1 teaspoon olive oil. Place the sweet potato cubes in the slow cooker.

2. Mix the remaining olive oil with the brown sugar, nutmeg, and cinnamon in a small bowl. Add to the slow cooker and mix well. Cover and cook on low for 6–8 hours.

3. Stir in lemon juice and pomegranate seeds. Crush sea salt with a mortar and pestle and sprinkle over the potatoes. Serve immediately.

PER SERVING: Calories: 136 | Fat: 5g | Protein: 1.5g | Sodium: 628mg | Fiber: 3g | Carbohydrates: 22g | Sugar: 10g

CHAPTER 10

Sauces and Pasta

Demi-Glace Reduction Sauce

When you taste something a little magical in a sauce, chances are it's because there's demi-glace in it. A demi-glace is a rich brown sauce made by concentrating the flavors of meat and vegetables until they completely meld. It can be used on its own as sauce or as the base for another sauce.

INGREDIENTS | MAKES 4 CUPS

3 pounds beef, chicken, or lamb bones, or a combination

2 large onions, peeled and chopped

2 large carrots, peeled and chopped

2 large stalks of celery, chopped

2 tablespoons olive oil

1 teaspoon kosher salt

1 teaspoon freshly ground black pepper

8 cups Roasted Beef Stock (see recipe in Chapter 11)

1 cup dry red wine

2 tablespoons tomato paste

1 bay leaf

1 tablespoon chopped fresh thyme

1. Preheat oven to 400°F. In a large roasting pan, toss bones and vegetables with olive oil and season with salt and pepper. Roast for 30 minutes; turn and roast for another 30 minutes.

2. Transfer bones and vegetables to a 6-quart slow cooker.

3. In a large pot, bring the stock, red wine, tomato paste, bay leaf, and thyme to a gentle boil over medium-high heat. Pour over bones and vegetables. Cover and heat on high for 1 hour.

4. Reduce heat to low and cook for 8 hours. Move lid slightly to allow the demi-glace to reduce. Cook for an additional 3 hours. Freeze in ice cube trays and store cubes in resealable plastic bags for up to 3 months.

PER SERVING (¼ CUP): Calories: 67 | Fat: 3g | Protein: 3g | Sodium: 412mg | Fiber: 0.5g | Carbohydrates: 5g | Sugar: 2g

Ghee

With a high smoke point and stable saturated bonds, ghee is unlikely to burn during cooking, keeping your food free from cancer-causing free radicals. Ghee is composed primarily of short-chain fatty acids, which are quickly and readily metabolized by the body. Store ghee in glass jars in the refrigerator. If the recipe you're using it in calls for liquid ghee, warm the ghee before using.

INGREDIENTS | SERVES 36

2 pounds unsalted butter

1. Cut the butter into large cubes. Place in a 4- to 5-quart slow cooker.

2. Cover and cook on low for 2–3 hours. The butter should separate. Don't let it brown.

3. Skim off the clear liquid on the top; this is ghee. Store refrigerated and covered. Discard the butter solids, or use in cooking as a butter substitute.

PER SERVING: Calories: 112 | Fat: 12g | Protein: 0g | Sodium: 0mg | Fiber: 0g | Carbohydrates: 0g | Sugar: 0g

Fresh Tomato Sauce

With this fresh tomato sauce in your repertoire, you'll never want to buy sauce in a can again.

INGREDIENTS | MAKES 1 GALLON

20 large plum tomatoes

1 tablespoon olive oil

½ teaspoon kosher salt

½ teaspoon ground red pepper

2 large red onions, peeled and diced

1 medium shallot, peeled and diced

8 cloves garlic, minced

½ teaspoon packed light brown sugar

½ cup dry red wine

10 large fresh basil leaves, chopped

3 sprigs fresh oregano leaves, chopped

¼ bunch fresh parsley, chopped

Remove the Skins or Not?

While the extra step of removing the skins from tomatoes may seem like a waste of a few minutes, it's really not. When tomato skins cook, they come off in unappetizing little strips. Plus, it's actually kind of fun to get your hands a little messy!

1. Bring a large pot of water to a boil. Fill a large bowl with cold water and ice. Gently make a small "x" in the bottom of each tomato, just piercing the skin with a small paring knife. Gently drop the tomatoes into the boiling water using a slotted spoon. Cook for 1 minute. Remove the tomatoes from the boiling water and place them in the ice bath. Let cool and remove the skins. Roughly chop the tomatoes and place in a 4- to 5-quart slow cooker.

2. Heat the oil over medium heat in a saucepan until it shimmers, about 1 minute. Add the salt, red pepper, onions, and shallot and cook until softened, about 5 minutes. Add garlic and brown sugar; cook for 1 minute.

3. Remove from heat and add wine, basil, oregano, and parsley. Transfer mixture to the slow cooker. Stir well.

4. Cook on low for 4–6 hours. Sauce will keep in the refrigerator for up to 3 days or the freezer for up to 6 months.

PER SERVING (½ CUP): Calories: 38 | Fat: 0.5g | Protein: 1g | Sodium: 43mg | Fiber: 1.5g | Carbohydrates: 6g | Sugar: 3.5g

Long-Cooking Traditional Tomato Sauce

Slow cooking tomato sauce gives a chance for all of the flavors to completely meld, becoming the perfect mix of slightly sweet and savory.

INGREDIENTS | MAKES 1 GALLON

1 pound sweet Italian sausage, sliced into ½" rounds

1 tablespoon olive oil

2 large onions, peeled and diced

2 medium shallots, peeled and diced

2 garlic cloves, diced

4 (28-ounce) cans plum tomatoes

1 cup dry red wine

1 cup water

½ teaspoon dried basil

½ teaspoon dried oregano

½ teaspoon dried parsley

½ teaspoon fennel seeds

½ teaspoon kosher salt

½ teaspoon freshly ground black pepper

½ teaspoon red pepper flakes

1. In a large nonstick skillet over medium heat, cook the sausage until browned, about 5–8 minutes. Remove sausage with a slotted spoon and place in a 6-quart slow cooker.

2. Heat oil over medium heat in a Dutch oven and add onions and shallots. Cook until softened, about 5–8 minutes. Stir in garlic and cook for 1 minute.

3. Add the tomatoes, and cook for 5 minutes. Break tomatoes down with potato masher as they cook.

4. Pour tomato mixture over sausage in the slow cooker. Add remaining ingredients and stir well. Simmer on low heat for 6–8 hours.

5. Serve immediately with pasta, or cool in an ice bath and freeze for up to 3 months.

PER SERVING (½ CUP): Calories: 76 | Fat: 4g | Protein: 3g | Sodium: 131mg | Fiber: 1.5g | Carbohydrates: 5g | Sugar: 3g

Dry It Yourself!

Drying parsley yourself is a cost-efficient way to make the herb last longer. Simply wash it well and run it through a salad spinner. Strip the parsley from the stem, and place the leaves on a large rimmed cookie sheet and bake for 10–15 minutes in a 250°F oven. Store in a jar or in a resealable plastic bag in the freezer.

Slow Cooker Bolognese

*The wonderful flavor of this sauce comes from slow cooking, which can be
a little tricky on the stovetop. But in a slow cooker, it's a breeze.*

INGREDIENTS | SERVES 8

2 tablespoons olive oil

1 large carrot, peeled and diced

1 large onion, peeled and diced

1 large celery stalk, diced

½ teaspoon kosher salt

½ teaspoon freshly ground black pepper

1 pound ground sirloin

1 pound ground pork

2 tablespoons tomato paste

½ cup dry red wine

2 teaspoons chopped fresh thyme

⅔ cup whole milk

2 (28-ounce) cans crushed tomatoes

1. In a large skillet or Dutch oven, heat the oil over medium heat until hot but not smoking. Add the carrot, onion, and celery. Season with salt and pepper. Cook until softened, about 5–8 minutes.

2. Using a slotted spoon, transfer the vegetables to a 4- to 5-quart slow cooker.

3. Add the ground sirloin and pork to the pan and brown, about 10 minutes. Add the tomato paste and stir well. Cook for 2 minutes. Spoon the meat into the slow cooker.

4. Turn the heat off under the pan and add the wine. Deglaze the pan well, making sure to get up all of the browned bits on the bottom. Pour the wine into the slow cooker.

5. Add the thyme, milk, and tomatoes and stir well. Cover and cook on low for 8 hours.

PER SERVING: Calories: 323 | Fat: 19g | Protein: 24g | Sodium: 553mg | Fiber: 3g | Carbohydrates: 13g | Sugar: 7g

Italian Tomato Sauce with Turkey Meatballs

Using roasted garlic eliminates the need for sautéing, making this recipe a snap to put together.

INGREDIENTS | SERVES 4

12 frozen turkey meatballs

1½ tablespoons minced fresh basil

1 medium onion, peeled and minced

1 head roasted garlic (about 2 tablespoons), peels removed

1 (28-ounce) can fire-roasted tomatoes

1 teaspoon crushed red pepper flakes

Defrost the meatballs according to package instructions. Place in a 4- to 5-quart slow cooker with the remaining ingredients. Stir. Cook on low for 3–6 hours. Stir before serving.

PER SERVING: Calories: 327 | Fat: 14g | Protein: 33g | Sodium: 174mg | Fiber: 3.5g | Carbohydrates: 21g | Sugar: 6g

Pink Tomato Sauce

Try this creamier version of classic spaghetti sauce over linguine or fettuccini.

INGREDIENTS | SERVES 8

1 tablespoon olive oil

1 large onion, peeled and diced

2 cloves garlic, minced

1 tablespoon minced fresh basil

1 tablespoon minced fresh Italian parsley

⅔ cup fat-free evaporated milk

1 stalk celery, diced

1 (15-ounce) can whole tomatoes in purée

1 (28-ounce) can crushed tomatoes

1. Heat the olive oil in a medium-sized nonstick skillet over medium-high heat. Sauté the onion and garlic until the onion is soft, about 5 minutes.

2. Transfer onion and garlic to a 6-quart slow cooker. Add basil, parsley, evaporated milk, celery, and tomatoes. Stir well. Cook on low for 10–12 hours.

PER SERVING: Calories: 80 | Fat: 3.5g | Protein: 3g | Sodium: 45mg | Fiber: 2g | Carbohydrates: 10g | Sugar: 7g

Celery, the Star

Celery is often overlooked as an ingredient. It is perfect for slow cooking because it has a high moisture content but still remains crisp through the cooking process. Celery is also very low in calories and high in fiber.

Tomato and Chicken Sausage Sauce

Sausage is a delicious alternative to meatballs in this rich tomato sauce.

INGREDIENTS | SERVES 6

4 Italian chicken sausages, sliced

2 tablespoons tomato paste

1 (28-ounce) can crushed tomatoes

3 cloves garlic, minced

1 medium onion, peeled and minced

3 tablespoons minced basil

1 tablespoon minced Italian parsley

¼ teaspoon crushed rosemary

¼ teaspoon freshly ground black pepper

1. Quickly brown the sausage slices on both sides in a nonstick skillet over medium-high heat. Remove sausages with a slotted spoon and place in a 4- to 5-quart slow cooker, along with the remaining ingredients. Stir.

2. Cook on low for 8 hours.

PER SERVING: Calories: 184 | Fat: 8g | Protein: 9.5g | Sodium: 547mg | Fiber: 2g | Carbohydrates: 8g | Sugar: 5g

Rosemary-Mushroom Sauce

Try this sauce with egg noodles. Add 8 ounces of dried egg noodles to the slow cooker at the end of the cooking time and cook on high for 15 minutes or until the noodles are tender.

INGREDIENTS | SERVES 4

1 teaspoon butter

1 large onion, peeled and thinly sliced

8 ounces sliced mushrooms

1 tablespoon crushed rosemary

3 cups Roasted Chicken Broth (see recipe in Chapter 11)

1. Melt the butter in a nonstick skillet over medium heat. Add the onion and mushrooms and sauté until the onion is soft, about 5 minutes.

2. Place the onion and mushrooms into a 4- to 5-quart slow cooker. Add the rosemary and broth. Stir. Cook on low for 6–8 hours or on high for 3 hours.

PER SERVING: Calories: 67 | Fat: 3g | Protein: 5g | Sodium: 599mg | Fiber: 1.5g | Carbohydrates: 14g | Sugar: 2.5g

Save Time!

Buy sliced mushrooms instead of slicing them yourself. Most stores carry several varieties in the produce section. Cremini and button are popular small mushrooms. Portobello mushrooms are large and meaty enough to use as a meat substitute.

Artichoke Sauce

Cooking artichokes slowly gives them a velvety texture.

INGREDIENTS | SERVES 4

1 teaspoon olive oil

8 ounces frozen artichoke hearts, defrosted

3 cloves garlic, minced

1 medium onion, peeled and minced

2 tablespoons capote capers

1 (28-ounce) can crushed tomatoes

1. Heat the oil in a nonstick skillet over medium heat. Sauté the artichokes, garlic, and onion until the onion is translucent and most of the liquid has evaporated, about 8 minutes. Put the mixture into a 4- to 5-quart slow cooker. Stir in the capers and crushed tomatoes.

2. Cook on high for 4 hours or on low for 8 hours.

PER SERVING: Calories: 85 | Fat: 2g | Protein: 4g | Sodium: 300mg | Fiber: 5.5g | Carbohydrates: 16g | Sugar: 6g

Cleaning Slow Cookers

Do not use very abrasive tools or cleansers on a slow cooker insert. They may scratch the surface, allowing bacteria and food to be absorbed. Use a soft sponge and baking soda for stubborn stains.

Fennel and Caper Sauce

Try this sauce over boneless pork chops or boneless, skinless chicken breasts and egg noodles.

INGREDIENTS | SERVES 4

2 fennel bulbs with stalks

2 tablespoons nonpareil capers

½ cup Roasted Chicken Broth (see recipe in Chapter 11)

2 shallots, peeled and thinly sliced

2 cups diced fresh tomatoes

¼ teaspoon kosher salt

½ teaspoon freshly ground black pepper

⅓ cup minced fresh parsley

Cut off fennel stalks and freeze for soup stock. Reserve 2 tablespoons of the fennel fronds. Thinly slice the fennel bulbs. Place the fennel, capers, broth, shallots, tomatoes, salt, and pepper in a 4- to 5-quart slow cooker. Cook on low for 2 hours, and then add the parsley. Cook an additional 15–30 minutes on high. Garnish with reserved fronds.

PER SERVING: Calories: 76 | Fat: 0.5g | Protein: 4g | Sodium: 444mg | Fiber: 5g | Carbohydrates: 15g | Sugar: 2.5g

Regal Caper Sauce

This savory sauce is excellent on Royal Meatballs (see recipe in Chapter 7), rabbit, fish, or other delicately flavored meats. Replace the chicken stock with one that corresponds with the meat you choose, if you like.

INGREDIENTS | MAKES 3 CUPS

2 tablespoons butter
2 tablespoons all-purpose flour
3 cups chicken stock
½ teaspoon kosher salt
½ teaspoon black peppercorns
1 large egg yolk
1 tablespoon butter
6 tablespoons capers

1. Spray a 4- to 5-quart slow cooker with nonstick olive oil cooking spray.

2. Melt the butter in a saucepan over medium heat and mix in the flour, stirring until the flour is well mixed and slightly browned. Add the stock and mix well, then transfer to the slow cooker.

3. Add salt and peppercorns. Cover and cook on low for 1–2 hours.

4. Half an hour before serving, skim with a strainer. Stir in the yolk and butter, then add the capers.

PER SERVING (½ CUP): Calories: 114 | Fat: 8g | Protein: 4g | Sodium: 625mg | Fiber: 0.5g | Carbohydrates: 6g | Sugar: 2g

Easy Italian Spaghetti

It doesn't get any easier than this. Because this meal cooks so quickly, you can put it together as soon as you get home from work.

INGREDIENTS | SERVES 4

1 pound ground beef, browned
1 (16-ounce) jar marinara sauce
1 cup water
8 ounces uncooked pasta
½ cup grated Parmesan cheese

1. Add ground beef, marinara sauce, and water to a greased 4- to 5-quart slow cooker. Cook on high for 2 hours or on low for 4 hours.

2. Forty-five minutes prior to serving, stir dry pasta into meat sauce. The pasta will cook in the sauce.

3. Serve with Parmesan cheese sprinkled on top.

PER SERVING: Calories: 556 | Fat: 18g | Protein: 36g | Sodium: 475mg | Fiber: 5g | Carbohydrates: 57g | Sugar: 8g

Garlic and Artichoke Pasta

Artichoke hearts give this sauce a unique and savory flavor perfect for pasta or rice.

INGREDIENTS | SERVES 6

2 (14½-ounce) cans diced tomatoes with basil, oregano, and garlic

2 (14-ounce) cans artichoke hearts, drained and quartered

6 cloves garlic, minced

½ cup heavy cream

3 cups cooked pasta

1. Pour tomatoes, artichokes, and garlic into a 4- to 5-quart slow cooker. Cook on high for 3–4 hours or on low for 6–8 hours.

2. Twenty minutes prior to serving, stir in cream.

3. Serve over hot pasta.

PER SERVING: Calories: 286 | Fat: 8g | Protein: 10g | Sodium: 576mg | Fiber: 8g | Carbohydrates: 40g | Sugar: 4.5g

Can't Find Seasoned Canned Tomatoes?

If you can't find diced tomatoes with herbs and spices in your grocery store, use regular diced tomatoes and add 2 teaspoons of Italian seasoning to your sauce.

Lasagna with Spinach

There is no need to precook the lasagna noodles in this recipe.

INGREDIENTS | SERVES 10

28 ounces low-fat ricotta cheese

1 cup defrosted and drained frozen cut spinach

1 large egg

½ cup part-skim shredded mozzarella cheese

8 cups (about 2 jars) marinara sauce

½ pound uncooked lasagna noodles

1. In a medium bowl, stir the ricotta, spinach, egg, and mozzarella.

2. Ladle a quarter of the marinara sauce along the bottom of a greased 6-quart slow cooker. The bottom should be thoroughly covered in sauce. Add a single layer of lasagna noodles on top of the sauce, breaking noodles if needed to fit in the cooker.

3. Ladle an additional quarter of sauce over the noodles, covering all of the noodles. Top with half of the cheese mixture, pressing firmly with the back of a spoon to smooth. Add a single layer of lasagna noodles on top of the cheese, breaking noodles if needed to fit in the sides.

4. Ladle another quarter of the sauce on top of the noodles, and top with the remaining cheese. Press another layer of noodles onto the cheese and top with the remaining sauce. Take care that the noodles are entirely covered in sauce.

5. Cover and cook for 4–6 hours on low until cooked through.

PER SERVING: Calories: 421 | Fat: 17g | Protein: 17g | Sodium: 840mg | Fiber: 6g | Carbohydrates: 47g | Sugar: 18g

Creamy Chicken in a Mushroom and White Wine Sauce

Many traditional slow cooker recipes call for using canned cream soups. For a healthier version, this recipe shows you how to make a simple homemade cream soup using cornstarch and milk.

INGREDIENTS | SERVES 4

4 (4-ounce) boneless, skinless chicken breasts, cut into chunks

3 tablespoons cornstarch

1 cup 2% milk

½ cup white wine

½ teaspoon kosher salt

½ teaspoon ground black pepper

1½ teaspoons poultry seasoning

½ teaspoon garlic powder

½ teaspoon salt-free all-purpose seasoning

2 (4-ounce) cans sliced mushrooms, drained and rinsed

1½ cups frozen peas

2 cups cooked pasta

1. Grease a 4- to 5-quart slow cooker with nonstick cooking spray. Place chicken into the slow cooker.

2. In a saucepan, whisk together the cornstarch, milk, and white wine. Whisk in salt, pepper, poultry seasoning, garlic powder, and all-purpose seasoning. Cook over medium heat, whisking constantly until sauce thickens. Pour sauce over chicken in the slow cooker.

3. Add mushrooms on top of the chicken. Cook on low for 6 hours or on high for 3 hours.

4. One hour before serving, stir in the frozen peas.

5. Serve over pasta.

PER SERVING: Calories: 382 | Fat: 6g | Protein: 33g | Sodium: 784mg | Fiber: 5.5g | Carbohydrates: 41g | Sugar: 8g

CHAPTER 11

Stock, Broth, and Soup

Roasted Beef Stock

The trick to creating a wonderful beef stock is slow-roasting the meat and slow-cooking the stock.

INGREDIENTS | MAKES 1 GALLON

3 pounds meaty beef bones filled with marrow

2 pounds stew meat, cubed

3 large onions, peeled and quartered

½ pound carrots, peeled and chopped

3 stalks celery, chopped

2 tablespoons olive oil

1½ teaspoons kosher salt

1½ teaspoons freshly ground black pepper

¼ cup dry red wine

3 gallons water

1 bunch fresh parsley stems

4 stems fresh thyme

2 dried bay leaves

10–20 peppercorns

Ice Cube Trays Aren't Just for Ice!

Pour cooled stock into an ice cube tray, freeze it, then remove the cubes and place them in a resealable plastic bag. That way, if you need a small amount for a sauce you don't need to defrost a large container of stock.

1. Preheat oven to 400°F.

2. Place the bones, stew meat, onions, carrots, and celery in a large rimmed sheet pan. Toss with olive oil, salt, and pepper. Roast for 25 minutes, then flip meat and vegetables. Bake for an additional 20 minutes.

3. Transfer meat and vegetables to a 6-quart slow cooker.

4. Pour wine into sheet pan while still hot, and gently deglaze the pan. Pour the wine and drippings over meat and vegetables.

5. Add the water, parsley, thyme, bay leaves, and peppercorns. Cook on low heat for 8 hours.

6. Strain stock and discard solids. Refrigerate at least 2 hours. Skim fat that solidifies at the surface before using or freezing. Freeze for up to 3 months.

PER SERVING (1 CUP): Calories: 38 | Fat: 4g | Protein: 6g | Sodium: 289mg | Fiber: 0g | Carbohydrates: 1g | Sugar: 1g

Fish Stock

It can be hard to find a good fish stock in the store. But making it yourself from leftover bits and pieces of shells and fish bones creates a wonderful and inexpensive stock that bursts with flavor.

INGREDIENTS | MAKES 1 GALLON

2 pounds cooked fish bones

1 pound shrimp shells

1 pound red or white onions, peeled and quartered

1 pound celery stalks, chopped

1 pound carrots, peeled and chopped

1 bunch flat-leaf parsley

1 leek, chopped

2 garlic cloves, peeled and halved

1 large fennel bulb, quartered

2 tablespoons dry white wine

1½ gallons water

10 peppercorns

1. Place all ingredients in the slow cooker. Cover and cook on low for 5 hours.

2. Strain stock and discard solids. Refrigerate at least 2 hours. Skim fat that solidifies at the surface before using or freezing. Freeze for up to 3 months.

PER SERVING (1 CUP): Calories: 19 | Fat: 0g | Protein: 5g | Sodium: 15mg | Fiber: 0g | Carbohydrates: 1g | Sugar: 1g

Save, Save, and Save!

Whenever you cook seafood, toss the bones and shells in a plastic bag and freeze them until you're ready to make stock. A varied collection of bones and shells will result in an even more delicious stock.

Roasted Chicken Broth

Roasting chicken and vegetables and then slow cooking them with herbs and seasoning creates a broth that's incredibly rich and full of flavor. Use it as a base for rice dishes, soups, and stews.

INGREDIENTS | MAKES 8 CUPS

Bones from 1 whole chicken carcass

1 large onion, peeled and quartered

2 celery stalks, chopped

3 large carrots, unpeeled

1 tablespoon olive oil

8½ cups water

1 bunch flat-leaf parsley, chopped

1 bunch dill

1 tablespoon sea salt

1 teaspoon black peppercorns

Did You Know?

Roasting chicken bones along with vegetables helps to create a darker and richer broth. However, when using a broth for soup remember that clear broths are better for delicate dishes, and roasted broths are better for hearty dishes.

1. Preheat oven to 350°F.

2. Place chicken bones, onion, celery, and carrots on a large rimmed sheet pan. Drizzle with olive oil and roast for 1 hour.

3. Place bones and vegetables in a 6-quart slow cooker along with 8½ cups water. Add parsley, dill, salt, and peppercorns.

4. Cook on low for 8 hours.

5. Strain broth through a colander and discard solids. Store in refrigerator for 3 days or freeze for up to 2 months.

PER SERVING (1 CUP): Calories: 28 | Fat: 1.5g | Protein: 0g | Sodium: 799mg | Fiber: 0g | Carbohydrates: 0g | Sugar: 0g

Turkey Stock

The parsnips in this stock gives it a slightly sweet and peppery flavor.

INGREDIENTS | MAKES 1 GALLON

1 pound celery, chopped, leaves reserved

1 small turkey carcass

1½ pounds yellow or red onions, peeled and quartered

½ pound carrots, peeled and chopped

½ pound parsnips, peeled and chopped

¼ pound shallots, peeled and halved

1 bunch fresh flat-leaf parsley stems

4 stems fresh thyme

1 rosemary stem

1½ gallons water

2 dried bay leaves

10–20 peppercorns

1. Set aside celery leaves and place all other ingredients in a 6-quart slow cooker. Cover and cook on low for 7½ hours.

2. Add celery leaves and cook for 30 minutes longer.

3. Strain stock and discard solids. Refrigerate at least 2 hours. Skim fat that solidifies at the surface before using or freezing. Freeze for up to 3 months.

PER SERVING (1 CUP): Calories: 26 | Fat: 1g | Protein: 5g | Sodium: 20mg | Fiber: 0g | Carbohydrates: 1g | Sugar: 1g

Roasted Vegetable Stock

Use this in vegetarian recipes as a substitute for chicken stock or in other recipes as a flavorful alternative to water.

INGREDIENTS | MAKES 5 QUARTS

3 large carrots, peeled

3 large parsnips, peeled

3 large onions, peeled and quartered

3 whole turnips

3 medium rutabagas, quartered

3 medium bell peppers, halved and seeded

2 medium shallots

1 whole head garlic

1 bunch fresh thyme

1 bunch parsley

3½ quarts water

1. Preheat oven to 425°F. Arrange the vegetables and herbs on a 9" × 13" baking pan lined with parchment paper. Roast for 30 minutes or until browned.

2. Transfer the vegetables to a 4- to 5-quart slow cooker. Add water and cover. Cook on low for 8–10 hours. Strain the stock, discarding the solids. Freeze or refrigerate the stock until ready to use.

PER SERVING (1 CUP): Calories: 15 | Fat: 0g | Protein: 3g | Sodium: 9mg | Fiber: 0g | Carbohydrates: 1g | Sugar: 1g

Savory Vegetable Stock

Mushrooms add a surprising "meaty" bite to this stock and will please vegetarians and meat lovers alike.

INGREDIENTS | MAKES 10 CUPS

2 pounds yellow onions, peeled and quartered

1 pound carrots, washed, unpeeled, and chopped

1 pound celery, chopped

½ pound button mushrooms, cleaned and halved

1 bunch fresh parsley stems

1 bunch dill

4 stems fresh thyme

10 cups water

2 bay leaves (fresh or dried)

1 tablespoon sea salt

10–20 peppercorns

1. Place all ingredients in a 4- to 5-quart slow cooker and cook on low for 8 hours.

2. Remove the solids with a slotted spoon, and discard. Refrigerate for up to 3 days or freeze and store for up to 3 months.

PER SERVING (1 CUP): Calories: 19 | Fat: 0g | Protein: 0g | Sodium: 700mg | Fiber: 0g | Carbohydrates: 0g | Sugar: 0g

White Wine Vegetable Stock

Wine brings a lovely brightness and an extra layer of flavor to stock that will carry through to finished soup or stews.

INGREDIENTS | MAKES 1 GALLON

1½ teaspoons olive oil

1½ pounds yellow or red onions, peeled and quartered

¼ pound shallots, peeled and halved

1 large leek, chopped

½ pound carrots, peeled and chopped

1 pound celery, leaves reserved

1 cup pinot grigio (or other light white wine)

1½ gallons water

1 bunch fresh parsley stems

4 stems fresh thyme

2 bay leaves (fresh or dried)

10–20 peppercorns

Don't Discard the Leaves!

Celery leaves can be an overlooked ingredient. They can be dried and mixed with kosher salt to create your own celery salt, which adds a fresh flavor to soups, stews, and sauces. Also, fresh chopped celery leaves are wonderful to use as a final step to finish dishes.

1. Heat the olive oil in a Dutch oven over medium heat. Add the onions, shallots, leek, carrots, and celery. Sauté until vegetables have softened, about 5–8 minutes. Pour in the wine and cook for 5 minutes, until slightly reduced.

2. Transfer the vegetable mixture to a 4- to 5-quart slow cooker. Add water.

3. Stir in parsley, thyme, bay leaves, and peppercorns, and cook on low heat for 7½ hours. Add celery leaves, and cook for an additional 30 minutes.

4. Strain the stock, discarding the solids. Freeze or refrigerate the stock until ready to use.

PER SERVING (1 CUP): Calories: 24 | Fat: 1g | Protein: 3g | Sodium: 20mg | Fiber: 0g | Carbohydrates: 2g | Sugar: 2g

Red Wine and Tomato Vegetable Stock

Use your favorite Mediterranean dry red wine. The more complex the wine, the more flavorful the stock will be. Remember the cardinal rule of cooking with wine—never cook with anything you wouldn't drink.

INGREDIENTS | MAKES 1 GALLON

½ pound tomatoes

1½ teaspoons olive oil

1½ pounds yellow onions, peeled and quartered

¼ pound shallots, peeled and halved

½ pound carrots, peeled and chopped

1 pound celery, chopped

½ pound portobello mushrooms, chopped

4 cloves garlic, chopped

1 cup dry red wine

1½ gallons water

1 bunch fresh parsley stems

4 stems fresh thyme

2 bay leaves (fresh or dried)

10–20 peppercorns

1. Bring a large pot of water to a boil. Fill a large bowl with cold water and ice. Gently cut a small "x" in the bottom of each tomato, just piercing the skin. Place tomatoes one at a time on a slotted spoon and gently drop into boiling water. Repeat until all tomatoes are in the pot. Cook the tomatoes for 1 minute and remove with slotted spoon. Place the tomatoes in the ice bath to cool. Remove skins of tomatoes when cooled, and roughly chop.

2. Heat the olive oil in a Dutch oven over medium heat. Add the onions, shallots, carrots, and celery. Sauté until softened, 5–8 minutes. Add the tomatoes, mushrooms, and garlic. Stir for 1 minute.

3. Pour in the wine and cook until almost completely evaporated, about 10 minutes.

4. Transfer the vegetable mixture to a 4- to 5-quart slow cooker and add water. Stir in parsley, thyme, bay leaves, and peppercorns and cook on low for 8 hours.

5. Strain the stock, discarding the solids. Freeze or refrigerate the stock until ready to use.

PER SERVING (1 CUP): Calories: 24 | Fat: 1g | Protein: 3g | Sodium: 20mg | Fiber: 0g | Carbohydrates: 1g | Sugar: 1g

Basic Bean Soup

This hearty vegetarian bean soup serves a crowd. If using cooked beans, the soup looks beautiful with a mélange of beans including white Northern beans, black beans, and pinto beans.

INGREDIENTS | SERVES 8

1 (16-ounce) bag dried mixed beans or 2¼ cups cooked beans

1 (14½-ounce) can diced tomatoes, with juice

6 cups vegetable broth

2 cups finely diced carrots

1½ cups finely diced celery

1 cup finely chopped onions

2 tablespoons tomato paste

1 teaspoon Italian seasoning

½ teaspoon ground black pepper

1 teaspoon kosher salt

1. If using dried beans, soak them according to package directions. Rinse and place in a 4-quart or larger slow cooker.

2. Add remaining ingredients to the slow cooker.

3. Cover and cook on high for 5–6 hours or on low for 10–12 hours until beans are tender.

PER SERVING: Calories: 290 | Fat: 1g | Protein: 15g | Sodium: 450mg | Fiber: 16g | Carbohydrates: 41g | Sugar: 5g

Simple Tomato Soup

This healthy, kid-friendly soup is made with canned tomatoes, which are available year-round at affordable prices. You can also make this soup with about 4 pounds of chopped fresh tomatoes if you prefer.

INGREDIENTS | SERVES 8

1 small sweet onion, peeled and finely diced

3 tablespoons butter

3 (14½-ounce) cans low-sodium diced tomatoes

1 tablespoon honey

1 (15-ounce) can chicken broth

½ teaspoon kosher salt

1. In a small glass or microwave-safe bowl, cook onion and butter in the microwave on high for 1 minute to soften them.

2. Add onion and butter to a greased 4- to 5-quart slow cooker. Stir in tomatoes, honey, and chicken broth. Cook on high for 4 hours or on low for 8 hours.

3. Turn off slow cooker and add salt to the soup. Allow soup to cool for about 20 minutes and then blend using an immersion blender or by pouring the soup (a little at a time) into a kitchen blender.

PER SERVING: Calories: 96 | Fat: 5g | Protein: 3g | Sodium: 190mg | Fiber: 2g | Carbohydrates: 11g | Sugar: 6g

Dandelion and White Bean Soup

This soup has a delicate flavor that will please meat eaters and vegetarians alike.

INGREDIENTS | SERVES 6

1 teaspoon olive oil

2 large red onions, peeled and chopped

3 large carrots, peeled and diced

3 stalks celery, diced

½ teaspoon freshly ground black pepper

1 clove garlic, minced

2 quarts Roasted Vegetable Stock (see recipe in this chapter)

1 dried bay leaf

1 cup cooked cannellini beans

¼ bunch flat-leaf parsley, chopped

4 sprigs fresh thyme, stripped from the stalk

2 cups fresh dandelion greens

¼ cup shredded Parmesan cheese

Dandelion Greens

Depending on where you live, dandelion greens may be a seasonal treat. If you can't find them, substitute arugula in the soup.

1. Heat the oil in a medium skillet or Dutch oven over medium heat until hot but not smoking. Add the onions, carrots, and celery and season with pepper. Sauté until softened, about 5–8 minutes. Add garlic and cook for 1 minute.

2. Place the vegetable mixture in a 4- to 5-quart slow cooker. Add the stock and bay leaf. Cover and cook on low heat for 3 hours.

3. Add the beans, parsley, thyme, and dandelion greens and cook for 30 minutes more.

4. Serve with shredded cheese.

PER SERVING: Calories: 102 | Fat: 1.5g | Protein: 4g | Sodium: 194mg | Fiber: 5g | Carbohydrates: 16g | Sugar: 5g

Winter Borscht

Borscht is a bright red soup, made with beets. This recipe uses the traditional spices of Mediterranean cooking and a bit of lean beef to add beautiful variety to the classic version.

INGREDIENTS | SERVES 6

¾ pound cubed lean top round beef

3½ cups shredded Roasted Beets (see recipe in Chapter 13)

1 medium onion, peeled and diced

1 medium carrot, peeled and grated

½ teaspoon kosher salt

½ teaspoon sugar

3 tablespoons red wine vinegar

½ teaspoon freshly ground black pepper

½ teaspoon cumin

¼ teaspoon coriander

1 clove garlic, minced

1 cup shredded green cabbage

2 cups Roasted Vegetable Stock (see recipe in this chapter)

2 cups water

1. In a nonstick skillet over medium-high heat, sauté the beef for 1 minute. Remove beef from skillet with a slotted spoon and place in a 4- to 5-quart slow cooker.

2. Add remaining ingredients to the slow cooker. Cook on low for 8 hours. Stir before serving.

PER SERVING: Calories: 149 | Fat: 3g | Protein: 15g | Sodium: 303mg | Fiber: 3g | Carbohydrates: 12g | Sugar: 7g

Pumpkin Soup

Sugar pumpkins are delicious in this autumnal soup. Fresh ginger gives it a little spice, too.

INGREDIENTS | SERVES 6

1 medium sugar pumpkin, halved and seeded (seeds reserved)

1 tablespoon plus 2 teaspoons olive oil, divided

1½ teaspoons kosher salt, divided

1 teaspoon freshly ground black pepper, divided

2 quarts Savory Vegetable Stock (see recipe in this chapter)

3 large leeks (white and pale green parts only), sliced

1½ teaspoons minced fresh ginger

1 teaspoon grated fresh lemon zest

1 teaspoon fresh lemon juice

Zesting

If you don't own a zester, simply use your hand-held cheese grater to zest a lemon. However, only grate the yellow rind. If you hit white, you've gone too far. The white pith is bitter, and you want to avoid it if you can.

1. Preheat oven to 375°F.

2. Wash the pumpkin seeds well, and pat them dry with paper towels. Place the seeds on a rimmed cookie sheet and toss with 1 tablespoon olive oil. Season with ½ teaspoon salt and ½ teaspoon pepper. Stir well and bake for 7–9 minutes, or until light golden brown. Set aside.

3. Place the pumpkin halves, cut-side up, in a baking dish, and drizzle each half with a teaspoon of olive oil. Season with remaining salt and pepper. Roast for 45 minutes to 1 hour, or until the flesh is easily pierced with a knife. Let cool slightly and scoop the pumpkin flesh into a 4- to 5-quart slow cooker.

4. Add the stock, leeks, ginger, zest, and lemon juice.

5. Cover and cook on low for 3–4 hours.

6. Carefully ladle half of the soup into a blender and process to desired consistency. Pour the blended soup back into the slow cooker, and stir well to combine.

7. To serve, divide the soup between six bowls and top with pumpkin seeds.

PER SERVING: Calories: 119 | Fat: 4g | Protein: 5g | Sodium: 589mg | Fiber: 2g | Carbohydrates: 14g | Sugar: 4g

Lentil and Barley Soup

For these as for all soup bones, ask your butcher for bones that have some meat remaining. This adds flavor and nutrients.

INGREDIENTS | SERVES 8

1 medium onion, peeled and coarsely chopped

3 cloves garlic, chopped

1½ pounds lamb bones

8 cups water

½ teaspoon kosher salt

2 bay leaves

¼ teaspoon ground black pepper

1 cup brown lentils, rinsed

½ cup pearl barley

1 bunch fresh parsley, coarsely chopped

A Garlic Project

Some evening while you're sitting at home talking on the phone or watching television, peel a dozen or so cloves of garlic and put them in a small jar of olive or vegetable oil. This will keep the garlic fresh and give the oil a nice flavor for future use in recipes or salad dressings.

1. Spray a 4- to 5-quart slow cooker with nonstick olive oil cooking spray.

2. Combine the onion, garlic, bones, water, salt, bay leaves, and pepper in the slow cooker. Stir in the lentils and barley.

3. Cover and cook on low for 4–5 hours. Remove the bay leaves and bones.

4. Top individual servings of soup with parsley.

PER SERVING: Calories: 139 | Fat: 1g | Protein: 8g | Sodium: 162mg | Fiber: 10g | Carbohydrates: 26g | Sugar: 1g

Onion-Garlic Soup

Garlic and five types of onions give this soup a complex and unique flavor.

INGREDIENTS | SERVES 6

1 tablespoon olive oil

2 large red onions, peeled and sliced

1 large yellow onion, peeled and sliced

1 large Vidalia onion, peeled and sliced

1 large leek (white and pale green parts only), chopped

1 shallot, peeled and diced

3 cloves garlic, chopped

1 ounce anisette or sambuca

2 quarts Red Wine and Tomato Vegetable Stock (see recipe in this chapter)

6 thin slices French bread

6 ounces Asiago or Parmesan cheese, grated

½ bunch scallions, sliced

1. Heat the oil in a large Dutch oven over medium heat. Add the red, yellow, and Vidalia onions and reduce heat to low. Let the onions cook down until lightly caramelized, about 25 minutes, stirring occasionally. Add the leek, shallot, and garlic. Cook for 5 minutes, stirring frequently.

2. Place the onion mixture in a 4- to 5-quart slow cooker.

3. Add the anisette to the Dutch oven, and stir well to pick up any browned pieces. Pour anisette mixture over the onions in the slow cooker. Add the stock and stir well. Cover the slow cooker, and cook on low for 3 hours.

4. When the soup has half an hour to continue cooking, start making the croutons. Preheat the oven to broil. Place the bread on a baking sheet, and divide cheese between toasts. Broil until the cheese is melted, about 3–5 minutes.

5. Ladle soup into six serving bowls. Top the soup with the cheese croutons and garnish with scallions.

PER SERVING: Calories: 285 | Fat: 10g | Protein: 15g | Sodium: 664mg | Fiber: 3g | Carbohydrates: 31g | Sugar: 5g

Old-Fashioned Onion Soup

Make your own croutons to serve with this soup. Cut thick slices of black bread into cubes.
Sprinkle with grated Parmesan cheese and freshly ground black pepper, then broil until browned.

INGREDIENTS | SERVES 8

6 tablespoons butter

6 medium onions, peeled and thinly sliced

4 cups beef broth

½ teaspoon kosher salt

½ teaspoon black peppercorns

¼ pound Parmesan cheese, grated, divided

1. Spray a 4- to 5-quart slow cooker with nonstick olive oil cooking spray.

2. Heat butter in a medium skillet over low heat. Slowly sauté onions in butter until browned, about 25 minutes.

3. Add onions, broth, salt, and peppercorns to the slow cooker.

4. Cover and cook on low for 3–4 hours.

5. Before serving, stir ¼ cup cheese into the soup. Set out the remainder to garnish individual servings.

PER SERVING: Calories: 139 | Fat: 12g | Protein: 7g | Sodium: 764mg | Fiber: 0g | Carbohydrates: 0g | Sugar: 0g

Leek, Potato, and Carrot Potage

Potage is a classic French home-style soup with minimal spices that derives its flavor from letting
a few simple ingredients shine. With crusty bread, it's perfect for a cold winter evening.

INGREDIENTS | SERVES 6

4 cups sliced leeks (white and pale green parts only)

4 medium russet potatoes, peeled and cubed

2 medium carrots, peeled and diced

2 celery stalks, diced

5 cups Roasted Chicken Broth (see recipe in this chapter)

¼ teaspoon kosher salt

½ teaspoon ground white pepper

1. Place all ingredients into a 4- to 5-quart slow cooker. Cook on low for 7 hours.

2. Use a potato masher to break down the vegetables to desired consistency. Serve piping hot.

PER SERVING: Calories: 227 | Fat: 3g | Protein: 8g | Sodium: 606mg | Fiber: 5g | Carbohydrates: 40g | Sugar: 5g

Forest Mushroom Soup

Using both fresh and dried mushrooms adds more texture as well as more flavor to this dish. Try using fresh wild mushrooms, if available.

INGREDIENTS | SERVES 8

½ cup dried mushrooms, cut into ½" strips

¾ cup Madeira wine

½ cup butter

2 medium onions, peeled and finely diced

2 pounds fresh mushrooms, sliced

5 cups chicken stock

½ teaspoon kosher salt

¼ teaspoon ground black pepper

½ cup heavy cream

Flour for Thickening

To thicken a thin sauce or soup, add ½ tablespoon all-purpose flour per cup of liquid. Mix the flour first with cold water or melted butter to make a paste, and then gradually stir into the hot liquid and let it swell while cooking.

1. Spray a 4- to 5-quart slow cooker with nonstick olive oil cooking spray.

2. Rinse the dried mushroom strips under cold water and soak in the wine for an hour. Transfer the dried mushrooms to a 4- to 5-quart slow cooker with a slotted spoon, setting aside the wine.

3. Melt butter in a medium skillet over medium heat. Reduce heat to low and sauté the onions in butter until the onions are soft, about 10 minutes. Add fresh mushrooms and sauté for another 5–10 minutes, until mushrooms are soft. Transfer the onions and mushrooms to the slow cooker.

4. Add the chicken stock, salt, and pepper to the slow cooker. Cover and cook on low for 3–4 hours.

5. An hour before serving, ladle out 1 cup of the mushrooms and onions and purée with the cream in a blender or food processor. Add the creamed mixture and the reserved wine to the slow cooker.

PER SERVING: Calories: 360 | Fat: 19g | Protein: 10g | Sodium: 381mg | Fiber: 4g | Carbohydrates: 35g | Sugar: 8g

Spring Soup

This delicious vegetable-packed soup is perfect for springtime, when fresh asparagus is readily available and affordable at local grocers.

INGREDIENTS | SERVES 6

3 pounds fresh asparagus

1 pound cauliflower

½ pound carrots, peeled and sliced

½ pound turnips, peeled and cut into 2" strips

½ pound string beans, cut diagonally

1 cup green peas

2 cups chicken broth

¼ teaspoon kosher salt

¼ teaspoon ground black pepper

½ cup chopped cilantro

1. Spray a 4- to 5-quart slow cooker with nonstick olive oil cooking spray. Cut 2" tips from the asparagus and the florets from the cauliflower and place in slow cooker; set aside the asparagus stalks and cauliflower stems for use in other recipes.

2. Stir in carrots, turnips, beans, peas, broth, salt, and pepper. Cover and cook on low for 3½ hours.

3. Stir in the cilantro and cook for 30 minutes more.

PER SERVING: Calories: 153 | Fat: 2g | Protein: 10g | Sodium: 228mg | Fiber: 10g | Carbohydrates: 28g | Sugar: 11g

Caraway Soup

Caraway has a distinctive flavor that is delicious in soup. Serve this with warm rye bread on the side.

INGREDIENTS | SERVES 6

1 cube chicken bouillon

3 cups chicken broth

3 pounds cabbage, coarsely chopped

½ cup diagonally sliced celery

1 tablespoon kosher salt

½ tablespoon caraway seeds

¼ tablespoon ground black pepper

1 tablespoon tapioca

1 cup heavy cream

1. Spray a 4- to 5-quart slow cooker with nonstick olive oil cooking spray. Dissolve the bouillon cube in the broth and pour into slow cooker.

2. Stir in cabbage, celery, salt, caraway seeds, pepper, and tapioca. Cover and cook on low for 4½ hours.

3. Stir in cream and cook for 30 minutes more.

PER SERVING: Calories: 254 | Fat: 17g | Protein: 7g | Sodium: 1,002mg | Fiber: 6g | Carbohydrates: 22g | Sugar: 7g

Greek-Style Orzo and Spinach Soup

Lemon zest adds a bright, robust flavor to this simple soup.

INGREDIENTS | SERVES 6

2 cloves garlic, minced

3 tablespoons lemon juice

1 teaspoon lemon zest

5 cups Roasted Chicken Broth (see recipe in this chapter)

1 small onion, peeled and thinly sliced

1 cup cubed cooked chicken breast

⅓ cup dried orzo

4 cups fresh baby spinach

1. Add the garlic, lemon juice, zest, broth, and onion to a 4- to 5-quart slow cooker. Cover and cook on low for 6–8 hours.

2. Stir in the chicken and cook for 30 minutes on high. Add the orzo and spinach. Stir and continue to cook on high for an additional 15 minutes. Stir before serving.

PER SERVING: Calories: 90 | Fat: 1g | Protein: 9g | Sodium: 237mg | Fiber: 1g | Carbohydrates: 10g | Sugar: 0g

Rajah's Apple Curry Soup

Curry comes in a variety of different heats—from sweet and mild to blazingly spicy. If you are making this dish for children or picky adults, stick to the ground yellow curry powder which is commonly available at most grocery stores.

INGREDIENTS | SERVES 12

2 tablespoons olive oil

3 pounds sliced fresh mushrooms

5 tablespoons all-purpose flour

½ cup dried mushrooms, sliced into strips

3 medium tart apples, peeled, cored, and coarsely chopped

7½ cups chicken broth

1½ teaspoons turmeric

2¼ teaspoons ground ginger

2¼ teaspoons ground cumin

2¼ teaspoons curry powder

¾ teaspoon ground coriander

1 cup sherry

¼ cup heavy cream

1. Spray a 4- to 5-quart slow cooker with nonstick olive oil cooking spray. Heat oil in a large skillet over medium heat. Sauté fresh mushrooms for 5–10 minutes, until soft. Stir in the flour. Transfer mushroom mixture to the slow cooker.

2. Add dried mushrooms, apples, broth, turmeric, ginger, cumin, curry powder, and coriander to the slow cooker. Cover and cook on low for 4½ hours.

3. Stir in sherry and cream and cook for 30 minutes more.

PER SERVING: Calories: 246 | Fat: 7g | Protein: 9g | Sodium: 667mg | Fiber: 4g | Carbohydrates: 36g | Sugar: 8g

Chicken Vegetable Soup

This soup is healthy and filling without a lot of calories. It's also a very frugal recipe, using ingredients you probably have in your pantry right now. If you like, add some cooked rice or pasta to the soup before serving.

INGREDIENTS | SERVES 4

½ cup chopped onions

1 (14½-ounce) can Italian-seasoned diced tomatoes

1 (14½-ounce) can low-sodium mixed vegetables

1 (14½-ounce) can low-sodium chicken broth

1 (10-ounce) can chunk chicken, drained

1. Spray a 4- to 5-quart slow cooker with nonstick olive oil cooking spray.

2. Place onions in a small glass or microwave-safe bowl. Cover with plastic wrap and cook on high for 1–2 minutes until onions are soft.

3. Add softened onions, tomatoes, mixed vegetables, and chicken broth to prepared slow cooker. Cook on high for 4 hours or on low for 8 hours.

4. Thirty minutes prior to serving add chicken to the slow cooker. Stir to warm through.

PER SERVING: Calories: 245 | Fat: 7g | Protein: 23g | Sodium: 522mg | Fiber: 4g | Carbohydrates: 20g | Sugar: 5g

Herbed Chicken and Pasta Soup

This slow-cooked chicken soup is filled with herbs and lemon to warm you on the coldest winter night. Serve it with crusty bread.

INGREDIENTS | SERVES 4

1 tablespoon olive oil

2 pounds boneless, skinless chicken breasts, pounded to 1" thickness

1 teaspoon kosher salt

1 teaspoon freshly ground black pepper

2 large red onions, peeled and diced

2 medium carrots, peeled and diced

2 stalks celery, diced

¼ bunch flat-leaf parsley, chopped

1 tablespoon chopped fresh dill, divided

10 cups Roasted Chicken Broth (see recipe in this chapter)

½ cup chopped fresh spinach

1 teaspoon fresh thyme

2 teaspoons lemon juice

1 cup uncooked orzo

1. Heat olive oil in a large skillet over medium heat until it shimmers, about 1 minute. Season both sides of chicken with salt and pepper. Cook chicken on one side for 5 minutes; flip and cook for an additional 3 minutes.

2. Place chicken in a 4- to 5-quart slow cooker with onions, carrots, celery, parsley, and half the dill. Stir in broth.

3. Simmer for 7½ hours on low heat. Add spinach, thyme, lemon juice, orzo, and remaining dill.

4. Cook for an additional 15–20 minutes or until orzo is plump.

PER SERVING: Calories: 542 | Fat: 15g | Protein: 57g | Sodium: 2,100mg | Fiber: 3g | Carbohydrates: 69g | Sugar: 5g

Healthy Dill

Did you know that dill is chock-a-block with antioxidants? And it contains vitamins like niacin, folic acid, vitamin A, and vitamin C. So keep fresh dill on hand for soups, stews, sauces, and even just as a snack with cucumber and a little vinegar. You can't go wrong with dill!

Matzo Ball Soup

*Although it is not strictly traditional, adding dill to the matzo balls
adds a fresh note to this slow-cooked soup.*

INGREDIENTS | SERVES 6

8 cups chicken stock

1 stalk celery, diced

2 medium carrots, peeled and thinly sliced

1 medium parsnip, peeled and diced

1 large onion, peeled and diced

1½ cups diced cooked chicken

1 cup boiling water

1 cup matzo meal

1 large egg

1½ tablespoons minced dill

1. Put the stock, celery, carrots, parsnip, and onion into a 4- to 5-quart slow cooker. Cook on low for 6 hours.

2. Add the chicken and cook for 1 hour.

3. Mix the boiling water, matzo meal, egg, and dill in a large bowl until smooth. Form into 2" balls. Drop them into the soup, cover, and cook for 15 minutes.

PER SERVING: Calories: 376 | Fat: 7g | Protein: 23g | Sodium: 323mg | Fiber: 3g | Carbohydrates: 51g | Sugar: 8g

Matzo Meal Facts

Matzo meal, a product similar to bread crumbs, is made from crushed matzo. While it is available year-round, it is particularly easy to find near Passover. You can make matzo meal at home by pulsing matzo (flat unleavened crackers) in a food processor until small crumbs form. It is a necessary ingredient in matzo balls and can be used as a substitute for bread crumbs in many recipes.

Chicken, Mushroom, and Barley Soup

This is a wonderful hearty but light soup. Mushrooms and vegetables cook in a seasoned roasted chicken stock, and cooked chicken is added at the end for even greater ease of preparation.

INGREDIENTS | SERVES 8

1 ounce dried porcini mushrooms

1 cup boiling water

2 tablespoons olive oil

2 medium carrots, peeled and diced

3 stalks celery, diced

1 large onion, peeled and diced

1 clove garlic, minced

6 cups Roasted Chicken Broth (see recipe in this chapter), divided

⅔ cup medium pearl barley

¼ teaspoon ground black pepper

2 cups cooked shredded chicken

1. Place the dried mushrooms in a medium heat-safe bowl. Pour the boiling water over the mushrooms. Soak for 15 minutes.

2. Heat olive oil in a large skillet set over medium-high heat. Sauté the carrots, celery, and onion together until the vegetables have softened and have some color, about 7–10 minutes. Drain mushrooms and add to vegetables in the skillet. Sauté for 5 minutes. Add garlic and sauté for 2 minutes. Transfer mixture to a 4- to 5-quart slow cooker.

3. Using 1 cup of the chicken broth, deglaze the pan, making sure to scoop up all the browned bits. Pour deglazed broth over vegetables along with the remaining 5 cups of broth.

4. Add barley and pepper and stir well. Cook for 6 hours on low heat. Add cooked chicken and cook for another 30 minutes or until chicken is heated through.

PER SERVING: Calories: 245 | Fat: 9g | Protein: 15g | Sodium: 741mg | Fiber: 4g | Carbohydrates: 25g | Sugar: 2g

Greek Lemon-Chicken Soup

*Lemon juice and egg yolks give this soup a lovely yellow color.
It's a unique soup that's perfect for a spring luncheon.*

4 cups chicken broth

¼ cup fresh lemon juice

¼ cup shredded carrots

¼ cup chopped onion

¼ cup chopped celery

⅛ teaspoon ground white pepper

2 tablespoons butter, softened

2 tablespoons all-purpose flour

4 large egg yolks

½ cup cooked white rice

½ cup diced, cooked, boneless, skinless chicken breast

8 slices lemon

1. In a greased 4- to 5-quart slow cooker, combine the chicken broth, lemon juice, carrots, onion, celery, and pepper. Cover and cook on high for 3–4 hours or on low for 6–8 hours.

2. One hour before serving, blend the butter and the flour together in a medium bowl with a fork. Remove 1 cup of hot broth from the slow cooker and whisk with the butter and flour. Add mixture back to the slow cooker.

3. In a small bowl, beat the egg yolks until light in color. Gradually add 1 cup of the hot soup to the egg yolks, stirring constantly. Return the egg mixture to the slow cooker.

4. Add the rice and cooked chicken. Cook on low for an additional hour. Ladle hot soup into bowls and garnish with lemon slices.

PER SERVING: Calories: 249 | Fat: 14g | Protein: 11g | Sodium: 389mg | Fiber: 1g | Carbohydrates: 24g | Sugar: 1g

Tuscan Potato, Kale, and Sausage Soup

Here's an easy and delicious version of a popular soup at a well-known Italian restaurant chain. This soup is so good you won't miss the breadsticks!

INGREDIENTS | SERVES 6

1 tablespoon olive oil

3 slices bacon, diced

1 pound Italian sausage, cut into bite-sized pieces

1 medium onion, peeled and chopped

2 cloves garlic, minced

3 tablespoons white wine

2 large russet potatoes, peeled and diced

4 cups chicken broth

¼ teaspoon red pepper flakes

½ teaspoon kosher salt

½ teaspoon ground black pepper

2 cups chopped fresh kale

1 cup heavy cream

Instead of Kale . . .

If you aren't fond of kale, try adding 2 cups fresh baby spinach to the soup in the last hour of cooking.

1. In a large skillet, heat olive oil over medium-high heat and cook bacon and sausage until crisp and fat has been rendered, about 5 minutes. Remove bacon and sausage with a slotted spoon and add to a greased 4- to 5-quart slow cooker.

2. Sauté onion and garlic in the bacon fat until softened, 3–5 minutes.

3. Deglaze the pan with wine. Scrape the pan to remove all bits of vegetables and meat. Add all of the pan contents to the slow cooker.

4. Add potatoes, broth, pepper flakes, salt, and ground pepper. Cover and cook on high for 4 hours or on low for 8 hours, until potatoes are very tender.

5. An hour before serving, stir in the kale and the cream. Continue to cook for 45 minutes to an hour until kale has softened and cream is warmed through. Be careful not to overcook at this point, as the cream can curdle and separate if heated for too long.

PER SERVING: Calories: 616 | Fat: 44g | Protein: 20g | Sodium: 1,240mg | Fiber: 3g | Carbohydrates: 35g | Sugar: 1g

CHAPTER 12

Hearty Stew, Chili, and Chowder

Beef and Guinness Stew

This stew is filled with vegetables and is very flavorful. The small amounts of sugar and cocoa eliminate the bitterness occasionally found in similar stews.

INGREDIENTS | SERVES 8

2 teaspoons olive oil

1 large onion, peeled and diced

2 medium parsnips, peeled and diced

2 medium carrots, peeled and diced

2 stalks celery, diced

3 cloves garlic, minced

2 large russet potatoes, peeled and diced

2 tablespoons minced fresh rosemary

2 pounds lean top round roast, cut into 1" cubes

1 tablespoon honey

¼ teaspoon kosher salt

½ teaspoon freshly ground black pepper

1 tablespoon baking cocoa

1 cup water

½ cup Guinness Extra Stout

1. Spray a 4- to 5-quart slow cooker with nonstick olive oil cooking spray.

2. Heat the oil in a large skillet over medium-high heat. Sauté the onion, parsnips, carrots, celery, garlic, and potatoes until softened, about 10 minutes. Stir in rosemary and beef. Sauté until the beef is browned, about 5 minutes more. Drain any excess fat.

3. Add beef and vegetables to the slow cooker. Drizzle with honey and sprinkle with salt, pepper, and cocoa. Pour in the water and Guinness. Stir. Cook for 8–9 hours on low.

4. Stir before serving to fully mix the cooked ingredients together.

PER SERVING: Calories: 279 | Fat: 6g | Protein: 28g | Sodium: 171mg | Fiber: 5g | Carbohydrates: 26g | Sugar: 6g

Choosing Cuts of Beef

Leaner cuts like top round are excellent choices for slow cooking because the long cooking time tenderizes them. Look for cuts that have minimal marbling and trim off any excess fat before cooking. Searing and sautéing are good ways to cook off some external fat before adding the meat to the slow cooker. Drain any excess fat.

Spanish Beef Stew

For extra flavor, use wrinkled Turkish or other olives,
instead of the standard stuffed olives found in the grocery store.

INGREDIENTS | **SERVES 6**

1 tablespoon olive oil
2 cloves garlic, sliced
1 medium onion, peeled and sliced
3 slices bacon, cut into 1" pieces
1 pound stew beef, cubed
3 large Roma tomatoes, diced
1 bay leaf, crumbled
¼ teaspoon sage
¼ teaspoon marjoram
½ teaspoon paprika
½ teaspoon curry powder
1 teaspoon kosher salt
2 tablespoons vinegar
1 cup beef stock
½ cup white wine
4 medium potatoes, peeled and sliced
⅓ cup pitted, sliced olives
2 tablespoons chopped parsley

1. Spray a 4- to 5-quart slow cooker with nonstick olive oil cooking spray. Heat oil in a large skillet over medium heat. Sauté the garlic, onion, bacon, and beef until the bacon and beef are done and the onion softened. Drain and transfer the meat mixture to the slow cooker.

2. Add the tomatoes, bay leaf, sage, marjoram, paprika, curry powder, salt, vinegar, stock, and wine to the slow cooker. Cover and on low for 5 hours.

3. Add the potatoes, olives, and parsley to the slow cooker and cook for 1 hour more.

PER SERVING: Calories: 333 | Fat: 13g | Protein: 21g | Sodium: 622mg | Fiber: 5g | Carbohydrates: 29g | Sugar: 5g

Royal Stew

This classic recipe is a thrifty way to get the most use out of juicy soup bones.
Ask your butcher to crack them for you.

INGREDIENTS | SERVES 6

2 tablespoons olive oil

1 large onion, peeled and thinly sliced

1 large leek (white and pale green parts only), thinly sliced

1 stalk celery, thinly sliced

½ cup butter

¼ cup all-purpose flour

2 large carrots, peeled and sliced

1 cup green peas

5 pounds fresh beef bones

3 cups water

2 large stems fresh thyme

2 large stems fresh sage

2 large stems fresh rosemary

½ cup sherry

Be Patient—Don't Peek

Keeping the lid on is the whole trick to slow cooking. The steam has to build up inside the cooker, and it takes time (about 15 minutes) to do so. Each time you lift the lid, the steam escapes, adding another 15 minutes to cooking time.

1. Spray a 4- to 5-quart slow cooker with nonstick olive oil cooking spray. Heat oil in a medium skillet over medium heat. Sauté onion, leek, and celery until soft, about 10 minutes. Transfer vegetables to the slow cooker.

2. Melt the butter in the same skillet over medium heat. Add the flour to the melted butter and stir until the flour is lightly browned. Transfer to the slow cooker; stir into the onion mixture.

3. Add the carrots, peas, bones, and water to the slow cooker. Tie the thyme, sage, and rosemary stems together with kitchen twine to make a bouquet garni. Add bouquet garni to the slow cooker. Cover and cook on low for 4–6 hours.

4. Remove and discard the beef bones and bouquet garni, then add the sherry. Cook for 30 minutes more.

PER SERVING: Calories: 283 | Fat: 19g | Protein: 4g | Sodium: 54mg | Fiber: 3g | Carbohydrates: 17g | Sugar: 5g

Thick and Hearty Lancashire Lamb Stew

Make a double recipe and freeze half for another busy day.
Cook beans the old-fashioned way or use canned cannellini beans instead.

INGREDIENTS | SERVES 6

¼ cup olive oil

½ cup all-purpose flour

1 teaspoon kosher salt

½ teaspoon ground black pepper

2 pounds lamb stew meat

2 slices bacon, chopped

4 cloves garlic

2 large onions, peeled and chopped

2 large carrots, peeled and chopped

2 bay leaves

2 cups chicken broth

1 cup dry white wine

½ bunch parsley

2 tablespoons dried rosemary

Juice and zest of ½ lemon

2 teaspoons Worcestershire sauce

1 (1-pound) bag great northern beans, soaked overnight and then simmered for 5 hours, or 2½ (15-ounce) cans white beans, drained

1. Heat the olive oil in a large skillet over medium-high heat.

2. In a shallow bowl, combine the flour, salt, and pepper. Dredge the lamb in the flour mixture. Brown the meat in the hot oil, about 1 minute on each side. Remove from pan and drain.

3. In the same pan, cook the bacon until crisp. Place lamb and bacon in a 6-quart slow cooker. Add remaining ingredients to the slow cooker.

4. Cover and cook on high for 4 hours or on low for 8 hours.

PER SERVING: Calories: 612 | Fat: 23g | Protein: 44g | Sodium: 702mg | Fiber: 12g | Carbohydrates: 48g | Sugar: 7g

Tuscan Chicken and Sausage Stew

You don't need a lot of ingredients to create a stew full of hearty and warm Tuscan flavors.

INGREDIENTS | SERVES 4

1 pound boneless, skinless chicken thighs, cut into bite-sized pieces

8 ounces turkey sausage, cut into ½" slices

1 (26-ounce) jar pasta sauce

1 can green beans, drained

1 teaspoon dried oregano

Place all ingredients in a greased 4- to 5-quart slow cooker. Stir to combine and cook on high for 4 hours or on low for 8 hours.

PER SERVING: Calories: 417 | Fat: 15g | Protein: 39g | Sodium: 604mg | Fiber: 6g | Carbohydrates: 28g | Sugar: 16g

Change It Up

Don't like green beans or don't have them available in your pantry? Use navy beans, cannellini beans, or even black beans.

Herbed Tilapia Stew

Any type of white fish fillets (such as haddock or cod) will also work in this recipe. Fish cooks very quickly, even on the low setting in a slow cooker, so this is one recipe you will need to set a timer for. Serve this stew over cooked rice or pasta.

INGREDIENTS | SERVES 6

2 pounds frozen boneless tilapia fillets

2 tablespoons butter

2 tablespoons olive oil

1 (14½-ounce) can diced tomatoes, with juice

4 cloves garlic, minced

½ cup sliced green onions

2 teaspoons Worcestershire sauce

2 tablespoons chopped fresh thyme or 1 teaspoon dried thyme

1. Grease a 4- to 5-quart slow cooker with nonstick cooking spray. Place all ingredients in the slow cooker.

2. Cover and cook on high for 1½–2 hours or on low for 2½–3 hours. Watch the cooking time. If the fish fillets are very thin you may need to reduce the cooking time.

3. When fish is cooked through, fillets will easily separate and flake with a fork. Break the fish up into the tomatoes and cooking liquids.

PER SERVING: Calories: 221 | Fat: 9g | Protein: 29g | Sodium: 410mg | Fiber: 1g | Carbohydrates: 4g | Sugar: 2g

Rosemary-Thyme Stew

Lots of rosemary and thyme give this surprisingly light stew a distinctive flavor.

INGREDIENTS | SERVES 4

1 teaspoon canola oil

1 large onion, peeled and diced

1 tablespoon all-purpose flour

1 large carrot, peeled and diced

2 stalks celery, diced

2 cloves garlic, minced

1 cup diced Yukon Gold potatoes

3½ tablespoons minced fresh thyme

3 tablespoons minced fresh rosemary

1 pound boneless, skinless chicken breast, cut into 1" cubes

¼ teaspoon kosher salt

½ teaspoon freshly ground black pepper

1½ cups water

½ cup frozen or fresh corn kernels

1. Heat the oil in a large skillet over medium heat. Sauté the onion, flour, carrots, celery, garlic, potatoes, thyme, rosemary, and chicken until the chicken is white on all sides, about 10 minutes. Using a slotted spoon, transfer to a 4- to 5-quart slow cooker.

2. Stir in salt, pepper, and water. Cook for 8–9 hours on low.

3. Add the corn. Cover and cook an additional 30 minutes on high. Stir before serving.

PER SERVING: Calories: 221 | Fat: 4g | Protein: 26g | Sodium: 313mg | Fiber: 4g | Carbohydrates: 18g | Sugar: 3g

Aromatic Paella

This is a fun dish for a slow cooker. The mussels and clams open during the cooking and flavor the rice.

INGREDIENTS | SERVES 12

3 tablespoons olive oil, divided

2 medium onions, peeled and thinly sliced

1 pound bulk spicy sausage

4 cloves garlic, crushed

2 pounds tomatoes, diced

16 ounces clam juice

2 cups chicken broth

1 cup dry vermouth

2½ cups uncooked rice

2 teaspoons coriander

½ teaspoon cumin

1 teaspoon saffron

¼ teaspoon ground white pepper

¼ teaspoon kosher salt

1 pound firm white fish, cubed

1 pound shrimp

1 pound fresh mussels, scrubbed and rinsed

1 pound fresh clams, scrubbed and rinsed

1 large green pepper, cored and diced

1 cup fresh green peas

1. Spray a 4- to 5-quart slow cooker with nonstick olive oil spray.

2. Heat 1 tablespoon olive oil in a large skillet over low heat. Sauté onions and sausage until the sausage is crumbled and browned (about 10 minutes), then drain and transfer to the slow cooker.

3. Stir in garlic, tomatoes, clam juice, broth, vermouth, rice, coriander, cumin, saffron, white pepper, and salt.

4. Cover and cook on low for 4 hours.

5. Heat remaining olive oil in a separate large skillet. Sauté the fish and shrimp in oil for 6 minutes. Transfer all the seafood to slow cooker. Stir in green pepper and peas.

6. Cover and cook on low for 1 hour.

PER SERVING: Calories: 480 | Fat: 17g | Protein: 34g | Sodium: 690mg | Fiber: 2g | Carbohydrates: 40g | Sugar: 4g

All about Aroma

Once they're opened, slow cookers full of food will release a strong aroma. Try putting different slow cookers in different areas of your entertaining space, even in separate rooms. Have a "dessert room," a "spicy room," and a "bakery" room and let your guests move freely between them.

Fish Chili with Beans

Play with different types of peppers for different levels of heat.

INGREDIENTS | SERVES 4

2 tablespoons olive oil

1 large leek (white and pale green parts only), sliced

1 medium onion, peeled and diced

4 ounces firm tofu, drained and chopped

1 medium jalapeño pepper, sliced

1 medium serrano chili, sliced

1 teaspoon chili powder

¼ teaspoon cayenne pepper

½ teaspoon freshly ground black pepper

6 large plum tomatoes, diced

½ cup dry red wine

1 cup Fish Stock (see recipe in Chapter 11)

½ cup brewed strong coffee

1 teaspoon packed light brown sugar

1 tablespoon honey

2 cups cooked pinto, cannellini, or red kidney beans

2 pounds firm-fleshed fish (Chilean sea bass, halibut, or red snapper), sliced on the bias

1. Heat the oil in a large Dutch oven over medium-high heat until hot but not smoking. Add the leek, onion, tofu, jalapeño, and serrano to the pan. Season with the chili powder, cayenne, and black pepper. Cook until softened, about 5–8 minutes.

2. Pour the onion and tofu mixture into a 4- to 5-quart slow cooker. Add the tomatoes.

3. Whisk together the wine, stock, coffee, brown sugar, and honey in a small bowl. Pour into the slow cooker.

4. Cover and cook on low for 3½ hours. Stir in the beans and fish and cook for 30 minutes more.

PER SERVING: Calories: 531 | Fat: 14g | Protein: 53g | Sodium: 633mg | Fiber: 10g | Carbohydrates: 42g | Sugar: 15g

Skinny Slow Cooker Chowder

Hearty vegetables and seafood cook together in a rich, hearty sauce and create a dinner you'll love to share. Makes enough for a crowd! Serve over Arborio rice or pasta for a delicious dish.

INGREDIENTS | SERVES 4

1 large onion, peeled and chopped

2 cloves garlic, finely chopped

2 medium red potatoes, peeled and diced

2 cups sliced carrots

4 stalks celery, chopped

2 (14½-ounce) cans chicken broth

1 teaspoon sea salt

1 (1-pound) package frozen seafood mix, thawed

1 (12-ounce) can fat-free evaporated milk

3 tablespoons fresh Italian parsley, chopped

1. Place onion, garlic, potatoes, carrots, celery, chicken broth, and salt in a 4- to 5-quart slow cooker. Cover and cook on high for 4–6 hours.

2. Stir thawed seafood mix and evaporated milk into the slow cooker. Cover and cook for 1 hour. Garnish with parsley and serve.

PER SERVING: Calories: 413 | Fat: 11g | Protein: 35g | Sodium: 1,238mg | Fiber: 5g | Carbohydrates: 46g | Sugar: 14g

Can't Find Seafood Mix?

If you're having trouble locating a seafood mix in the frozen section of your grocer, you can replace the mix with ⅓ pound each of scallops, shrimp, and diced halibut.

CHAPTER 13

Vegetarian

Savory Cauliflower Custard

*Use this recipe as a guide for unique custards using other
vegetables and herbs. Have fun and experiment!*

INGREDIENTS | SERVES 6

½ pound fresh cauliflower, cored and cut
into bite-sized pieces
1 tablespoon olive oil, divided
½ teaspoon freshly ground black pepper
1 teaspoon kosher salt, divided
2 large eggs
1 cup skim milk
1 teaspoon all-purpose flour
Leaves from 1 sprig rosemary, chopped
1 teaspoon sea salt

Herbed Sea Salt

Sea salt is a great beginning to creating
small (or large) amounts of your own herbed salt. Crush salt and dried herbs
together in a mortar and pestle and use it
to finish anything from a salad to a dessert.
Try finishing Savory Cauliflower Custard
with crushed dill seeds and sea salt.

1. Preheat oven to 375°F. Pour 1 inch of water into a 4- to 5-quart slow cooker, cover, and turn on high for 40 minutes.

2. In a large bowl, toss cauliflower in 2 teaspoons of oil. Season with pepper and ½ teaspoon kosher salt. Transfer cauliflower to a large baking sheet and roast for 20 minutes. Set aside to cool.

3. Whisk the eggs, milk, flour, remaining kosher salt, and rosemary in a large bowl. Roughly chop the cooled cauliflower and add to the egg mixture.

4. Grease six (6-ounce) ramekins with remaining olive oil. Divide cauliflower mixture between the ramekins. Carefully place the ramekins into the hot water in the slow cooker, stacking them if necessary. Cover and cook on high for 5–6 hours, or until set.

5. Season with sea salt.

PER SERVING: Calories: 72 | Fat: 4g | Protein: 4g |
Sodium: 823mg | Fiber: 1g | Carbohydrates: 5g | Sugar: 3g

Corn Pudding

*Grilled corn and long, slow cooking create a succulent main dish
that would be perfect with a simple side salad.*

INGREDIENTS | SERVES 6

1 tablespoon olive oil, divided

1 medium shallot, minced

¼ teaspoon dried red pepper flakes

½ teaspoon kosher salt

½ teaspoon freshly ground black pepper

3 medium ears corn, husked

3 large eggs

1 cup skim milk

1. Preheat a grill to medium. Pour 1 inch of water into a 4- to 5-quart slow cooker, cover, and turn heat to high. Heat for 40 minutes.

2. Combine 2 teaspoons of the oil, shallot, pepper flakes, salt, and black pepper in a small bowl. Brush the corn with the seasoned oil. Reserve any leftover oil. Grill the corn for 3–5 minutes, turning frequently. Set the corn aside to cool.

3. Grease six (6-ounce) ramekins with remaining oil.

4. In a large bowl, whisk together the eggs and milk. Add any remaining seasoned oil to the egg mixture.

5. Cut the kernels from the cobs and stir them into the egg mixture. Divide the corn pudding between the ramekins.

6. Carefully place the ramekins into the hot water in the slow cooker, stacking them if necessary. Cover and cook on high for 5–6 hours, or until set.

PER SERVING: Calories: 135 | Fat: 5g | Protein: 7g | Sodium: 252mg | Fiber: 2g | Carbohydrates: 17g | Sugar: 4g

Zucchini Parmesan

Layers of onion and herbs would be a good addition to this classic.

INGREDIENTS | SERVES 6

2 teaspoons olive oil, divided

2 egg whites (from large eggs)

1 cup skim milk

½ cup bread crumbs

3 medium zucchini, sliced

6 ounces mozzarella cheese, shredded

2 cups Long-Cooking Traditional Tomato Sauce (see recipe in Chapter 10)

Make Your Own Seasoned Bread Crumbs

Customizing your own bread crumbs is incredibly simple and fun. Place stale bread in a food processor with dried basil, oregano, onion flakes, or any other dried spices that you think would be delicious in the recipe. Just process the mixture until it's the desired consistency.

1. Preheat oven to 350°F. Brush a nonstick baking sheet with 1 teaspoon olive oil.

2. In a shallow bowl, whisk the egg whites and add in the milk. Place bread crumbs in another shallow bowl. Dip the zucchini into the egg mixture, then roll in the bread crumbs, making sure to cover completely. Place the zucchini on the prepared baking sheet and bake for 12–15 minutes.

3. Grease a 4- to 5-quart slow cooker with remaining olive oil. Ladle ⅓ cup of sauce on the bottom of the slow cooker. Cover with a single layer of zucchini. Top with a quarter of the cheese and sauce. Repeat the process until the ingredients have been used. Cook on low for 4 hours.

PER SERVING: Calories: 191 | Fat: 9g | Protein: 12g | Sodium: 394mg | Fiber: 3g | Carbohydrates: 16g | Sugar: 8g

Ratatouille

Ratatouille is as limitless as your imagination. There are endless amounts of vegetables and herbs you can add for extra flavor.

INGREDIENTS | SERVES 6

1 small eggplant, diced into 1" pieces

1 teaspoon kosher salt

1 small zucchini squash, diced into 1" pieces

1 small yellow squash, diced into 1" pieces

1 leek (white and pale green parts only), sliced

1 large plum tomato, diced

1 medium shallot, diced

2 cloves garlic, diced

2 sprigs marjoram, chopped

¼ cup Kalamata olives, chopped

½ teaspoon olive oil

1 cup Savory Vegetable Stock (see recipe in Chapter 11)

½ teaspoon freshly ground black pepper

Place eggplant in a colander and sprinkle with salt. Let the colander rest over the sink for 15 minutes. Rinse the salt off. Place all of the ingredients in a 4- to 5-quart slow cooker. Cover and cook on high for 3–4 hours.

PER SERVING: Calories: 60 | Fat: 1g | Protein: 2g | Sodium: 402mg | Fiber: 5g | Carbohydrates: 12g | Sugar: 5g

Salting the Eggplant

It's always a good idea to "salt" eggplant before cooking with it. The salt draws out the bitter juices, and if frying the eggplant, it keeps it from absorbing too much oil.

Roasted Beets

Fresh roasted beets are delicious—and beautiful. They are a wonderful addition to salads, or even just as a snack with sea salt. To make for an even prettier presentation, use yellow beets as well.

INGREDIENTS | SERVES 6

3 large beets, trimmed (greens reserved)

3 tablespoons plus 2 teaspoons olive oil, divided

1 teaspoon kosher salt

1 teaspoon freshly ground black pepper

¼ cup golden raisins

2 tablespoons balsamic vinegar

¼ cup slivered almonds

Skinning Beets

Beets have many things going for them. They're full of antioxidants and vitamins. However, once you remove the skins, clean your work surface quickly! Beet juice will stain a neutral-colored surface—especially wood.

1. Place each beet in a large square of foil and drizzle with a tablespoon of olive oil. Season with salt and pepper. Wrap the foil tightly.

2. Place the beets in a 4- to 5-quart slow cooker and cook on high for 3–5 hours.

3. When the beets are fork tender, unwrap them and let them cool.

4. In a medium skillet, heat remaining olive oil over medium heat. Once the oil is hot but not smoking, add the greens and sauté until wilted, about 2 minutes. Reduce heat to low and add the raisins and balsamic vinegar. Stir and cook for 1 minute.

5. Using a paper towel, rub the beets to remove skins. Thinly slice the beets and fan into a large circle on a platter or serving plate. Mound the warm greens mixture in the center and top with almonds.

PER SERVING: Calories: 148 | Fat: 10g | Protein: 2g | Sodium: 440mg | Fiber: 2g | Carbohydrates: 13g | Sugar: 9g

Butternut Squash with Walnuts and Vanilla

Butternut squash has a very mild and slightly sweet flavor. Often people who don't like sweet potatoes enjoy this alternative side dish. Many grocery stores now sell butternut squash that has been peeled and precut into cubes, which can make meal preparation a breeze.

INGREDIENTS | SERVES 4

1 (2-pound) butternut squash, peeled, seeded, and cut into 1" cubes

½ cup water

½ cup packed light brown sugar

1 cup walnuts, chopped

1 teaspoon cinnamon

4 tablespoons butter

2 teaspoons grated ginger

1 teaspoon vanilla

1. Grease a 4- to 5-quart slow cooker with nonstick cooking spray. Add squash and water to slow cooker.

2. In a small bowl, mix together brown sugar, walnuts, cinnamon, butter, ginger, and vanilla. Sprinkle brown sugar mixture evenly over butternut squash.

3. Cook on high for 4 hours or on low for 6–8 hours, or until butternut squash is fork tender.

PER SERVING: Calories: 501 | Fat: 30g | Protein: 7g | Sodium: 20mg | Fiber: 7g | Carbohydrates: 58g | Sugar: 32g

Classic Minestrone

A traditional vegetarian Italian soup, minestrone can withstand long cooking periods. It tastes even better on the second day.

INGREDIENTS | SERVES 12

3 tablespoons olive oil

1 cup minced onion

3 stalks celery, chopped

4 cloves garlic, minced

1 small zucchini, chopped

4 cups vegetable broth

2 (14-ounce) cans diced tomatoes, drained

2 (15-ounce) cans red kidney beans, drained

2 (15-ounce) cans cannellini (white) beans, drained

1 (28-ounce) can Italian-style green beans

½ cup julienned carrots

1 cup red wine (Chianti or Cabernet Sauvignon)

2 (6-ounce) cans tomato paste

2 tablespoons minced fresh parsley

1½ teaspoons dried oregano

2 teaspoons kosher salt

½ teaspoon ground black pepper

1 teaspoon garlic powder

½ teaspoon Italian seasoning

4 cups fresh baby spinach

1 cup cooked small pasta

1. In a large skillet, heat the olive oil over medium heat. Sauté onion, celery, garlic, and zucchini in the oil for 3–5 minutes until the onion is translucent.

2. Add sautéed vegetables and vegetable broth to a 6-quart slow cooker, along with tomatoes, red and white beans, green beans, carrots, wine, tomato paste, parsley, oregano, salt, pepper, garlic powder, and Italian seasoning.

3. Cover and cook on high for 8 hours.

4. One hour prior to serving, stir in spinach. Add 1 tablespoon of cooked pasta to each bowl of soup.

PER SERVING: Calories: 245 | Fat: 4g | Protein: 11g | Sodium: 1,214mg | Fiber: 11g | Carbohydrates: 38g | Sugar: 9g

Classic Polenta with Herbs and Parmesan

*By using the slow cooker to make this creamy homemade polenta,
you don't have to stand over the stove for nearly 2 hours stirring the pot.*

INGREDIENTS | SERVES 6

7 cups water

2 teaspoons kosher salt

2 cups yellow cornmeal

2–4 ounces unsalted butter

1 teaspoon dried basil

1 teaspoon dried parsley

1 teaspoon crushed rosemary

½ teaspoon freshly ground black pepper

½ cup freshly grated Parmesan cheese

1. Add all ingredients except cheese into a greased 4- to 5-quart slow cooker.

2. Whisk together thoroughly. Cover and cook on low for 6–7 hours or on high for 3–4 hours.

3. Thirty minutes prior to serving, stir in Parmesan cheese.

PER SERVING: Calories: 242 | Fat: 9g | Protein: 5g | Sodium: 726mg | Fiber: 3g | Carbohydrates: 36g | Sugar: 1g

Classic Italian Risotto

*Risotto should be very creamy on the outside, with just a bit
of toothsome resistance on the inside of each grain of rice.*

INGREDIENTS | SERVES 4

2 tablespoons butter

2 tablespoons olive oil

½ cup finely chopped sweet onion

2 stalks celery, finely chopped

¼ cup celery leaves, chopped

1½ cups Arborio rice

1 teaspoon kosher salt

5 cups Roasted Vegetable Stock (see recipe in Chapter 11)

¼ cup chopped parsley

½ teaspoon freshly ground black pepper

⅔ cup freshly grated Parmesan cheese

1. Place the butter and oil in a heavy-bottomed pot, melt butter, and add the onion, celery, and celery leaves. Cook for 3–5 minutes, until vegetables are softened.

2. Add the rice and stir to coat with butter and oil. Stir in salt. Add rice mixture to a greased 4- to 5-quart slow cooker.

3. Add remaining ingredients, except cheese, to the slow cooker. Cover and cook on high for 3 hours or on low for 6 hours.

4. Twenty minutes before serving, stir in Parmesan cheese.

PER SERVING: Calories: 391 | Fat: 20g | Protein: 14g | Sodium: 1,921mg | Fiber: 1g | Carbohydrates: 62g | Sugar: 1g

Eggplant "Lasagna"

This no-noodle dish makes for a hearty vegetarian meal. Serve it with a side salad.

INGREDIENTS | SERVES 8

2 (1-pound) eggplants

1 tablespoon plus ¼ teaspoon kosher salt

30 ounces skim-milk ricotta

2 teaspoons olive oil, divided

1 medium onion, peeled and diced

3 cloves garlic, minced

1 tablespoon minced Italian parsley

1 tablespoon minced basil

1 (28-ounce) can crushed tomatoes

1 medium shallot, diced

4 ounces fresh spinach

1 tablespoon dried mixed Italian seasoning

½ teaspoon freshly ground black pepper

½ cup shredded mozzarella

Do-It-Yourself Italian Herb Mix

While most spice companies make an Italian mix of dried herbs, it is easy to make your own. Mix 1 teaspoon each of oregano, basil, marjoram, thyme, savory, and crushed rosemary. Store in an airtight container.

1. Slice the eggplants lengthwise into ¼"-thick slices. Place in a bowl or colander and sprinkle with 1 tablespoon of the salt. Allow slices to sit for 15 minutes. Rinse off the salt, pat dry, and set aside. Line a colander with cheesecloth or paper towels. Pour the ricotta into the colander and drain for 15 minutes.

2. Heat 1 teaspoon olive oil in a large nonstick skillet. Sauté the onion and garlic until just softened. Add the parsley, basil, and crushed tomatoes. Sauté until the sauce thickens and the liquid has evaporated.

3. In a second nonstick pan, heat the remaining oil. Sauté the shallot and spinach until the spinach has wilted, about 5 minutes. Drain off any extra liquid. Stir this mixture and the Italian seasoning, remaining ¼ teaspoon salt, and pepper into a bowl with the ricotta. Set aside.

4. Preheat the oven to 375°F. Place the eggplant slices on baking sheets. Bake for 10 minutes. Cool slightly.

5. To Assemble: Pour ⅓ of the sauce onto the bottom of a 4- to 5-quart slow cooker. Top with a single layer of eggplant, half of the cheese mixture, and ⅓ of the sauce. Repeat. Cook for 4 hours on low and remove lid. Top with mozzarella and cook 30 minutes on high uncovered.

PER SERVING: Calories: 249 | Fat: 15g | Protein: 14g | Sodium: 865mg | Fiber: 6g | Carbohydrates: 15g | Sugar: 6g

Portobello Barley

This method of cooking barley makes it as creamy as risotto but with the bonus of being high in fiber.

INGREDIENTS | SERVES 8

1 teaspoon olive oil

2 medium shallots, minced

2 cloves garlic, minced

3 large portobello mushroom caps, sliced

1 cup pearl barley

3¼ cups water

¼ teaspoon kosher salt

½ teaspoon freshly ground black pepper

1 teaspoon crushed rosemary

1 teaspoon dried chervil

¼ cup grated Parmesan

1. Heat the oil in a medium nonstick skillet. Sauté the shallots, garlic, and mushrooms until softened.

2. Place the mushroom mixture into a 4- to 5-quart slow cooker. Add the barley, water, salt, pepper, rosemary, and chervil. Stir. Cook on low for 8–9 hours or on high for 4 hours.

3. Turn off the slow cooker and stir in the Parmesan. Serve immediately.

PER SERVING: Calories: 117 | Fat: 2g | Protein: 5g | Sodium: 130mg | Fiber: 5g | Carbohydrates: 21g | Sugar: 1g

Caramelized Onions

Caramelized onions are a great addition to roasts, dips, and sandwiches.
They are also the perfect filling for a tart on a cold winter evening.

INGREDIENTS | MAKES 1 QUART

4 pounds red onions, peeled and sliced

1 tablespoon butter, cut into small pieces

2 teaspoons packed dark brown sugar

1 tablespoon balsamic vinegar

2 tablespoons olive oil

½ teaspoon kosher salt

1 teaspoon freshly ground black pepper

Storing Caramelized Onions

Store the onions in an airtight container. They will keep up to 2 weeks refrigerated or up to 6 months frozen. If frozen, defrost overnight in the refrigerator before using. They also make a wonderful addition to a holiday food gift basket along with olives, baguette, and cheese.

1. Place onions in a 4- to 5-quart slow cooker. Scatter butter slices over top of the onions.

2. Drizzle the onions with brown sugar, vinegar, and olive oil. Add salt and pepper and stir well. Cover and cook on low for 10 hours.

3. If after 10 hours the onions are still wet, turn the slow cooker up to high and cook uncovered for an additional 30 minutes or until the liquid evaporates.

PER SERVING (2 TABLESPOONS): Calories: 34 | Fat: 1g | Protein: 1g | Sodium: 39mg | Fiber: 1g | Carbohydrates: 6g | Sugar: 3g

Steamed Artichokes

The flavors in this dish mimic the heavier artichoke hearts packed in oil. But when slow cooked with lemon, dried herbs, and spicy red pepper flakes, these artichokes are succulent and addictive. Choose artichokes that are all roughly the same size for consistent cooking time.

INGREDIENTS | SERVES 4

4 large artichokes

1 cup water

1 medium lemon, cut into eighths

2 tablespoons lemon juice

1 teaspoon dried oregano

1 teaspoon dried basil

½ teaspoon red pepper flakes

1. Place the artichokes stem-side down in an oval 4- to 5-quart slow cooker. Pour the water into the bottom of the slow cooker. Add the lemons, lemon juice, oregano, basil, and red pepper flakes.

2. Cook on low for 6 hours or until the leaves are tender.

PER SERVING: Calories: 77 | Fat: 0g | Protein: 5g | Sodium: 155mg | Fiber: 8.5g | Carbohydrates: 17g | Sugar: 2g

Wine-Braised Leeks with Artichokes and Lemon

Leeks love wine, and artichokes love wine and lemon. And they both love plenty of herbs, too.

INGREDIENTS | SERVES 4

4 leeks (white and pale green parts only)

1 (14-ounce) can artichoke hearts, rinsed

¼ cup chopped flat-leaf parsley, divided

½ cup dry white wine

1½ cups Savory Vegetable Stock (see recipe in Chapter 11)

1 tablespoon lemon juice

1 teaspoon chopped fresh rosemary

1 teaspoon chopped fresh oregano

½ teaspoon kosher salt

Wash Them Well!

Leeks need to be washed extremely well because dirt is often trapped inside. One method is to cut them in half lengthwise and let them soak in water to remove grit. Another is to run them under cold water and gently fan the layers so that each gets cleaned.

1. Halve leeks lengthwise and wash well. Place leeks in the bottom of a 4- to 5-quart slow cooker and top with artichoke hearts and half of the parsley. Add remaining ingredients. (Note, if leeks are very large you may need to cut them in half for them to fit comfortably in a 4-quart slow cooker.)

2. Cook on low heat for 6 hours. Scatter remaining parsley on leeks and artichokes before serving.

PER SERVING: Calories: 123 | Fat: 0.5g | Protein: 4.5g | Sodium: 499mg | Fiber: 6g | Carbohydrates: 22g | Sugar: 4.5g

Slow-Cooked Carrots in Dill and Wine

This delicious side dish is both light and elegant.

INGREDIENTS | SERVES 6

1 large red onion, peeled and diced

2 medium shallots, peeled and diced

2 garlic cloves, peeled and diced

8 medium carrots, peeled and cut into matchsticks

½ cup Roasted Vegetable Stock (see recipe in Chapter 11)

¼ bunch dill, chopped and divided

¼ teaspoon kosher salt

1 tablespoon lemon juice

½ cup dry white wine

2 tablespoons cornstarch

2 tablespoons cold water

1. Combine the onion, shallots, garlic, carrots, stock, half of the dill, salt, lemon juice, and wine in the slow cooker.

2. Cover and cook on high for 2½ hours.

3. In a small bowl, mix the cornstarch into the cold water; stir into the carrot mixture, and turn the temperature to low. Cover and cook for 1 hour more. Garnish with remaining fresh dill.

PER SERVING: Calories: 74 | Fat: 0g | Protein: 1g | Sodium: 157mg | Fiber: 3g | Carbohydrates: 14g | Sugar: 5g

Sweet Potatoes with Cranberries and Pine Nuts

This sweet potato recipe is sweet and crunchy, and will become a family favorite.

INGREDIENTS | SERVES 6

6 medium sweet potatoes, peeled and cut into 1" pieces

1½ cups water

2 tablespoons olive oil

¼ cup packed light brown sugar

2 tablespoons dried cranberries, chopped

2 tablespoons pine nuts

1. Place sweet potatoes and water in slow cooker. Cover and cook on low for 5–6 hours.

2. Stir in olive oil, brown sugar, cranberries, and pine nuts. Serve immediately.

PER SERVING: Calories: 255 | Fat: 10g | Protein: 3g | Sodium: 84mg | Fiber: 5g | Carbohydrates: 39g | Sugar: 16g

Goat Cheese Stuffed Baked Potatoes

These baked and stuffed potatoes aren't the usual fare. Normally twice-baked potatoes are loaded with heavy flavors, but these are light and creamy.

INGREDIENTS | SERVES 6

6 large baked potatoes

1 (4-ounce) container crumbled goat cheese

1 cup low-fat plain Greek yogurt

1 tablespoon lemon juice

1 teaspoon dried basil

1 teaspoon dried oregano

½ teaspoon kosher salt

½ teaspoon freshly ground black pepper

Stock Up!

Did you know that you can freeze goat cheese? Simply place it in a resealable plastic bag and store for up to 6 months.

1. Halve the potatoes. Scoop most of the insides of the potatoes into a large bowl. Set potato halves aside.

2. Stir the remaining ingredients into the potatoes. Divide the mixture between the potato skins.

3. Wrap the potatoes in foil and place on a trivet in a 4- to 5-quart slow cooker. Pour water around the base of the trivet.

4. Cover and cook on high for 1–2 hours.

PER SERVING: Calories: 256 | Fat: 16g | Protein: 9g | Sodium: 347mg | Fiber: 0g | Carbohydrates: 21g | Sugar: 2g

Tomato and Roasted Red Pepper Pinto Beans

The combination of smoky red peppers and tomatoes with hearty beans makes this recipe irresistible.

INGREDIENTS | SERVES 9

2 cups dry pinto beans

1 large red onion, peeled and chopped

1 garlic clove, diced

4 cups Savory Vegetable Stock (see recipe in Chapter 11)

¼ teaspoon ground white pepper

1 teaspoon kosher salt

1 teaspoon dried oregano

1 roasted red pepper, diced

1 (28-ounce) can crushed tomatoes

1. Cover the beans with water and soak overnight. Drain beans and place them in a 4- to 5-quart slow cooker. Add onion, garlic, stock, pepper, salt, and oregano.

2. Cover and cook on low for 6 hours.

3. Add the red pepper and tomatoes to the slow cooker and cook for 2 hours more.

PER SERVING: Calories: 115 | Fat: 2g | Protein: 7g | Sodium: 540mg | Fiber: 4.5g | Carbohydrates: 19g | Sugar: 4.5g

Spiced Orange Vegetables with Chives

To make this dish even more impressive, garnish with dried orange peel.

INGREDIENTS | SERVES 6

1 tablespoon olive oil

2 pounds baby carrots, chopped into 1" pieces

½ pound sweet potato, peeled and cubed into 1" pieces

1 large red onion, peeled and diced

1 tablespoon butter

3 tablespoons packed light brown sugar

1 teaspoon ground cinnamon

½ teaspoon ground cumin

½ teaspoon nutmeg

½ teaspoon kosher salt

¼ teaspoon ground black pepper

1¼ cups orange juice

2 tablespoons chives, chopped

1. Heat the olive oil in a large skillet over medium heat until it shimmers, about 1 minute. Add the carrots, sweet potato, and onion. Sauté until vegetables are softened, about 10 minutes.

2. In another large skillet, melt the butter over medium heat and stir in the brown sugar, cinnamon, cumin, nutmeg, salt, and pepper. Add the sweet potato mixture to the skillet. Stir well to coat.

3. Transfer the vegetables to a 4- to 5-quart slow cooker and add the orange juice.

4. Cover and cook on low for 5–6 hours. Serve garnished with chives.

PER SERVING: Calories: 159 | Fat: 4.5g | Protein: 2g | Sodium: 337mg | Fiber: 6g | Carbohydrates: 29g | Sugar: 16g

Sweet and Sour Beans

With just a few simple ingredients, you can make these wonderfully sweet and tart beans that are perfect for dinner along with a simple salad.

INGREDIENTS | SERVES 8

1 pound cooked kidney beans

1 medium onion, peeled and diced

1 clove garlic, minced

¼ cup packed dark brown sugar

1 teaspoon kosher salt

2 tablespoons sherry vinegar

Place all ingredients in a 4- to 5-quart slow cooker. Cover and cook on low for 3–4 hours.

PER SERVING: Calories: 222 | Fat: 0.5g | Protein: 12g | Sodium: 307mg | Fiber: 10g | Carbohydrates: 43g | Sugar: 12g

CHAPTER 14

Vegan

Apricot Peach Chutney

Chutney is a wonderful condiment because it's sweet and tangy. It also makes a hearty snack when spread on rustic bread. If you're a meat eater, try it with pork, chicken, or lamb.

INGREDIENTS | MAKES 2½ CUPS

1 tablespoon olive oil

1 large red onion, peeled and diced

½ teaspoon kosher salt

½ teaspoon freshly ground black pepper

½ cup chopped dried apricots

½ cup raisins

1 cup peach marmalade

½ cup apple vinegar

½ cup packed dark brown sugar

1 tablespoon mustard seeds

½ cup water

1. Heat olive oil in a medium skillet over medium-low heat. Sauté onion until softened, about 8 minutes. Season with salt and pepper and transfer to a 4- to 5-quart slow cooker.

2. Stir in remaining ingredients.

3. Cover and cook on low for 2–3 hours.

PER SERVING (¼ CUP): Calories: 181 | Fat: 1.5g | Protein: 1g | Sodium: 141mg | Fiber: 1.5g | Carbohydrates: 43g | Sugar: 38g

Brandy Sauce

Apples, apricots, pears, and raisins work well in this recipe, but use what you love.

INGREDIENTS | MAKES 5 CUPS

2 cups mixed dried fruit, chopped

2 cups water

1 cup packed light brown sugar

1 cup granulated sugar

1 cup brandy

1. Place all ingredients in a 4- to 5-quart slow cooker and mix well.

2. Cover and cook on low for 3–4 hours.

PER SERVING (¼ CUP): Calories: 106 | Fat: 0g | Protein: 0g | Sodium: 4mg | Fiber: 0g | Carbohydrates: 20g | Sugar: 20g

Cranberry Bean Paste

Use this savory dip for crudités or crackers or as a base for sandwiches.

INGREDIENTS | MAKES 2 CUPS

1 pound cranberry beans

2 quarts water

1 large red onion, peeled and quartered

2 dried bay leaves

3 sprigs flat-leaf parsley

1 sprig thyme

2 quarts Savory Vegetable Stock (see recipe in Chapter 11)

1 teaspoon virgin olive oil

1. Soak the beans overnight in the water; rinse and drain.

2. Place all the ingredients except the oil in a 4- to 5-quart slow cooker and bring to a slow simmer on low heat. Cook on high until the beans are very tender, about 5 hours.

3. Drain and reserve the liquid. Remove the bay leaves, parsley, and thyme stalk.

4. Purée the bean mixture in a blender or food processor until smooth. Add a few spoonfuls of the reserved liquid and the oil to thin the mixture to a paste.

PER SERVING (2 TABLESPOONS): Calories: 76 | Fat: 1g | Protein: 5g | Sodium: 623mg | Fiber: 3.5g | Carbohydrates: 9g | Sugar: 0g

Lentil-Stuffed Peppers

No meat, no problem! These peppers are so filling and delicious, no one will notice that they're vegan.

INGREDIENTS | SERVES 6

1 tablespoon olive oil

2 medium red onions, peeled and diced

2 large carrots, peeled and diced

2 stalks celery, diced

½ teaspoon kosher salt

½ teaspoon ground black pepper

2 cups White Wine Vegetable Stock (see recipe in Chapter 11), divided

3 cups red lentils

6 sprigs oregano

6 large bell peppers

1. Heat the oil over medium heat in a Dutch oven until hot but not smoking. Add the onions, carrots, and celery. Season with salt and pepper. Sauté until softened, about 5–8 minutes.

2. Add 1 cup of stock and the lentils. Reduce heat to medium-low and simmer for 15–20 minutes, until the lentils are fully cooked. Strip oregano leaves from the stem and roughly chop. Stir oregano into lentil mixture.

3. Cut off the tops of the peppers, leaving the stems attached. Set tops aside. Remove the seeds and ribs. Stuff the peppers with the lentil mixture.

4. Pour remaining stock into a 4- to 5-quart slow cooker. Stand peppers in the stock and cover the slow cooker. Cook on low for 3½ hours.

5. Remove peppers from slow cooker. Gently place reserved pepper tops over the cooked peppers for a colorful presentation.

PER SERVING: Calories: 458 | Fat: 6g | Protein: 28g | Sodium: 328mg | Fiber: 34g | Carbohydrates: 72g | Sugar: 9g

Grilled and Slow-Cooked Braised Fennel

The combination of grilling and braising fennel creates an amazingly sweet and savory side dish.

INGREDIENTS | SERVES 6

3 large bulbs fennel
1 tablespoon olive oil
½ teaspoon kosher salt
1 teaspoon freshly ground black pepper
1 cup White Wine Vegetable Stock (see recipe in Chapter 11)

Versatile Fennel Tops

When cooking with fennel, be sure to save the tops! The stalks can be used in stocks or added to a sauté. And both the stalks and fronds are freezer-friendly. So when you're looking for a flavorful garnish, pull some fronds out of the freezer and chop them up. They will defrost by the time they hit the plate.

1. Remove the tops from the fennel and reserve for another use. Cut the bulbs into 1½"-thick slices vertically.

2. Preheat grill to medium. Mix the oil, salt, and pepper together in a shallow bowl. Dip the fennel in the seasoned oil. Grill for 2 minutes, then flip.

3. Place fennel in a 1½- to 2-quart slow cooker. Pour stock over the fennel. Cover and cook on low for 4 hours.

PER SERVING: Calories: 72 | Fat: 3g | Protein: 3.5g | Sodium: 457mg | Fiber: 4g | Carbohydrates: 9g | Sugar: 0g

Succotash

Frozen lima beans can be found in almost every grocery store. However, if you can't find frozen, you can substitute canned. Just drain and rinse them and add them during the last hour of cooking. Although the recipe calls for frozen beans, you could certainly substitute dry beans. Just make sure to soak them overnight and adjust the cooking time.

INGREDIENTS | SERVES 6

1 teaspoon olive oil

1 large red onion, peeled and diced

1 medium red pepper, seeded and diced

1 teaspoon kosher salt

½ teaspoon freshly ground black pepper

1 tablespoon all-purpose flour

1 cup Roasted Vegetable Stock (see recipe in Chapter 11)

½ cup frozen lima beans, thawed

2 cups frozen corn, thawed

1. In a Dutch oven, heat the oil over medium heat until hot but not smoking. Add the onion and red pepper. Season with salt and pepper. Cook until the vegetables are softened, about 5–8 minutes.

2. Sprinkle vegetable mixture with flour and cook for 1 minute. Whisk in stock. Simmer for 3 minutes, or until thickened.

3. Add the beans and corn. Stir well.

4. Pour the mixture into a 4- to 5-quart slow cooker. Cover and cook on high for 4 hours.

PER SERVING: Calories: 205 | Fat: 2g | Protein: 11g | Sodium: 411mg | Fiber: 9g | Carbohydrates: 39g | Sugar: 5g

Spiced Tomatoes

These tomatoes are excellent as a side dish warm or cold, and they're also a fun addition to a sandwich.

INGREDIENTS | SERVES 6

2 pounds red, yellow, and orange cherry tomatoes

1 teaspoon ground cloves

1 teaspoon ground allspice

1 teaspoon freshly ground black pepper

½ teaspoon kosher salt

1 tablespoon packed dark brown sugar

2 cups cider vinegar

1. Pierce the tomatoes with a paring knife and place them in a 4- to 5-quart slow cooker.

2. Sprinkle the tomatoes with the cloves, allspice, black pepper, and salt. Stir well. Place the brown sugar and vinegar in a bowl and whisk well to combine. Pour the vinegar mixture over the tomatoes.

3. Cover and cook on low for 2–3 hours.

PER SERVING: Calories: 55 | Fat: 1g | Protein: 2g | Sodium: 209mg | Fiber: 2g | Carbohydrates: 9.5g | Sugar: 6.5g

Simple Beans

These beans live up to their name. They're simple to make, but full of flavor.
Simple Beans are the perfect accompaniment to any meal.

INGREDIENTS | SERVES 6

1 cup dried cannellini beans

2 cups water

2 bay leaves

½ teaspoon kosher salt

½ teaspoon freshly ground black pepper

1. Soak the cannellini beans in water overnight. Drain and rinse them and place them in a 4- to 5-quart slow cooker.

2. Pour the water over the beans; add the bay leaves, salt, and pepper. Stir well.

3. Cover the slow cooker and cook on low for 8–10 hours.

PER SERVING: Calories: 101 | Fat: 0.5g | Protein: 7g | Sodium: 204mg | Fiber: 6g | Carbohydrates: 19g | Sugar: 2.5g

Red Cabbage with Wine

Red cabbage is irresistible when slow cooked with red wine.
Its deep, rich color makes it perfect for a holiday table.

INGREDIENTS | SERVES 6

1 head red cabbage, very thinly sliced

1 teaspoon kosher salt

½ teaspoon freshly ground black pepper

2 cups vegetable stock

1 tablespoon olive oil

1 cup dry red wine

1. Place the cabbage, salt, pepper, stock, and oil in a 4- to 5-quart slow cooker. Stir well.

2. Cover and cook on low for 3 hours.

3. Add the wine and stir well again. Cook for 1 hour more.

PER SERVING: Calories: 124 | Fat: 3.5g | Protein: 4g | Sodium: 570mg | Fiber: 4g | Carbohydrates: 13g | Sugar: 5g

Nomad's Fruit and Nut Dish

This stunning dish is delicious on its own, but it's also fantastic on rice.

INGREDIENTS | SERVES 6

¼ cup shelled pistachio nuts

¼ cup roasted almonds

1 tablespoon finely chopped dried orange rind

¼ cup raisins

¼ cup chopped dried apricots

4 medium carrots, peeled and thinly sliced

¼ cup sugar

2 cups water

1. Place the pistachio nuts in a small dry skillet. Cook over low heat, stirring constantly, until they become fragrant, about 1 minute.

2. Combine pistachios with the remaining ingredients in a 4- to 5-quart slow cooker.

3. Cover and heat on low for 4–5 hours.

PER SERVING: Calories: 132 | Fat: 4g | Protein: 3g | Sodium: 29mg | Fiber: 3g | Carbohydrates: 22g | Sugar: 17g

Mountain Garden Stew

This is an excellent stew, and you probably have everything you need for it in your pantry. You could also substitute pumpkin for the squash, and pinto beans for the navy beans.

INGREDIENTS | SERVES 10

2 tablespoons olive oil

3 medium onions, peeled and diced

½ teaspoon kosher salt

½ teaspoon freshly ground black pepper

3 cloves garlic, diced

1 pound butternut squash, peeled and cubed

2 cups chopped tomatoes, canned or fresh

1 teaspoon dried basil

1 teaspoon dried oregano

½ cup Roasted Vegetable Stock (see recipe in Chapter 11)

4 cups cooked navy beans

1 cup frozen corn kernels

1. Heat olive oil in a large skillet over medium heat. Sauté the onions until soft, about 5–8 minutes. Season with salt and pepper. Add the garlic and cook for 1 minute.

2. Remove the onion mixture with a slotted spoon and transfer to a 4- to 5-quart slow cooker. Add the squash, tomatoes, basil, and oregano.

3. Pour the stock in the skillet, and stir well to remove all of the browned pieces. Pour the stock over the vegetables.

4. Cover and heat on low for 3 hours.

5. Add the beans and corn kernels to the slow cooker. Cook for 1 hour more.

PER SERVING: Calories: 140 | Fat: 4g | Protein: 7g | Sodium: 295mg | Fiber: 6g | Carbohydrates: 23g | Sugar: 4g

Braised Cabbage

Braising brings out the subtly sweet flavor of cabbage.

INGREDIENTS | SERVES 6

1 teaspoon olive oil

1 large head cabbage (savoy, red, or white), shredded

2 large red onions, peeled and quartered

1 quart White Wine Vegetable Stock (see recipe in Chapter 11)

2 tablespoons whole-grain mustard

½ teaspoon kosher salt

½ teaspoon freshly ground black pepper

1. Heat olive oil in a Dutch oven over medium heat. Sauté cabbage and onions until softened and light brown, about 5–8 minutes.

2. Spoon the cabbage and onions into a 4- to 5-quart slow cooker. Add the stock, mustard, salt, and pepper. Stir well.

3. Cover and cook on high for 4 hours.

PER SERVING: Calories: 88 | Fat: 1g | Protein: 4g | Sodium: 584mg | Fiber: 5g | Carbohydrates: 14g | Sugar: 7g

Roasted Winter Vegetables

To make sure all the vegetables cook evenly, cut into small cubes that are similar in size. If you find the vegetables are becoming too dry, add in about ½ cup vegetable broth a little at a time until they are as moist as you would like them to be.

INGREDIENTS | SERVES 4

2 cups peeled cubed potatoes

2 cups chopped carrots

2 large onions, peeled and chopped

2 tablespoons olive oil

½ teaspoon kosher salt

1 teaspoon freshly ground pepper

1. Place vegetables in a greased 4- to 5-quart slow cooker. Drizzle with olive oil and sprinkle with salt and pepper.

2. Cover and cook on high for 3½–4 hours or on low for 7–8 hours until vegetables are fork tender. Stir vegetables every hour or so to prevent them from overbrowning on the bottom.

PER SERVING: Calories: 165 | Fat: 7g | Protein: 3g | Sodium: 340mg | Fiber: 5g | Carbohydrates: 24g | Sugar: 7g

Winter Root Vegetables

Use a variety of your favorite root vegetables such as carrots, turnips, sweet potatoes, white potatoes, parsnips, or onions. If using turnips, rutabagas, or sweet potatoes, make sure to peel the tough skin off before adding to the other vegetables.

Steamed Spaghetti Squash

People are often intimidated by cooking spaghetti squash, but by using your slow cooker it's an incredibly easy process. Serve this freshly cooked squash instead of pasta for a healthy gluten-free main dish. Or top it with butter, salt, and pepper for a delicious side dish.

INGREDIENTS | SERVES 4

1 large spaghetti squash

¾ cup water

Safely Cutting Winter Squashes

You can cook any type of winter squash (such as acorn squash, butternut squash, or pumpkins) whole using this method with the slow cooker. Because these squashes are rock hard when fresh, they can be extremely hard to cut, even with a very sharp knife. The possibility of cutting yourself once they are soft after being cooked is much less likely.

1. Place whole spaghetti squash and water in a 4-quart or larger greased slow cooker.

2. Cook on high for 4 hours or on low for 8 hours until squash is fork tender or a knife can be inserted in the center easily. Remove the squash carefully from the slow cooker. Allow to cool for several minutes.

3. With a sharp knife cut top and bottom off of squash, then cut in half lengthwise. Scoop seeds out of the center of the squash and use a fork to remove the noodle-like threads of the spaghetti squash.

PER SERVING: Calories: 82 | Fat: 1g | Protein: 2g | Sodium: 47mg | Fiber: 4g | Carbohydrates: 20g | Sugar: 8g

Herb-Stuffed Tomatoes

Serve these Italian-influenced stuffed tomatoes with a simple salad for an easy, light meal.

INGREDIENTS | SERVES 4

4 large tomatoes

1 cup cooked quinoa

1 stalk celery, minced

1 tablespoon minced fresh garlic

2 tablespoons minced fresh oregano

2 tablespoons minced fresh Italian parsley

1 teaspoon dried chervil

1 teaspoon fennel seeds

¾ cup water

1. Cut out the core of each tomato and discard. Scoop out the seeds, leaving the walls of the tomato intact.

2. In a small bowl, stir together the quinoa, celery, garlic, oregano, parsley, chervil, and fennel seeds. Divide into four even portions, and stuff one portion into the center of each tomato.

3. Place the filled tomatoes in a single layer in a 4- to 5-quart slow cooker. Pour the water into the bottom of the slow cooker. Cook on low for 4 hours.

PER SERVING: Calories: 105 | Fat: 1.5g | Protein: 4g | Sodium: 22mg | Fiber: 4g | Carbohydrates: 18g | Sugar: 5g

White Bean Cassoulet

*The longer you cook this cassoulet, the creamier the beans become.
Try serving this meal with toasted croutons on top.*

INGREDIENTS | SERVES 8

1 pound dried cannellini beans

2 large leeks (white and pale green parts only)

1 teaspoon canola oil

2 large parsnips, peeled and diced

2 large carrots, peeled and diced

2 stalks celery, diced

1 cup sliced baby portobello mushrooms

2 cups Savory Vegetable Stock (see recipe in Chapter 11)

½ teaspoon ground fennel

1 teaspoon crushed rosemary

1 teaspoon dried parsley

⅛ teaspoon ground cloves

¼ teaspoon kosher salt

¼ teaspoon freshly ground black pepper

1. The night before making the soup, place the beans in a 4- to 5-quart slow cooker. Fill with water to 1" below the top of the insert. Soak overnight.

2. Drain the beans and return them to the slow cooker.

3. Slice only the white and pale green parts of the leek into ¼" rounds. Cut the rounds in half.

4. Heat the oil in a large nonstick skillet over medium-high heat. Add the leeks, parsnips, carrots, celery, and mushrooms. Sauté for 1 minute, just until the color of the vegetables brightens. Add vegetables to the slow cooker. Stir in stock, fennel, rosemary, parsley, cloves, salt, and pepper.

5. Cook on low for 8–10 hours.

PER SERVING: Calories: 240 | Fat: 1.5g | Protein: 13g | Sodium: 114mg | Fiber: 13g | Carbohydrates: 46g | Sugar: 8g

Eggplant and Pepper Casserole

This casserole is wonderfully savory, and the eggplant comes out remarkably crisp-tender once slow cooked.

INGREDIENTS | SERVES 6

1 medium onion, peeled and chopped

1 large unpeeled eggplant, cubed into ½" pieces

2 medium zucchini, sliced into ½" rounds

1 large green, red, or yellow bell pepper, seeded and sliced into thin strips

3 large tomatoes, cut into wedges

2 tablespoons minced fresh basil

2 tablespoons minced fresh Italian parsley

¼ teaspoon kosher salt

½ teaspoon freshly ground black pepper

3 ounces tomato paste

1 cup water

1. Grease a 4- to 5-quart slow cooker with nonstick cooking spray. Place the onion, eggplant, zucchini, pepper, and tomatoes into the slow cooker. Sprinkle with basil, parsley, salt, and black pepper.

2. Whisk the tomato paste and water in a small bowl. Pour the mixture over the vegetables. Stir to combine.

3. Cook on low for 4 hours or until the eggplant and zucchini are fork tender.

PER SERVING: Calories: 76 | Fat: 1g | Protein: 3.5g | Sodium: 222mg | Fiber: 6g | Carbohydrates: 16g | Sugar: 9g

Make Your Own Tomato Paste

Tomato paste is made by slowly cooking tomatoes to reduce them, straining the tomatoes, and then cooking them again until a rich paste is formed. As long as you have fresh tomatoes, you can always make tomato paste in a pinch.

Spiced "Baked" Eggplant

Serve this as a main dish over rice or as a side dish as-is.

INGREDIENTS | SERVES 4

1 pound peeled, cubed eggplant

⅓ cup sliced onion

½ teaspoon red pepper flakes

½ teaspoon crushed rosemary

¼ cup lemon juice

Place all ingredients in a 1½- to 2-quart slow cooker. Cook on low for 3 hours or until the eggplant is tender.

PER SERVING: Calories: 38 | Fat: 0.5g | Protein: 1.5g | Sodium: 6mg | Fiber: 4g | Carbohydrates: 9g | Sugar: 3.5g

Cold Snap

Take care not to put a cold ceramic slow cooker insert directly into the slow cooker. The sudden shift in temperature can cause it to crack. If you want to prepare your ingredients the night before use, refrigerate them in reusable containers, not in the insert.

Wild Mushroom Risotto

This makes a great side dish, or try it as a main course paired with a green salad.

INGREDIENTS | SERVES 6

1 teaspoon olive oil

1 medium shallot, peeled and minced

2 cloves garlic, minced

8 ounces sliced assorted wild mushrooms

2 cups Roasted Vegetable Stock (see recipe in Chapter 11), divided

2 cups Arborio rice

3 cups water

1. Heat the oil in a medium nonstick skillet over medium heat. Sauté the shallot, garlic, and mushrooms until soft.

2. Add ½ cup stock and cook until half of the stock has evaporated. Add the rice and cook until the liquid is fully absorbed.

3. Scrape the rice mixture into a 4- to 5-quart slow cooker. Add the water and remaining stock, and cook on low for 1 hour. Stir before serving.

PER SERVING: Calories: 259 | Fat: 1g | Protein: 6g | Sodium: 211mg | Fiber: 3g | Carbohydrates: 55g | Sugar: 0.5g

Zucchini Ragout

A ragout is either a main-dish stew or a sauce. This one can be served as either.

INGREDIENTS | SERVES 6

5 ounces fresh spinach, torn

3 medium zucchini, diced

½ cup diced red onion

2 stalks celery, diced

2 medium carrots, peeled and diced

1 medium parsnip, peeled and diced

3 tablespoons tomato paste

¼ cup water

¼ teaspoon kosher salt

1 teaspoon freshly ground black pepper

1 tablespoon minced basil

1 tablespoon minced Italian parsley

1 tablespoon minced oregano

Place all ingredients into a 4- to 5-quart slow cooker. Stir. Cook on low for 4 hours. Stir before serving.

PER SERVING: Calories: 63 | Fat: 0.5g | Protein: 3g | Sodium: 217mg | Fiber: 4g | Carbohydrates: 13g | Sugar: 6g

Stuffed Eggplant

This easy vegan dish is a complete meal in itself.

INGREDIENTS | SERVES 2

1 (1-pound) eggplant
½ teaspoon olive oil
2 tablespoons minced red onion
1 clove garlic, minced
⅓ cup cooked rice
1 tablespoon chopped fresh parsley
¼ cup corn kernels
¼ cup diced cremini mushrooms
1 (14½-ounce) can diced tomatoes with onions and garlic

1. Preheat oven to 375°F. Slice the eggplant in two equal halves lengthwise. Use an ice cream scoop or large spoon to remove the seeds. Place on a nonstick baking sheet, skin-side down. Bake for 8 minutes. Allow to cool slightly.

2. Heat the oil in a small skillet over medium heat. Sauté the onion and garlic until softened, about 5 minutes.

3. In a medium bowl, stir the onion mixture, rice, parsley, corn, and mushrooms. Divide mixture evenly among eggplant halves and spoon into the indentations.

4. Pour the tomatoes onto the bottom of an oval 4- or 6-quart slow cooker. Place the eggplant halves side by side. Cook on low for 3 hours.

5. Transfer eggplant halves to a serving dish. Top with tomatoes.

PER SERVING: Calories: 174 | Fat: 2g | Protein: 7g | Sodium: 299mg | Fiber: 11g | Carbohydrates: 37g | Sugar: 12g

Savory Rye Berries

This meal is wonderful on a cold evening. It's flavorful, comforting, and beautiful.

INGREDIENTS | SERVES 6

1 tablespoon olive oil

1 medium onion, peeled and diced

1 medium carrot, peeled and diced

1 celery stalk, diced

1 large leek (white and pale green parts only), chopped

1 cup rye berries

2 cups Savory Vegetable Stock (see recipe in Chapter 11)

1 teaspoon kosher salt

¼ bunch flat-leaf parsley, chopped

1. Heat olive oil in a large skillet over medium heat until it simmers, about 1 minute. Add onion, carrot, celery, and leek to the pan. Sauté until soft, about 5–8 minutes.

2. Place the vegetables, rye berries, stock, and salt in a 4- to 5-quart slow cooker. Stir well.

3. Cover and cook on low for 6–8 hours. Serve garnished with parsley.

PER SERVING: Calories: 158 | Fat: 3g | Protein: 4g | Sodium: 412mg | Fiber: 6g | Carbohydrates: 30g | Sugar: 2g

Try Something New!

Rye berries are high in dietary fiber, which makes them an excellent addition to your diet.

Farmer Peas

If at all possible, use new spring peas in this dish because of their delicate flavor.

INGREDIENTS | SERVES 6

2 large leeks (white and pale green parts only), chopped

6 small carrots, peeled and diced

1 head romaine lettuce, chopped

2 cups fresh green peas

12 asparagus tips

2 cups Savory Vegetable Stock (see recipe in Chapter 11)

1 teaspoon lemon juice

½ teaspoon dried basil

½ teaspoon kosher salt

1. Place all ingredients in a 4- to 5-quart slow cooker.

2. Cover and cook on high for 2–3 hours. Serve immediately.

PER SERVING: Calories: 98 | Fat: 1g | Protein: 5g | Sodium: 248mg | Fiber: 7g | Carbohydrates: 19g | Sugar: 7g

"Baked" Acorn Squash with Lemony Couscous and Spinach

Slow cooking acorn squash helps to bring out its natural sweetness. This makes an incredibly delicious side dish, with the benefit of making the whole house smell like autumn.

INGREDIENTS | SERVES 4

2 medium acorn squash, halved and seeded

1 tablespoon olive oil

½ teaspoon kosher salt, divided

1 teaspoon freshly ground black pepper, divided

½ cup Savory Vegetable Stock (see recipe in Chapter 11)

2 cups cooked couscous

2 teaspoons lemon juice

1 cup chopped fresh spinach

1. Place squash in a 4- to 5-quart slow cooker, cut-side up. Drizzle olive oil over squash halves and season with salt and pepper. Pour stock into slow cooker.

2. Cook on high for 1 hour. Reduce heat to low and cook for 5½ more hours.

3. In a large bowl, combine couscous with lemon juice and spinach. Stir well.

4. Divide couscous stuffing between squash halves. Cover and cook on high for an additional 30 minutes. Serve immediately.

PER SERVING: Calories: 210 | Fat: 4g | Protein: 5g | Sodium: 341mg | Fiber: 5g | Carbohydrates: 41g | Sugar: 0g

Mushroom and Chickpea Stew

This rich, tender stew is a satisfying dish, full of healthy protein.

INGREDIENTS | SERVES 6

Nonstick olive oil cooking spray

3 cups chopped cremini mushrooms

2 (14½-ounce) cans chickpeas, drained and rinsed

1 (15-ounce) can crushed tomatoes

3 cloves garlic, chopped

¼ cup olive oil

1 teaspoon salt

2 cups cooked brown rice

¼ cup chopped fresh basil

1. Spray a 4- to 5-quart slow cooker with nonstick cooking spray.

2. Add mushrooms, chickpeas, and tomatoes to the slow cooker. Sprinkle with garlic and drizzle with olive oil. Sprinkle salt on top.

3. Place lid on slow cooker, and cook on low for 4–6 hours, or until the mushrooms are tender.

4. Serve stew over rice, topped with fresh chopped basil.

PER SERVING: Calories: 396 | Fat: 13g | Protein: 15g | Sodium: 505mg | Fiber: 12g | Carbohydrates: 56g | Sugar: 8g

CHAPTER 15

Gluten-Free

Gluten-Free Breakfast Granola

Finding gluten-free granola can be a challenge in most grocery stores, but it's super easy to make your own in the slow cooker. Make sure to stir the ingredients every hour to prevent uneven cooking or overbrowning.

INGREDIENTS | SERVES 10

2½ cups gluten-free rolled oats

¼ cup ground flaxseeds

½ cup unsweetened shredded coconut

½ cup pumpkin seeds

½ cup walnuts, chopped

½ cup sliced almonds

1 cup dried cranberries

¾ cup packed light brown sugar

⅓ cup coconut oil

¼ cup honey

½ teaspoon kosher salt

1 teaspoon ground cinnamon

Change It Up

Don't like pumpkin seeds, walnuts, or dried cranberries? Use the seeds, nuts, and dried fruit that you prefer in your own granola. Use raisins, sunflower seeds, cocoa nibs, dried cranberries, or even dried bananas. The variations are endless. You can even add chocolate chips if you'd like, but only after the granola has been cooked and cooled!

1. Mix all ingredients together and place in a greased 4- to 5-quart slow cooker.

2. Cover slow cooker and vent with a wooden spoon handle or a chopstick. Cook on high for 4 hours, or on low for 8 hours, stirring every hour.

3. When granola is toasty and done, pour it onto a cookie sheet that has been lined with parchment paper. Spread the granola out evenly over the entire sheet of parchment paper. Allow granola to cool and dry for several hours.

4. Once cooled, break granola up and place in an airtight container or a tightly sealed glass jar and store in pantry for up to 1 month. For longer storage, keep granola in freezer for up to 6 months.

PER SERVING: Calories: 399 | Fat: 20g | Protein: 8g | Sodium: 125mg | Fiber: 5.5g | Carbohydrates: 51g | Sugar: 31g

Gluten-Free Cream of Mushroom Soup

Cream of mushroom soup is a simple and light main dish. It's also a perfect gluten-free base to use when a recipe calls for canned cream soup.

INGREDIENTS | SERVES 4

2 tablespoons olive oil

1 cup fresh mushrooms, finely diced

4 tablespoons cornstarch

2 cups skim milk

½ teaspoon kosher salt

½ teaspoon ground black pepper

Cream Soup Variations

You can make any number of homemade cream soups with this recipe. If you would rather have cream of celery soup, use 1 cup of finely diced celery instead of the mushrooms. For a cream of chicken soup, use 1 cup of finely diced chicken and 2 teaspoons of poultry seasoning. For a cheese sauce, add 1 cup of reduced-fat shredded sharp Cheddar cheese.

1. Heat olive oil in a deep saucepan over medium heat. Add mushrooms and cook until soft, approximately 4–5 minutes.

2. In a medium bowl, whisk cornstarch into the milk. Slowly add to the mushrooms and oil. Cook on medium heat for 5–10 minutes, whisking constantly, until slightly thickened.

3. Carefully pour cream soup into a greased 2½-quart slow cooker. Add salt, pepper, and any additional seasonings you would like. Cook on high for 2 hours or on low for 4 hours.

PER SERVING: Calories: 145 | Fat: 8g | Protein: 5g | Sodium: 350mg | Fiber: 0.5g | Carbohydrates: 14g | Sugar: 6g

Low-Carb Snack Mix

For this recipe, use raw almonds, cashews, pecans, shelled pumpkin seeds, shelled sunflower seeds, walnuts, and raw or dry-roasted peanuts. The amounts you use of each kind of nut is up to you, although because of their size, ideally the recipe shouldn't have more than 1 cup of sunflower seeds.

INGREDIENTS | SERVES 24

4 tablespoons butter, melted

3 tablespoons gluten-free Worcestershire sauce

1½ teaspoons garlic powder

2 teaspoons onion powder

½ teaspoon sea salt

8 cups raw nuts

Gluten-Free Worcestershire Sauce

Worcestershire sauce is gluten-free as long as it doesn't contain malt vinegar. Even though malt vinegar by definition contains some wheat, it's in very small amounts. However, people who are extremely sensitive to gluten should avoid it. Luckily two of the largest Worcestershire sauce companies (Lea & Perrins and French's) are gluten-free. But, when in doubt, always double check the label.

1. Add all ingredients to a 4- to 5-quart slow cooker. Stir to coat the nuts evenly. Cover and cook on low for 6 hours, stirring occasionally.

2. Uncover and continue to cook on low for 1 more hour to dry the nuts and seeds, stirring occasionally, then evenly spread them on a baking sheet lined with aluminum foil or parchment paper until completely cooled. Store in an airtight container in the pantry for up to 2 weeks.

PER SERVING: Calories: 201 | Fat: 17g | Protein: 7g | Sodium: 70mg | Fiber: 4g | Carbohydrates: 7.5g | Sugar: 1.5g

Four-Ingredient Marinara Sauce

Marinara sauce is full of authentic Italian flavor. This method proves you don't need a laundry list of ingredients for great flavor. Serve this sauce over steamed spaghetti squash or cooked gluten-free pasta.

INGREDIENTS | SERVES 6

2 teaspoons olive oil

2–3 cloves garlic, crushed

1 large sweet onion, peeled and finely diced

1 (28-ounce) can whole tomatoes with basil

Simmering Sauces All Day

Simple sauces like this can be simmered for long periods of time on low heat. The longer the sauce cooks, the better the flavor will be once it's time to eat.

1. In a medium skillet, heat oil over medium heat. Add garlic and onion and sauté for 3–5 minutes until golden and soft.

2. Pour sautéed onion and garlic into a 4- to 5-quart slow cooker. Add tomatoes. Using a fork or a potato masher, break up the tomatoes into the sauce. They will be a little bit chunky. If you prefer, use an immersion blender to blend until smooth.

3. Cover and cook on high for 4–5 hours or on low for 8–10 hours.

PER SERVING: Calories: 46 | Fat: 1.5g | Protein: 1.5g | Sodium: 188mg | Fiber: 2g | Carbohydrates: 7g | Sugar: 4g

Gluten-Free Millet Bread

Many people who are sensitive to gluten are also sensitive to other grains such as corn. This bread is free of gluten, corn, yeast, dairy/casein, soy, and rice and is a perfect alternative for those with multiple food sensitivities.

INGREDIENTS | SERVES 12

⅓ cup sorghum flour

⅓ cup arrowroot starch

1 cup millet flour

1 teaspoon xanthan gum

1 teaspoon baking soda

¼ teaspoon kosher salt

3 tablespoons sugar

3 tablespoons oil

2 large eggs

1 cup almond milk

1 tablespoon lemon juice or apple cider vinegar

Use Recycled Cans for Slow Cooker Baking

When using recycled aluminum cans for baking, make sure to carefully cut away sharp edges with wire cutters so that you do not chance cutting your fingers when filling or emptying the cans. Clean cans carefully between each use with a baby bottle cleaner.

1. In a large bowl, whisk together sorghum flour, arrowroot starch, and millet flour. Add xanthan gum, baking soda, salt, and sugar. Mix together thoroughly.

2. In a smaller bowl, mix together the oil, eggs, almond milk, and lemon juice or apple cider vinegar.

3. Mix wet ingredients into dry ingredients with a fork until you have a thick batter.

4. Grease three emptied and cleaned (15-ounce) aluminum cans and place ⅓ of the bread batter into each can. The cans will be about half full.

5. Place the cans in a 4- to 5-quart slow cooker. Pour ½ cup of water around the cans.

6. Cover the slow cooker and vent the lid with a chopstick. Cook on high for 3–3½ hours or on low for 6–7 hours. Bread should rise and double in size and become golden brown on top when done.

7. Remove cans of bread carefully from slow cooker and allow the bread to cool before removing from cans. Slice each loaf into four round pieces of bread. Serve warm.

PER SERVING: Calories: 145 | Fat: 5g | Protein: 3g | Sodium: 179mg | Fiber: 1g | Carbohydrates: 22g | Sugar: 4g

Gluten-Free Slow Cooker Yeast Bread

*Did you know you can make gluten-free sandwich bread right in your slow cooker?
If using the loaf pan for this bread, make sure to use the size recommended in the recipe.
Otherwise, your bread can rise too high and then fall while baking.*

INGREDIENTS | SERVES 12

⅓ cup arrowroot starch

⅓ cup blanched almond flour

3 tablespoons millet flour

1½ cups brown rice flour

1 teaspoon kosher salt

1 tablespoon xanthan gum

2 teaspoons bread machine yeast (try SAF, Red Star, or Fleischmann's)

3 tablespoons sugar

1 large egg, plus 2 egg whites, room temperature

1⅓ cups whole milk, heated to 110°F

3 tablespoons olive oil

Free-Form Oval Bread

If you don't have a large 6-quart slow cooker, simply line a 2½-quart or a 4- to 5-quart slow cooker with parchment paper. Spray it with nonstick cooking spray. Coat your hands or a large spoon with cooking spray or olive oil and shape the dough into an oval loaf. Place loaf in the middle of the parchment paper and bake as directed. You will need to keep a close eye on the loaf—it can burn around the edges since it's closer to the heating element.

1. In a large bowl, whisk together arrowroot starch, blanched almond flour, millet flour, brown rice flour, salt, xanthan gum, yeast, and sugar.

2. In a smaller bowl, whisk together the egg, egg whites, milk, and oil.

3. Pour wet ingredients into whisked dry ingredients. Stir with a wooden spoon or a fork for several minutes until dough resembles a thick cake batter. First it will look like biscuit dough, but after a few minutes it will appear thick and sticky.

4. Line an 8½" × 4½" metal or glass loaf pan with parchment paper or spray with nonstick cooking spray. Pour bread dough into the pan. Using a spatula that's been dipped in water or coated with oil or nonstick cooking spray, spread the dough evenly in the pan. Continue to use the spatula to smooth out the top of the bread dough. Place the loaf pan in a 6-quart or larger oval slow cooker.

5. Cover the slow cooker and vent the lid with a chopstick or the handle of a wooden spoon. Cook on high for 3½–4 hours. The bread will rise and bake at the same time. The bread should be about double in size and the sides should be a light golden brown; the bread will not "brown" as much as it would in the oven.

6. Remove the bread from the pan and cool on a wire rack. Slice and keep in an airtight plastic bag on the counter for 2 days. Freeze any remaining bread.

PER SERVING: Calories: 179 | Fat: 5g | Protein: 3g | Sodium: 222mg | Fiber: 3g | Carbohydrates: 29g | Sugar: 4g

Slow Cooker Gluten-Free Yeast Rolls

This recipe proves how versatile gluten-free yeast dough can be, even in the slow cooker!
You will need two (4-quart) slow cookers or one (6-quart) slow cooker for this recipe.

INGREDIENTS | SERVES 12

1 recipe Gluten-Free Slow Cooker Yeast Bread dough (see recipe in this chapter)

3 tablespoons olive oil or melted butter

½ teaspoon garlic powder

½ teaspoon toasted sesame seeds

½ teaspoon Italian seasoning

Drop Rolls

Instead of using cupcake liners, you can simply line the slow cooker with parchment paper. Spray the parchment paper with nonstick cooking spray and drop the scoops of dough onto the parchment paper. Bake as directed.

1. Using an ice cream scoop, scoop dough into twelve balls and place each ball in a greased cupcake liner. Place the cupcake liners on the bottom of one large (6-quart) or two smaller (4-quart) slow cookers.

2. Brush rolls with olive oil or melted butter and sprinkle garlic powder, sesame seeds, and Italian seasoning over the tops.

3. Cover and vent the lid with a chopstick or the handle of a wooden spoon. Cook on high for 1½–2½ hours until dough has almost doubled in size and the rolls are cooked through. You will need to watch the rolls at the end of the cooking period—they can get overdone on the edges since they are so close to the cooking element.

PER SERVING: Calories: 209 | Fat: 8g | Protein: 3g | Sodium: 222mg | Fiber: 3g | Carbohydrates: 29g | Sugar: 4g

Applesauce Cake

A lightly spiced cake that can be frosted with whipped vanilla icing or eaten plain, this cake would also be delicious with Spiced Winter Fruit Compote (see recipe in Chapter 16) spooned over each serving.

INGREDIENTS | SERVES 9

½ cup brown rice flour

½ cup plus 2 tablespoons arrowroot starch

½ cup sugar

1 teaspoon baking powder

½ teaspoon baking soda

½ teaspoon xanthan gum

¼ teaspoon kosher salt

1 teaspoon cinnamon

½ teaspoon ground nutmeg

¼ teaspoon ground cloves

2 tablespoons canola oil

1 cup applesauce

2 large eggs

Make a Round or Oval Cake

If you can't find any aluminum cans to use for this recipe, you can pour the batter into the bottom of a 4- to 5-quart slow cooker that's been lined with parchment paper. Cover, vent the lid, and cook on high for 2–2½ hours or until cake is cooked through in the middle. You'll have to watch the cake carefully, as it could burn on the edges and the bottom.

1. In a large bowl, whisk together flour, arrowroot starch, sugar, baking powder, baking soda, xanthan gum, salt, cinnamon, nutmeg, and cloves. Mix together thoroughly.

2. In a smaller bowl, mix together the oil, applesauce, and eggs.

3. Mix wet ingredients into dry ingredients with a fork until you have a thick batter.

4. Grease three emptied and cleaned (15-ounce) aluminum cans and place ⅓ of the cake batter into each can. Place the cans into a 4- to 5-quart slow cooker.

5. Cover the slow cooker and vent the lid with a chopstick. Cook on high for 3–3½ hours or on low for 6–7 hours. Cakes should rise and become a golden brown on top when done.

6. Remove cans of cake carefully from slow cooker and allow to cool before removing from cans. Slice each cake into three round pieces of cake. These pieces can be placed in cupcake liners and served as cupcakes.

PER SERVING: Calories: 163 | Fat: 4g | Protein: 2g | Sodium: 207mg | Fiber: 1g | Carbohydrates: 29g | Sugar: 13g

Easy Chocolate Cake

To make your own chocolate cake mix, simply whisk together all dry ingredients and place in a sanitized glass jar with a tight-fitting lid. Little jars of gluten-free cake mix make a nice homemade gift.

INGREDIENTS | SERVES 9

⅓ cup brown rice flour

⅓ cup arrowroot starch

⅓ cup sorghum flour

½ teaspoon xanthan gum

¾ cup sugar

¼ cup unsweetened baking cocoa

1 teaspoon baking powder

¼ teaspoon baking soda

¼ cup oil

¾ cup almond milk

½ teaspoon vanilla extract

2 large eggs, slightly beaten

Everybody Loves Chocolate Chips

Mini chocolate chips make a nice addition to this cake. The Enjoy Life company makes gluten-free and dairy-free mini chocolate chips.

1. In a large bowl, whisk together brown rice flour, arrowroot starch, sorghum flour, xanthan gum, sugar, cocoa, baking powder, and baking soda. Mix together thoroughly.

2. In a smaller bowl, whisk together the oil, almond milk, vanilla, and eggs.

3. Mix wet ingredients into dry ingredients with a fork until you have a thick cake batter.

4. Grease three emptied and cleaned (15-ounce) aluminum cans and place ⅓ of the cake batter into each can. Place the cans in a 4- to 5-quart slow cooker.

5. Cover the slow cooker and vent the lid with a chopstick. Cook on high for 3–3½ hours or on low for 6–7 hours. Cakes should rise and about double in size and become a dark brown on top when done.

6. Remove cans of cake carefully from slow cooker and allow to cool before removing from cans. Slice each cake into three round pieces of cake. These pieces can be placed in cupcake liners and served as cupcakes. Eat plain or frost with your favorite icing.

PER SERVING: Calories: 214 | Fat: 8g | Protein: 4g | Sodium: 118mg | Fiber: 2g | Carbohydrates: 34g | Sugar: 17g

Pear Clafoutis

*If you choose to use a larger slow cooker than the specified 2½-quart size,
you will need to reduce the cooking time. When the sides are golden brown
and a toothpick stuck in the middle comes out clean, the clafoutis is done.*

INGREDIENTS | SERVES 4

2 pears, stem and seeds removed, cut into chunks, and peeled if preferred

½ cup brown rice flour

½ cup arrowroot starch

2 teaspoons baking powder

½ teaspoon xanthan gum

¼ teaspoon kosher salt

⅓ cup sugar

1 teaspoon ground cinnamon

2 tablespoons vegetable shortening, melted

2 large eggs

¾ cup skim milk

1 tablespoon vanilla

Gluten-Free Baking Shortcut

Don't want to mix up all these ingredients? You can replace the brown rice flour, arrowroot starch, baking powder, and xanthan gum with 1 cup of Bob's Red Mill Gluten-Free Pancake Mix, or your favorite gluten-free pancake mix.

1. Place cut-up pears into a greased 4- to 5-quart slow cooker.

2. In a large bowl, whisk together the brown rice flour, arrowroot starch, baking powder, xanthan gum, salt, sugar, and cinnamon.

3. Make a well in the center of the dry ingredients and add melted shortening, eggs, milk, and vanilla. Stir to combine wet with dry ingredients.

4. Pour batter over pears. Cover slow cooker and vent lid with a chopstick or the handle of a wooden spoon.

5. Cook on high for 2½–3 hours or on low for 5–6 hours. Serve warm or cold drizzled with pure maple syrup.

PER SERVING: Calories: 368 | Fat: 9g | Protein: 6g |
Sodium: 451mg | Fiber: 4g | Carbohydrates: 63g | Sugar: 27g

Blueberry Cobbler

Blueberries are beloved not just for their flavor—they are also naturally high in antioxidants and naturally low in calories and sugars. A perfect way to indulge, without really indulging at all!

INGREDIENTS | SERVES 6

¾ cup water

6 tablespoons honey, divided

2 tablespoons cornstarch

3 cups fresh or frozen blueberries

½ cup brown rice flour

½ cup arrowroot starch

1 teaspoon baking powder

¼ teaspoon xanthan gum

⅓ cup 2% milk

1 tablespoon melted butter

½ teaspoon cinnamon mixed with 2 teaspoons sugar

2 tablespoons cold butter, cut into small pieces

Make It Easier

If you don't want to go to the trouble of making your own fruit filling, use a can of cherry pie filling, apple pie filling, or even a can of whole cranberry jelly. Make the cobbler even easier by replacing the brown rice flour, arrowroot starch, baking powder, and xanthan gum with 1 cup of Gluten-Free Bisquick.

1. Grease a 4- to 5-quart slow cooker.

2. In a small saucepan, add water, 3 tablespoons honey, and cornstarch. Whisk together and cook over high heat, stirring constantly until boiling. Allow to boil for 1 minute. The mixture will turn translucent and thicken. Remove from heat and add blueberries. Pour blueberry filling into the greased slow cooker.

3. In a small bowl, whisk together flour, arrowroot starch, baking powder, remaining honey, and xanthan gum. Make a well in the center of the dry ingredients and add milk and melted butter. Mix until you have a thick batter.

4. Drop batter by tablespoons on top of the blueberry filling and use a fork to spread evenly over the casserole.

5. Sprinkle cinnamon and sugar mixture over the top of the casserole. Dot with butter.

6. Cover and vent slow cooker lid with a chopstick or the handle of a wooden spoon. Cook on high for 2½–3 hours or until fruit filling is bubbling on the sides of the topping and the biscuit topping is cooked through.

PER SERVING: Calories: 268 | Fat: 6g | Protein: 2g | Sodium: 92mg | Fiber: 3g | Carbohydrates: 52g | Sugar: 26g

CHAPTER 16

Dessert

Apple and Pear Spread

This delicious combination of apples and pears is delicious on cake or even toast.

INGREDIENTS | MAKES 3 CUPS

4 medium Winesap apples, cored and sliced

4 medium Bartlett pears, cored and sliced

1 cup water

¼ cup packed light brown sugar

¼ cup granulated sugar

¼ teaspoon ginger

¼ teaspoon cinnamon

¼ teaspoon nutmeg

¼ teaspoon allspice

1. Place all ingredients in a 4- to 5-quart slow cooker. Cook on low for 10–12 hours.

2. Uncover slow cooker, and cook on low for an additional 10–12 hours or until thickened.

3. Let the spread cool and then process in a food processor. Pour into clean glass jars. Refrigerate for up to 6 weeks.

PER SERVING (2 TABLESPOONS): Calories: 47 | Fat: 0g | Protein: 0g | Sodium: 1.5mg | Fiber: 1.5g | Carbohydrates: 12g | Sugar: 10g

Make Your Own Brown Sugar

Brown sugar is simply granulated white sugar combined with molasses. You can make your own by combining 1 cup of granulated sugar with ¼ cup of molasses. Store in an airtight container for up to a month at room temperature.

Raspberry Coulis

A dessert coulis is a very thick sauce made from puréed fruits. Because the coulis is slow cooked, there's no need to purée the sauce at the end of cooking—the slow cooker does the work for you.

INGREDIENTS | SERVES 8

12 ounces fresh or frozen raspberries

1 teaspoon balsamic vinegar

2 tablespoons sugar

Place all ingredients into a 1½- to 2-quart slow cooker. Mash gently with a potato masher or large fork. Cook on low for 4 hours uncovered. Stir well before serving.

PER SERVING: Calories: 34 | Fat: 0g | Protein: 0.5g | Sodium: 0.6mg | Fiber: 3g | Carbohydrates: 8g | Sugar: 5g

Taste the Berries!

When using fresh berries in a recipe, it's important to taste-test them before adding sugar. One batch can be tart; another batch can be extremely sweet.

Strawberry-Rhubarb Compote

Try this over Greek yogurt, pancakes, or oatmeal.

INGREDIENTS | MAKES 1½ CUPS

1 pound strawberries, diced
½ pound rhubarb, diced
2 tablespoons lemon juice
1 tablespoon lemon zest

1. Place all ingredients into a 4- to 5-quart slow cooker. Cook on low for 2 hours.

2. Lightly mash with a potato masher.

3. Cook on high, uncovered, for 1 additional hour.

PER SERVING (¼ CUP): Calories: 33 | Fat: 0g | Protein: 1g | Sodium: 3mg | Fiber: 3g | Carbohydrates: 8g | Sugar: 4g

Chocolate Crème Brûlée

This dessert is incredibly elegant, and will please children and adults alike.

INGREDIENTS | SERVES 4

2 cups fat-free evaporated milk
2½ tablespoons cocoa
½ teaspoon vanilla extract
4 large egg yolks
½ cup granulated sugar
2 tablespoons packed light brown sugar

1. Pour 1" of water into the bottom of an oval 4- to 5-quart slow cooker. Heat on high for 40 minutes.

2. In a small bowl, whisk the evaporated milk, cocoa, vanilla, egg yolks, and granulated sugar until the sugar dissolves. Pour the mixture into a small saucepan and bring it to a boil over high heat. Remove the pan from the heat and allow the mixture to cool. Divide it among four (6-ounce) broiler-safe ramekins.

3. Place the ramekins in the hot water. Cover and cook on high for 3 hours or until the custard is set.

4. Sprinkle each crème brûlée with ½ tablespoon brown sugar. Place them under the broiler and broil until the sugar caramelizes.

PER SERVING: Calories: 355 | Fat: 14g | Protein: 12g | Sodium: 144mg | Fiber: 1g | Carbohydrates: 47g | Sugar: 44g

Strawberry Pandowdy

The pandowdy gets its name from its "dowdy" appearance. Don't let its looks fool you, though. The pandowdy is so delicious that you'll want to make it once a week.

INGREDIENTS | SERVES 4

4 cups whole strawberries, stems removed

½ teaspoon ground ginger

1½ tablespoons sugar

½ teaspoon cornstarch

¾ cup all-purpose flour

3 tablespoons cold butter, cubed

3 tablespoons cold water

⅛ teaspoon kosher salt

1. Place the strawberries, ginger, sugar, and cornstarch into a 1½- to 2-quart slow cooker. Stir well.

2. Place the flour, butter, water, and salt into a food processor fitted with a metal blade. Pulse until a solid ball of dough forms. Roll dough out on a clean surface until it is about ¼"–½" thick.

3. Drape the dough over the strawberries. Cover and cook on high for 40 minutes. Uncover the slow cooker. Using the tip of a paring knife, cut the dough into two halves without removing it from the slow cooker. Cook on high for an additional 40–45 minutes. Serve immediately.

PER SERVING: Calories: 228 | Fat: 9g | Protein: 4g | Sodium: 573mg | Fiber: 3.5g | Carbohydrates: 34g | Sugar: 11g

Carrot Nutmeg Pudding

Carrots aren't just for savory dishes! They're surprisingly sweet, and add a lovely color to the pudding.

INGREDIENTS | SERVES 4

4 large carrots, peeled and grated

2 tablespoons unsalted butter

½ teaspoon kosher salt

½ teaspoon freshly grated nutmeg

2 tablespoons sugar

1 teaspoon vanilla

1 cup milk

3 large eggs, beaten

1. Place carrots and butter in a large glass, microwavable bowl. Cover and cook on high for 3–4 minutes or until carrots have softened slightly.

2. Stir in salt, nutmeg, sugar, vanilla, milk, and eggs. Whisk well and pour into a greased 2½-quart slow cooker. Cook on high for 3 hours. Serve hot or cold.

PER SERVING: Calories: 200 | Fat: 11g | Protein: 7g | Sodium: 424mg | Fiber: 2g | Carbohydrates: 16g | Sugar: 13g

Spiced Winter Fruit Compote

Warm fruit spiced with ginger, cardamom, and nutmeg, this would be perfect spooned over toasted pound cake or even ice cream.

INGREDIENTS | SERVES 8

3 medium pears, peeled if desired, cored, and cubed

1 (15½-ounce) can pineapple chunks, undrained

1 cup dried apricots, quartered

½ cup dried cranberries

3 tablespoons frozen orange juice concentrate

2 tablespoons packed light brown sugar

3 tablespoons tapioca starch

½ teaspoon ground ginger

¼ teaspoon cardamom

½ teaspoon freshly grated nutmeg

2 cups frozen unsweetened pitted dark sweet cherries

½ cup toasted flaked coconut

½ cup toasted pecans

1. In a greased 4- to 5-quart slow cooker, combine pears, pineapple, apricots, and cranberries.

2. In a small bowl, whisk together orange juice concentrate, brown sugar, tapioca starch, ginger, cardamom, and nutmeg. Pour orange juice mixture over fruit in slow cooker.

3. Cover and cook on low for 6–8 hours or on high for 3–4 hours. Stir in cherries 1 hour prior to serving.

4. To serve, spoon warm compote into dessert dishes. Top with coconut and pecans.

PER SERVING: Calories: 265 | Fat: 7g | Protein: 3g | Sodium: 5mg | Fiber: 6g | Carbohydrates: 52g | Sugar: 39g

Maple-Orange Pears

These pears, coated with the sweet flavors of maple, ginger, and orange, make a delicious fruit dessert.

INGREDIENTS | SERVES 6

6 large pears

½ cup packed light brown sugar

⅓ cup maple-flavored pancake syrup

1 tablespoon butter, melted

1 teaspoon grated orange zest

⅛ teaspoon ground ginger

1 tablespoon cornstarch

2 tablespoons orange juice

1. Peel pears and place them upright in a 4- to 5-quart slow cooker.

2. In a small bowl, mix the brown sugar, syrup, butter, zest, and ginger; pour over pears.

3. Cover and cook on high for 2–2½ hours or on low for 4 hours, until tender.

4. Using a slotted spoon, carefully remove pears from the slow cooker and place upright in a serving dish or individual dessert dishes.

5. In a small bowl, mix cornstarch and orange juice together. Stir into sauce in cooker. Cover and cook on high for about 10 minutes or until sauce is thickened. Spoon orange sauce over pears.

PER SERVING: Calories: 274 | Fat: 2g | Protein: 1g | Sodium: 9mg | Fiber: 7g | Carbohydrates: 67g | Sugar: 51g

Crustless Apple Pie

You may need to adjust the cooking time depending on the type of apples you use. A softer Golden Delicious should be cooked through and soft in the recommended cooking times, but a crisper Granny Smith, Roma, or Gala apple may take longer.

INGREDIENTS | SERVES 8

8 medium apples, cored, peeled, and sliced

3 tablespoons orange juice

3 tablespoons water

½ cup pecans, chopped

⅓ cup packed light brown sugar

2 tablespoons butter, melted

½ teaspoon cinnamon

1 cup plain low-fat Greek yogurt

¼ cup honey

1. Treat a 4- to 5-quart slow cooker with nonstick spray. Arrange apple slices on the bottom of the slow cooker.

2. In a small bowl, combine the orange juice and water; stir to mix. Evenly drizzle over the apples.

3. In a separate bowl, combine the pecans, brown sugar, butter, and cinnamon. Mix well. Evenly crumble the pecan mixture over the apples. Cover and cook on high for 2 hours or on low for 4 hours.

4. Serve warm or chilled, topped with Greek yogurt and honey.

PER SERVING: Calories: 239 | Fat: 8g | Protein: 3g | Sodium: 25mg | Fiber: 3g | Carbohydrates: 42g | Sugar: 36g

Old-Fashioned Chocolate Cobbler

This chocolate dessert creates its own chocolate sauce underneath the thick, fudgy cake layer. Don't be alarmed if the appearance is not that of a normal cake. It's meant to be served with ice cream or whipped cream on top!

INGREDIENTS | SERVES 8

3 tablespoons olive oil

1 cup all-purpose flour

½ teaspoon baking powder

¼ teaspoon kosher salt

½ cup plus ⅓ cup sugar, divided

2 tablespoons plus ¼ cup cocoa powder, divided

1 teaspoon vanilla

¾ cup skim milk

1 large egg

1¼ cups boiling water

1. Drizzle olive oil in the bottom of a greased 4- to 5-quart slow cooker.

2. In a large bowl, whisk together the flour, baking powder, salt, ½ cup sugar, and 2 tablespoons cocoa powder. Stir in the vanilla, milk, and egg. Pour the batter into the slow cooker and spread it evenly. The olive oil will probably come up around the edges of the batter; this is okay.

3. Sprinkle ⅓ cup sugar and ¼ cup cocoa powder over the cake batter. Pour the boiling water over the entire cake.

4. Cook on low 2½–3 hours or on high for 1½–2 hours, or until a toothpick inserted in the middle of the cake portion comes out clean. Remove the slow cooker insert and set it on top of several pot holders or a heat-safe surface and allow to cool for 20–30 minutes. This will allow the pudding underneath to thicken and set.

5. Serve warm.

PER SERVING: Calories: 212 | Fat: 6g | Protein: 4g | Sodium: 125mg | Fiber: 2g | Carbohydrates: 36g | Sugar: 22g

Peach Crisp

Serve with frozen Greek yogurt on top and a drizzle of honey for a truly Mediterranean treat.

INGREDIENTS | SERVES 4

6 large peaches, peeled, pitted, and sliced

¼ cup granulated sugar

2 teaspoons garam masala or curry powder

¾ cup rolled oats

¼ cup all-purpose flour

½ cup packed light brown sugar

2 tablespoons butter

2 tablespoons olive oil

1 cup pecans, chopped

Quicker and Easier Fruit Crisp

Fruit crisp is a super versatile dessert. You don't have to limit yourself to fresh fruit. If you need to throw together a dessert in a hurry, you can thaw some frozen peaches or open a can of any pie filling and use that instead.

1. Toss peaches with granulated sugar and garam masala.

2. Grease a 4- to 5-quart slow cooker with nonstick cooking spray. Arrange the peaches on the bottom of the slow cooker.

3. In a medium bowl, mix together the oats, flour, brown sugar, butter, olive oil, and pecans with a fork until you have a crumbly topping mixture. Sprinkle the topping evenly over the fruit in the slow cooker.

4. Cover, vent the lid with a chopstick or the handle of a wooden spoon, and cook on high for 2 hours or on low for 4 hours or until the peaches are tender and the topping is crisp. The peach mixture may start to bubble up around the topping. Serve warm or chilled.

PER SERVING: Calories: 640 | Fat: 33g | Protein: 8g | Sodium: 9mg | Fiber: 8g | Carbohydrates: 84g | Sugar: 62g

Cinnamon-Vanilla Tapioca Pudding

Tapioca pudding is a favorite among children. This dessert can be made overnight and placed in the refrigerator to serve as a cold afternoon snack.

INGREDIENTS | SERVES 4

4 cups skim milk
¼ cup honey
2 large eggs, lightly beaten
½ cup small pearl tapioca
½ teaspoon cinnamon
1 tablespoon vanilla

1. In a greased 2½-quart or 4- to 5-quart slow cooker, whisk together all ingredients.

2. Cover and cook on high for 2½–3 hours or on low for 6 hours, stirring occasionally.

3. Serve warm or cold.

PER SERVING: Calories: 280 | Fat: 5g | Protein: 12g | Sodium: 143mg | Fiber: 0g | Carbohydrates: 47g | Sugar: 31g

Crustless Lemon Cheesecake

Cheesecake bakes perfectly in the slow cooker. In this recipe, the slow cooker is lined with parchment paper, which makes for a very easy cleanup!

INGREDIENTS | SERVES 8

16 ounces cream cheese, softened
⅔ cup sugar
2 large eggs
1 tablespoon cornstarch
1 teaspoon fresh lemon zest
2 tablespoons fresh lemon juice

1. In a large bowl, beat cream cheese and sugar together until smooth.

2. Beat in eggs, and continue beating with a hand-held electric mixer on medium speed for about 3 minutes.

3. Beat in remaining ingredients and continue beating for about 1 minute.

4. Line a 4- to 5-quart slow cooker with parchment paper. Pour batter onto the parchment paper.

5. Cover and cook on high for 2½–3 hours or until cheesecake is set. Remove slow cooker insert and let it cool to room temperature. Then place in fridge to chill for 2–6 hours. Slice to serve.

PER SERVING: Calories: 159 | Fat: 8g | Protein: 3g | Sodium: 85mg | Fiber: 0g | Carbohydrates: 18g | Sugar: 17g

Poached Figs

These poached figs are perfect for a snack or dessert.

INGREDIENTS | SERVES 4

½ cup water

½ cup apple juice

2 teaspoons honey

2 teaspoons sugar

1 vanilla bean, split

8 ounces fresh figs

Shopping for Figs

Look for figs that are plump and soft (but not squishy) with unbroken skin. Store figs in the refrigerator or in a cool dark place until ready to use.

1. In a small saucepan over medium heat, combine the water, apple juice, honey, sugar, and vanilla bean. Heat through until hot but not boiling, about 5 minutes.

2. Place the figs into a 2-quart slow cooker. Pour hot water/apple juice mixture over them. Cook on low for 5 hours or until the figs are cooked through and starting to split.

3. Remove the figs from the poaching liquid and serve.

PER SERVING: Calories: 74 | Fat: 0g | Protein: 0.5g | Sodium: 3mg | Fiber: 1.5g | Carbohydrates: 19g | Sugar: 17g

Challah Bread Pudding

*This slimmed-down bread pudding is a wonderful way to use up leftover,
even slightly stale, challah. Use dried cranberries if you can't find dried cherries.*

INGREDIENTS | SERVES 10

4 cups cubed challah

⅓ cup dried tart cherries

2⅓ cups fat-free evaporated milk

2 large eggs

⅓ cup packed dark brown sugar

1 teaspoon vanilla extract

1 teaspoon cinnamon

½ teaspoon ground ginger

¼ teaspoon nutmeg

1. Spray a 4- to 5-quart slow cooker with cooking spray. Add the bread cubes and dried cherries. Stir.

2. In a medium bowl, whisk the evaporated milk, eggs, brown sugar, vanilla, cinnamon, ginger, and nutmeg. Pour over the bread crumbs and dried fruit.

3. Cook for 5 hours on low or until the pudding no longer looks liquid.

PER SERVING: Calories: 200 | Fat: 4g | Protein: 8g | Sodium: 230mg | Fiber: 1g | Carbohydrates: 28g | Sugar: 14g

Breaking Bread

It is important to cut the bread used for bread pudding into uniform 1"–2" cubes for maximum absorption and distribution of liquid. Slightly stale bread cuts easily and can be used in bread puddings or stuffing. Bread cubes can even be frozen for future use.

Orange-Scented Custard

Orange blossom water is a common Middle Eastern ingredient that adds a fruity, floral note to this custard.

INGREDIENTS | SERVES 10

1 tablespoon orange blossom water, or ½ teaspoon orange extract

2 cups fat-free evaporated milk

5 large eggs

⅓ cup sugar

Place all ingredients into a large bowl. Whisk until smooth. Pour into a 4- to 5-quart slow cooker. Cook on low for 8 hours, or until the center looks set and does not jiggle.

PER SERVING: Calories: 129 | Fat: 4g | Protein: 6.5g | Sodium: 88mg | Fiber: 0g | Carbohydrates: 12g | Sugar: 11g

Vanilla Poached Pears

Slow poaching makes these pears meltingly tender and infuses them with a rich vanilla flavor.

INGREDIENTS | SERVES 4

4 medium Bosc pears, peeled

1 vanilla bean, split

2 tablespoons vanilla extract

2 cups water

Stand the pears up in a 4-quart oval slow cooker. Add the remaining ingredients. Cook on low for 2 hours or until the pears are tender. Discard all cooking liquid prior to serving.

PER SERVING: Calories: 121 | Fat: 0g | Protein: 1g | Sodium: 6mg | Fiber: 5.5g | Carbohydrates: 28g | Sugar: 18g

"Baked" Apples

Serve these lightly spiced apples as a simple dessert or a breakfast treat.

Baking with Apples

When baking or cooking, choose apples with firm flesh such as Granny Smith, Jonathan, McIntosh, Cortland, Pink Lady, Pippin, or Winesap. They will be able to hold up to long cooking times while keeping the body of the apple intact. Leaving the skin on adds fiber and flavor.

1. Drizzle ½ teaspoon lemon juice in each apple.

2. In a small bowl, combine brown sugar, walnuts, cranberries, cinnamon, dried ginger, and salt. Divide mixture between apples and press down gently. Chop butter into pieces and divide between apples.

3. Place the apples in a simple layer on the bottom of a 4- or 6-quart slow cooker. Add water around the base. Cook on low for 6–8 hours or until the apples are tender and easily pierced with a fork.

4. Use a slotted spoon to remove the apples from the insert. Serve immediately.

PER SERVING: Calories: 248 | Fat: 6g | Protein: 1.5g | Sodium: 105mg | Fiber: 3.5g | Carbohydrates: 50g | Sugar: 43g

Additional Resources

Slow Cookers

Most of the recipes in this book have been made with a 4- to 5-quart slow cooker. Whether you're ready to buy your first slow cooker, need to upsize or downsize your current model, or simply want to purchase a second to have in your kitchen, these online stores offer incredible variety and make shopping for slow cookers simple!

Amazon.com

www.amazon.com

If you are an Amazon Prime member, free shipping makes Amazon.com one particularly good site for online shopping. The organization of the site is another good reason to purchase slow cookers through Amazon.com. Customer reviews make it easy to understand the pros and cons of each product, and windows that let you see what other items customers looking for slow cookers also viewed connect you to additional accessories or brands worth considering for your own kitchen.

Crock-pot.com

www.crock-pot.com

Crock-Pot, the original slow cooker, offers hundreds of slow cookers in every size from large to small through their brand website. If design is an important element in your kitchen, you'll find dozens of styles and colors, including team logos, sleek modern styles, and Crock-Pots covered in flower designs. The site often offers free or discounted shipping, also sells accessories and parts, and offers a large archive of slow-cooker-friendly recipes.

ConsumerReports.org

www.consumerreports.org

You won't be able to purchase a slow cooker straight from the Consumer Reports website, but it's a vital resource if you're invested in obtaining the best slow cooker unit on the market. Consumer Reports offers a Consumer Buying Guide and detailed reports on their product tests from all the major brands, and specifies the features worth considering when looking to purchase a slow cooker.

Slow Cooker Brands

The companies that create slow cookers usually sell them through their company websites. There are several benefits to buying units directly from the supplier of the product. Deals or discounts are often offered on units—particularly refurbished or retired-model slow cookers. Many companies extend and track warranties when items are ordered directly from their sites, as well, making it easy to order replacement parts, return faulty units, and receive refunds for unwanted items. If you'd prefer to shop for a slow cooker directly, here's a list of companies known for their quality slow cooking units.

- All-Clad
- Aroma Housewares
- Black & Decker
- Breville
- Crock-Pot
- Cuisinart
- Hamilton Beach
- Oster
- Proctor Silex
- West Bend

Other Major Retailers

Several of these corporations offer slow cookers for purchase on their sites, and slow cookers can be purchased in person at local stores, as well.

Walmart

www.walmart.com

The website and box stores carry a variety of shapes, sizes, colors, and prices. Most stores carry 1- to 3-unit slow cookers, so several Crock-Pot recipes can be cooking at once. Prices online and in stores range from $25 to $80.

Target

www.target.com

With a limited number of units offered in stores, Target online carries more than seventy-two slow cooker unit options, in a variety of sizes, styles, colors, and brand names. Prices range from $12 to $160.

Bed Bath & Beyond

www.bedbathandbeyond.com

Perhaps the highest number of crockpot brands are carried here. With more than seven different companies offered through this retailer, shoppers can expect to find great variety in price—and feature options as well. Prices range from $49 to $200.

Williams-Sonoma

www.williams-sonoma.com

This high-end kitchen store offers high-end slow cookers. Well-designed units with high-quality brand names (like Breville and All-Clad) are offered at prices ranging from $129 to $300.

Accessories

www.crock-pot.com/accessories

Find slow cooker recipe books, premade sauces for easy recipe prep, and Crock-Pot tote bags, tongs, and spatulas created specifically by the Crock-Pot company in the accessories section of their website.

www.crock-pot.com/parts

Replacement parts for specific Crock-Pot models are available in the "parts" section of the Crock-Pot brand website. Just search for your crock, click on the photo, and you'll be taken directly to a page where the parts you need—lids, knobs, and stoneware pots—are clearly listed for your unit, making ordering new parts a cinch!

Mediterranean Ingredients

Mediterranean cooking is mainstream enough that most of the ingredients called for in this book can be quickly and easily located in the aisles of most grocery stores. However, if you're unable to find specific ingredients, are looking for better deals or prices than those found locally, or want to purchase authentic Mediterranean items for your mealtimes, the following online sites offer a variety of excellent ingredients and options.

Dayna's Market

www.daynasmarket.com

Perhaps the most robust online resource for Mediterranean and Middle Eastern foods and ingredients, Dayna's carries authentic foods. Their product list is geared specifically for the American crowd, importing authentic and national brands. With excellent customer service and hundreds of products to choose from, Dayna's is a popular way to shop Med online.

The Ethnic Grocer

www.theethnicgrocer.com

This website offers a unique shopping experience, inviting home-page visitors to choose the country or region they're seeking ingredients from. The Ethnic Grocer offers hundreds of authentic ingredients, and keeps the shipping costs surprisingly low.

Sadaf

www.sadaf.com

A well-designed online shopping market for Mediterranean foods and merchandise. Select the category and begin browsing through everything from baked goods, to herbs and spices, to authentic local coffees and teas. The site is easy to navigate and easy to order from.

Slow Cooking Websites

365 Days of Slow Cooking

www.365daysofcrockpot.com

With vibrant photography and a simple, searchable recipe index, this site is an incredible online resource for home cooks looking for simple recipes made in the slow cooker.

Crock-Pot

www.crock-pot.com

With hundreds of recipes sorted by course, cuisine, cooker size, or main ingredient, the Crock-Pot website makes it easy to find whatever recipe you're craving for dinner tonight.

Slow Cooker from Scratch

www.slowcookerfromscratch.com

A new website created by beloved blogger Kalyn Denny, this site boasts beautiful photos and an ongoing refresh of new slow cooker recipes daily. As the name suggests, healthy, whole-food ingredients are the focus of the recipes on this site. It's an excellent resource if you're looking for healthy recipes that are simple, accessible, and delicious.

Mediterranean Cooking Sites

The Italian Dish Blog

www.theitaliandishblog.com

The daughter of an Italian mother, Elaine McCardel shares traditional Italian cuisine using beautiful photos and clearly written recipes.

Mediterrasian

www.mediterrasian.com

With stunning photos and simple, mouthwatering recipe offerings, this website is a must-visit recipe resource for eaters looking for healthy, Mediterranean-style cuisine.

Standard U.S./Metric Measurement Conversions

VOLUME CONVERSIONS

U.S. Volume Measure	Metric Equivalent
⅛ teaspoon	0.5 milliliter
¼ teaspoon	1 milliliter
½ teaspoon	2 milliliters
1 teaspoon	5 milliliters
½ tablespoon	7 milliliters
1 tablespoon (3 teaspoons)	15 milliliters
2 tablespoons (1 fluid ounce)	30 milliliters
¼ cup (4 tablespoons)	60 milliliters
⅓ cup	90 milliliters
½ cup (4 fluid ounces)	125 milliliters
⅔ cup	160 milliliters
¾ cup (6 fluid ounces)	180 milliliters
1 cup (16 tablespoons)	250 milliliters
1 pint (2 cups)	500 milliliters
1 quart (4 cups)	1 liter (about)

WEIGHT CONVERSIONS

U.S. Weight Measure	Metric Equivalent
½ ounce	15 grams
1 ounce	30 grams
2 ounces	60 grams
3 ounces	85 grams
¼ pound (4 ounces)	115 grams
½ pound (8 ounces)	225 grams
¾ pound (12 ounces)	340 grams
1 pound (16 ounces)	454 grams

OVEN TEMPERATURE CONVERSIONS

Degrees Fahrenheit	Degrees Celsius
200 degrees F	95 degrees C
250 degrees F	120 degrees C
275 degrees F	135 degrees C
300 degrees F	150 degrees C
325 degrees F	160 degrees C
350 degrees F	180 degrees C
375 degrees F	190 degrees C
400 degrees F	205 degrees C
425 degrees F	220 degrees C
450 degrees F	230 degrees C

BAKING PAN SIZES

U.S.	Metric
8 × 1½ inch round baking pan	20 × 4 cm cake tin
9 × 1½ inch round baking pan	23 × 3.5 cm cake tin
11 × 7 × 1½ inch baking pan	28 × 18 × 4 cm baking tin
13 × 9 × 2 inch baking pan	30 × 20 × 5 cm baking tin
2 quart rectangular baking dish	30 × 20 × 3 cm baking tin
15 × 10 × 2 inch baking pan	30 × 25 × 2 cm baking tin (Swiss roll tin)
9 inch pie plate	22 × 4 or 23 × 4 cm pie plate
7 or 8 inch springform pan	18 or 20 cm springform or loose-bottom cake tin
9 × 5 × 3 inch loaf pan	23 × 13 × 7 cm or 2 lb narrow loaf or pâté tin
1½ quart casserole	1.5 liter casserole
2 quart casserole	2 liter casserole

Index